国际胜任力英语系列

国际胜任力英语教程
——通用

主　编　郝运慧
副主编　田永丰　高　歌
编　者（姓氏笔画）
　　　　王建荣　杜可心　苗　禾
　　　　姜玉珍　雷　瑜

清华大学出版社
北京

内 容 简 介

本书将国际胜任知识、技能、态度与价值观融为一体，以国际胜任力内涵、重要国际议题与相关国际组织、人类命运共同体建设为总体内容架构，每个单元由国际胜任知识阅读、国际胜任技能训练和"中国记事"三个维度组成。国际胜任知识维度涵盖全球和平、全球发展、全球健康、全球生态、全球性别平等、全球减贫等重要议题的相关知识；国际胜任能力维度包括如何写报告、如何写项目提案、如何写立场文件等重要写作能力以及如何在国际场合做正式汇报、如何在跨文化语境中进行有效沟通等重要口头沟通和综合能力。态度与价值观维度聚焦中国视角，通过与单元主题相匹配的案例学习突出全球治理中的中国智慧和方案，提升学生的中国情怀、国际视野与世界胸怀。

本书的使用对象为本科高阶拓展课程或者研究生英语课程学习者。

版权所有，侵权必究。举报：010-62782989，beiqinquan@tup.tsinghua.edu.cn。

图书在版编目（CIP）数据

国际胜任力英语教程：通用 / 郝运慧主编．
北京：清华大学出版社，2024.7. —（国际胜任力英语系列）．— ISBN 978-7-302-66638-7

I. H319.39

中国国家版本馆 CIP 数据核字第 2024FK0042 号

责任编辑：刘　艳
封面设计：李伯骥
责任校对：王荣静
责任印制：宋　林

出版发行：清华大学出版社
网　　址：https://www.tup.com.cn, https://www.wqxuetang.com
地　　址：北京清华大学学研大厦 A 座
邮　编：100084
社 总 机：010-83470000
邮　购：010-62786544
投稿与读者服务：010-62776969, c-service@tup.tsinghua.edu.cn
质量反馈：010-62772015, zhiliang@tup.tsinghua.edu.cn
印 装 者：三河市少明印务有限公司
经　　销：全国新华书店
开　　本：185mm×260mm
印　张：19.25
字　数：444 千字
版　　次：2024 年 8 月第 1 版
印　次：2024 年 8 月第 1 次印刷
定　　价：79.00 元

产品编号：103971-01

当前,世界之变、时代之变、历史之变正以前所未有的方式展开。我国作为当今世界最大的发展中国家,一直在积极致力于参与和推动全球治理向正确的方向发展。特别是近几年来,我国在国际舞台上先后发出全球发展倡议(2021)、全球安全倡议(2022)、全球文明倡议(2023)等重大倡议,推动新时代的全球治理理念不断走深走实。但是,实现这些国家重大倡议的挑战之一便是能够胜任全球治理的国际化人才的缺乏。我个人长期在外交外事领域工作,近些年通过学术会议、讲学等方式对高校的人才培养工作有不断深入的了解,我也一直在呼吁加强对学生国际胜任能力的培养。我很高兴地看到外语界在持续关注培养学生的国际胜任能力这一问题,《国际胜任力英语教程:通用》便是从教材建设和课程教学这一微观切口来推进和落实国家对这一类型人才培养的需求。因此,我很乐于为这部教材作序。

通读书稿,我发现该教材具有以下三个特点:

第一,立足外语教育教学规律与实践,回应国家对国际胜任人才培养的需求。 习近平总书记在全国教育大会上强调,要大力培养掌握党和国家方针政策、具有全球视野、通晓国际规则、熟练运用外语、精通中外谈判和沟通的国际化人才,有计划地培养选拔优秀人才到国际组织任职。这部教材立意高、定位清,通过内容和语言相融合的方式,将重要的国际性议题与相关国际组织和国际规则相结合,精准回应了习近平总书记在全国教育大会上的讲话精神。教材涵盖了经济、外交、文化、生态、健康、性别等重要和热点领域以及联合国、联合国教科文组织、亚太经合组织、世界卫生组织等重要国际组织,对于提升学生国际视野、了解国际规则、运用外语进行跨文化沟通将有重要促进作用。

同时，该教材配有丰富的语言能力练习，融通读与写、融通读与说，以阅读上的输入保障写作与口头表达的输出，以写作与表达的输出促进阅读的深化。

第二，选材精良、与时俱进，内容涵盖话题核心内容与新发展、新动态。这部教材的阅读语篇材料多选自国际组织官方网址、官方机构发布的皮书或报告以及相关话题的学术研究网站，内容权威、可靠，经适度改编处理后适用于教学的组织与安排。同时，这部教材将相关话题的新发展与新动态以不同的形式融入学习框架，让学生与时俱进地了解联合国 2030 可持续发展目标、全球文化政策、全球减贫问题、人类命运共同体理念、三大全球倡议等重要内容，这对提升学生理解和分析地区性、全球性重要议题，为集体福祉和可持续发展采取行动的能力培养具有重要意义，也是国际胜任能力的核心维度。

第三，全球视野与中国视角的统一、全球治理与中国方案的统一。这部教材立足国际胜任力知识、技能和态度与价值三重经典维度，强调全球性议题的阅读与理解能力、国际性文书写作与表达能力以及跨文化沟通等能力。值得一提的是，该教材的"中国记事"（Notes from China）部分，以案例形式讲述了新时代中国在世界维和、合作抗疫、教育公平、生态文明建设、世界文化多样性等问题上的视角、方案和贡献，不仅能够培养学生的全球胸怀和国际视野，而且对于培养学生讲好中国故事、传播好中国声音的能力以及担负起中外文化交流的信使职责具有重要作用。

总之，这部教材立足新时期的国家需求，对具有国际胜任能力的人才培养作出了十分有益的尝试，希望各院校和学子在使用中结合自身优势与特色，发挥出国际胜任能力人才培养的合力。

中国驻新西兰、瑞典前大使
中国翻译协会前副会长
外交部外语专家
2024 年 6 月

前言 FOREWORD

2010年颁布的《国家中长期教育改革和发展规划纲要（2010—2020）》指出，我国要积极参与和推动国际组织教育政策、规则、标准的研究和制定，要适应国家经济社会对外开放的要求，培养大批具有国际视野、通晓国际规则、能够参与国际事务和国际竞争的国际化人才。2018年，习近平总书记在全国教育大会上强调，要大力培养掌握党和国家方针政策、具有全球视野、通晓国际规则、熟练运用外语、精通中外谈判和沟通的国际化人才，有针对性地培养"一带一路"等对外急需的懂外语的各类专业技术和管理人才，有计划地培养选拔优秀人才到国际组织任职。党的二十大报告指出，中国积极参与全球治理体系改革与建设，践行共商共建共享的全球治理观，要增强新兴市场国家和发展中国家在全球事务中的代表性和发言权。可见，国家的系列规划都指出具有国际胜任能力的人才是时代之需和国家高质量发展之需。然而，中国新时期参与全球治理面临的显著困难与挑战之一便是具有国际胜任能力的人才的匮乏。虽然我国一直致力于与以联合国为核心的国际社会积极协作并承担充分的责任与义务，但是我国在国际组织的任职人员不仅数量不足，而且职级普遍不高，话语影响力有限。当下，全球化进程加速和全球治理体系的深度变革进一步凸显了国际胜任能力人才培养的重要性与紧迫性。

国际胜任力是21世纪，特别是21世纪第二个十年以来全球相关组织和教育界积极关注并在研究与实践中不断推进的重要领域。经济合作与发展组织、美国亚洲学会、中国教育发展战略学会国际胜任力专委会、中国教育国际交流协会等机构和哈佛大学、清华大学等高校分别对国际胜任力的内涵给出了不同的界定并推进了相应的人才培养项目，为国际胜任能力人才培养积累了宝贵的参考经验。

《国际胜任力英语教程：通用》对接我国国际胜任人才培养的战略需求，全面吸收借鉴国内外在这一领域的研究与实践成果，立足外语教学的规律与可行性，旨在为培养外语熟练、视野开阔、跨文化国际沟通能力卓越的人才添砖加瓦。本教材具有如下特色：

1. 立足国际胜任力内涵要素，将价值塑造、知识传授、能力培养相统一。本教材立足国际胜任力领域知名学者 Bill Hunter 提出的国际胜任力经典三要素——知识、技能、态度（KSA）模型来构建教材的内容与结构框架。在国际胜任知识维度，将全球性重要议题与对应的国际组织相结合，通过经济、外交、文化、生态、健康、性别等领域的语篇阅读来加强学生对国际胜任知识的掌握；同时，将我国提出的人类命运共同体理念以及"一带一路"倡议、三大全球倡议等重要内容与时俱进地融入国际胜任知识体系。国际胜任能力维度包括五个方面：如何写报告、如何写项目提案、如何写立场文件等重要写作能力以及如何在国际场合做正式汇报、如何在跨文化语境中进行有效沟通等重要口头沟通和综合能力。态度与价值观维度聚焦中国视角，通过与单元主题相匹配的案例学习突出全球治理中的中国智慧和中国方案，旨在于知识浸润和能力形成中提升学生的中国情怀、国际视野与世界胸怀。

2. 能力与思维并举，产出与互动并重。本教材在能力培养上聚焦两条主线，分别为蕴含国际胜任内涵的文章阅读分析和国际化场合的写作与表达产出，融通读与写、融通读与说，以阅读上的输入保障写作与口头表达的输出，以写作与表达的输出促进阅读的深化。在阅读主线上，每个单元由两篇文章组成，分别聚焦重要国际性议题的相关知识以及该领域的重要话题，力求使学生在学习过程中既能获取该领域的核心知识，又能在此基础上进行深度和广度的拓展与思考。在写作和表达能力输出的主线上，突出美国心理学家、教育家 Benjamin Bloom 的教育目标分类系统中的分析、评价、创造等高阶能力，遵循 OBE（Outcome-Based Education）模式，以报告、提案、立场文件书写以及做正式汇报等重要成果类型产出为导向来开展教与学。在任务设置上，以学生为中心，以项目式活动为依托，突出互动原则，力求达到学中做、做中学的效果。

3. 注重自身民族文化身份认同和中国价值立场，培养学生讲好中国故事的能力。 学者滕珺等（2018：100）立足国际胜任力教育权威机构经济合作与发展组织对国际胜任力的界定指出："中国教育工作者既要认识到全球胜任力的重要性，同时也要批判地思考全球胜任力与民族文化身份认同和中国价值立场的关系。"虽然国际胜任力的核心思想之一是理解和欣赏他人的观点，具有开放、包容的心态，但是实现这一目标的前提是有足够的民族文化自信和身份认同，同时对中国的历史和当今国际社会的多元文化格局有较多的理解和价值认同，唯有这样才能更积极、更自信地在国际社会发挥沟通作用。因此，本教材的重要宗旨之一也在于培养学生的民族身份和中国价值立场的认同，通过以人类命运共同体等章节的设置，通过模拟"理解当代中国"等主题活动设计，培养学生讲好中国故事、传播好中国声音的能力，担负起中外文化交流的信使职责。

教材配有习题参考答案和 PPT 课件。本教材的建议使用对象为本科高阶拓展课程、研究生基础课程或者各类对国际胜任力感兴趣的英语学习者，旨在以国际胜任力 KSA 框架为依托，全面提升学生的国际胜任力素养；以内容为依托强化学生的外语运用能力，为学生开拓国际视野和后续从事国际组织相关工作发挥启蒙和引路作用。

本教材的编写人员均具有多年不同类型英语课程的教学经验，主要编写人员对国际胜任力内涵有深入的理解，对学生拔尖创新人才培养项目有较为丰富的经验。同时，编写人员具有博士学位或高级职称，均具有海外学习或访学经历，有良好的国际视野和跨文化意识，对全球性议题有较为深入的理解。

由于编者水平有限，书中错漏之处在所难免，恳请广大读者批评指正。

编者

2024 年 6 月

CONTENTS 目录

Unit 1 Global Competence ... 1
Part I   Reading for GC Knowledge ... 2
Text A   Preparing for Global Competence ... 2
Text B   Developing Global Competence ... 10
Part II Drilling for GC Skills ... 17
How to Communicate Effectively in Cross-Cultural Contexts (I) ... 17
Part III Notes from China ... 25
Ancient Chinese Philosophy and Global Competence ... 25

Unit 2 Global Peace and the UN ... 27
Part I   Reading for GC Knowledge ... 28
Text A   The United Nations and Its Duties ... 28
Text B   The UN and the Maintenance of Global Security and Peace ... 36
Part II Drilling for GC Skills ... 43
How to Communicate Effectively in Cross-Cultural Contexts (II) ... 43
Part III Notes from China ... 52
UNMISS Peacekeepers from China Recognized for Their Contributions in South Sudan ... 52

Unit 3 Global Development and APEC ... 55
Part I   Reading for GC Knowledge ... 56
Text A   An Introduction to APEC ... 56
Text B   APEC, Creating a Resilient and Sustainable Future for All ... 64

Part II　Drilling for GC Skills 72
How to Write a Report (I) 72
Part III　Notes from China 82
China Contributes to APEC Sub-Fund to Combat COVID-19 Pandemic ... 82

Unit 4　Global Health and the WHO 85

Part I　Reading for GC Knowledge 86
Text A　Global Health—Key Concepts and Misperceptions 86
Text B　The Way Forward: WHO's Five Strategic Directions 93
Part II　Drilling for GC Skills 100
How to Write a Report (II) 100
Part III　Notes from China 105
The Globalization of Chinese Medicine 105

Unit 5　Global Ecology and the World Bank 107

Part I　Reading for GC Knowledge 108
Text A　Economy-Wide and Enabling Policies for Carbon Neutrality 108
Text B　Further Global Cooperation on Biodiversity Conservation 115
Part II　Drilling for GC Skills 121
How to Write a Project Proposal (I) 121
Part III　Notes from China 127
"Xiamen Solution" Exemplifies Harmonious Coexistence Between
　　Man and Nature 127

Unit 6　Global Gender Equality and the IAW 131

Part I　Reading for GC Knowledge 132
Text A　Gender Equality: The Unfinished Business of Our Time 132
Text B　Technology-Facilitated Gender-Based Violence in an Era of
　　　　Generative AI 141
Part II　Drilling for GC Skills 149
How to Write a Project Proposal (II) 149

Part III　Notes from China 155

Empowering Dreams: Free Education for Girls in Rural China 155

Unit 7　Global Culture and the UNESCO 159

Part I　Reading for GC Knowledge 160

Text A　1982-2022: Cultural Policies at the Heart of International Debate 160

Text B　Cultural Selection: The Diffusion of Tea and Tea Culture Along the Silk Roads 167

Part II　Drilling for GC Skills 173

How to Write a Position Paper (I) 173

Part III　Notes from China 183

Chinese Culture Pursues "Not King, But Jade" 183

Unit 8　A Community of Shared Future for Mankind (I) ... 187

Part I　Reading for GC Knowledge 188

Text A　The Belt and Road Initiative as a Strategy to Promote and Sustain Growth 188

Text B　The Chinese Express Train Running in East Africa 196

Part II　Drilling for GC Skills 203

How to Write a Position Paper (II) 203

Part III　Notes from China 209

President Xi's Reply Letters to Student Representatives from BRI Countries 209

Unit 9　A Community of Shared Future for Mankind (II) ... 211

Part I　Reading for GC Knowledge 212

Text A　Poverty Alleviation: China's Experience and Contribution 212

Text B　Poverty Reduction in Sub-Saharan Africa 219

Part II　Drilling for GC Skills 226

How to Give a Formal Presentation (I) 226

Part III　Notes from China 237

Anji Solution in China's Rural Revitalization 237

Unit 10 A Community of Shared Future for Mankind (III) ... 241

Part I Reading for GC Knowledge 242

Text A China's Three Global Initiatives 242

Text B The Influence of Ancient Chinese Cultural Classics in France 252

Part II Drilling for GC Skills 260

How to Give a Formal Presentation (II) 260

Part III Notes from China 277

Nishan Forum on World Civilizations 277

Glossary 279

Unit 1

Global Competence

Part I Reading for GC Knowledge

Text A Preparing for Global Competence

Warm-up

Self-Assessment of Global Competence

Directions: *Please rate yourself on a scale of 1 to 5, where 1 = Strongly Disagree; 2 = Disagree; 3 = Neutral; 4 = Agree; 5 = Strongly Agree. Then discuss the questions that follow.*

Self-Assessment Questionnaire	Scale				
Cultural Awareness					
I am curious about and interested in learning about different cultures.	1	2	3	4	5
I actively seek opportunities to engage with people from diverse cultural backgrounds.	1	2	3	4	5
I am aware of my own cultural biases and open to challenging and expanding my cultural perspectives.	1	2	3	4	5
Communication Skills					
I feel comfortable communicating with people who speak languages other than my native language.	1	2	3	4	5
I am mindful of non-verbal communication cues (body language, gestures) in cross-cultural interactions.	1	2	3	4	5
I adapt my communication style to be more inclusive and respectful of cultural differences.	1	2	3	4	5
Openness to Diversity					
I actively seek opportunities to engage with individuals from diverse ethnic groups, religions, and social backgrounds.	1	2	3	4	5
I am comfortable working in a team with people who have different perspectives and ideas.	1	2	3	4	5

(Continued)

Self-Assessment Questionnaire	Scale				
I believe that diversity enhances the learning and working environment.	1	2	3	4	5
Global Awareness					
I am knowledgeable about global issues such as climate change, poverty, and human rights.	1	2	3	4	5
I actively seek information about current events and international affairs.	1	2	3	4	5
I feel a sense of responsibility to contribute to addressing global challenges.	1	2	3	4	5

1. Based on your self-assessment, what do you think is global competence?

2. Considering your score, would you say that you possess a strong level of global competence?

Preparing for Global Competence[1]

❶ In the 21st century, students live in an **interconnected**, diverse, and rapidly changing world. Emerging economic, digital, cultural, **demographic**, and environmental forces are shaping young people's lives around the globe and increasing their intercultural encounters on a daily basis. This complex environment presents an opportunity and a challenge. Young people today must not only learn to participate in a more interconnected world but also appreciate and benefit from cultural differences. Developing global competence is a lifelong process.

What Is Global Competence?

❷ Global competence is a **multidimensional capacity**. Globally **competent** individuals can examine local, global, and intercultural issues, understand and appreciate the perspectives and world views of others, interact successfully and respectfully with others, and take responsible action toward **sustainability** and **collective** well-being.

---

[1] The text was adapted from "Preparing Our Youth for an Inclusive and Sustainable World: The OECD PISA Global Competence Framework". 2018. Organization for Economic Cooperation and Development (OECD, France).

❸ "Competence" here is not merely a specific skill but a combination of knowledge, skills, attitudes, and values successfully applied to face-to-face, virtual or **mediated** encounters with people who are **perceived** to be from a different cultural background, and to individuals' experiences of global issues (i.e. situations that require an individual to reflect upon and engage with global problems that have deep **implications** for current and future generations).

Why Do We Need Global Competence?

❹ Since the end of the Cold War, ethno-cultural **conflicts** have become the most common source of political violence in the world, and they show no sign of **abating**. The many episodes of **indiscriminate** violence in the name of a religious or **ethnic affiliation** challenge the belief that people with diverse cultures are able to live peacefully in close **proximity**, accept differences, find common solutions and resolve disagreements. Contemporary societies call for complex forms of belonging and **citizenship** where individuals must interact with distant regions, people, and ideas while also deepening their understanding of their local environment and the diversity within their own communities.

❺ Effective communication and appropriate behavior within diverse teams are also keys to success in many jobs and will remain so as technology continues to make it easier for people to connect across the globe. Employers increasingly seek to attract learners who easily adapt and are able to apply and **transfer** their skills and knowledge to new contexts. Work readiness in an interconnected world requires young people to understand the complex **dynamics** of globalization, be open to people from different cultural backgrounds, build trust in diverse teams, and demonstrate respect for others.

❻ Meanwhile, over the past two decades, **radical** transformations in digital technologies have shaped young people's outlook on the world, their interactions with others and their perception of themselves. Online networks, social media, and interactive technologies are giving rise to new types of learning, where young people exercise greater control over what and how they learn. At the same time, young people's digital lives can cause them to disconnect from themselves and the world, and ignore the impact that their actions may have on others. **Likewise**, access to an unlimited amount of information is often paired with insufficient media **literacy**, meaning that they are easily fooled by **partisan**, biased or fake news. In this context, cultivating global competence can help young people **capitalize** on digital spaces, better understand the world they live in, and responsibly express their voice online.

❼ Finally, developing global competence can help form new generations who care about global issues and engage in **tackling** social, political, economic, and environmental challenges. It is **imperative** to guarantee that every young person acquires the knowledge and skills **essential** for promoting **sustainable** development. This **encompasses** education for sustainable development, the adoption of sustainable lifestyles, the **advocacy** for human rights, the pursuit of gender equality, the **propagation** of a culture of peace and nonviolence, the cultivation of global citizenship, and a **profound** appreciation for cultural diversity, recognizing its significant contribution to sustainable development.

What Does Global Competence Include?

❽ The definition of "global competence" outlines four target dimensions that people need to apply successfully in their everyday life.

❾ **Dimension 1:** The capacity to examine issues and situations of local, global, and cultural significance (e.g. poverty, economic interdependence, **migration**, inequality, environmental risks, conflicts, cultural differences, and stereotypes). People who acquire a mature level of development in this dimension use higher-order thinking skills, such as selecting and weighing appropriate evidence to reason about global developments.

❿ **Dimension 2:** The capacity to understand and appreciate different perspectives and world views. It highlights that globally competent people are willing and capable of considering global problems and other people's perspectives and behavior from **multiple** viewpoints. As individuals acquire knowledge about other cultures' histories, values, communication styles, beliefs, and practices, they acquire the means to recognize that their perspectives and behavior are shaped by multiple influences, that they are not always fully aware of these influences, and that others have views of the world that are profoundly different from their own.

⓫ **Dimension 3:** The ability to establish positive interactions with people of different national, ethnic, religious, social or cultural backgrounds and genders. It describes what globally competent individuals are able to do when they interact with people from different cultures. They understand the cultural norms, interactive styles and degrees of formality of intercultural contexts, and they can flexibly adapt their behavior and communication to suit.

⓬ **Dimension 4:** The capacity and **disposition** to take constructive action toward sustainable development and collective well-being. It focuses on young people's role as active and responsible members of society and refers to individuals' readiness to respond to a given local, global or intercultural issue or situation. This dimension recognizes that young people have multiple **realms** of influence ranging from personal and local to digital and global.

⑬ These four dimensions are strongly interdependent and **overlapping**, justifying the use of the singular term "global competence". For example, students from two different cultural backgrounds who work together on a school project demonstrate global competence as they: get to know each other better (examine their cultural differences); try to understand how each perceives his or her role in the project and the other's perspective (understand perspectives); negotiate misunderstandings and clearly communicate expectations and feelings (interact openly, appropriately, and effectively); and take stock of what they learn from each other to improve social relationships in their classroom and school (act for collective well-being).

(1,034 words)

Glossary

interconnect	/ˌɪntəkə'nekt/	v.	相联系；相互连接
demographic	/ˌdemə'græfɪk/	adj.	人口的，人口统计的
multidimensional	/ˌmʌltɪdaɪ'menʃənl/	adj.	多维的；多面的
capacity	/kə'pæsəti/	n.	能力；生产量；生产能力
competent	/'kɒmpɪtənt/	adj.	能胜任的
sustainability	/səˌsteɪnə'bɪləti/	n.	耐久性，可持续性
collective	/kə'lektɪv/	adj.	集体的，共同的
mediate	/'miːdieɪt/	v.	调解
perceive	/pə'siːv/	v.	感知；认为
implication	/ˌɪmplɪ'keɪʃn/	n.	可能的影响（或作用、结果）
conflict	/'kɑːnflɪkt/	n.	冲突，争论
abate	/ə'beɪt/	v.	减弱，减轻
indiscriminate	/ˌɪndɪ'skrɪmɪnət/	adj.	任意而为的
ethnic	/'eθnɪk/	adj.	民族的，种族的
affiliation	/əˌfɪli'eɪʃn/	n.	紧密联系；官方联系
proximity	/prɒk'sɪməti/	n.	接近，靠近
citizenship	/'sɪtɪzənʃɪp/	n.	公民身份，国籍
transfer	/træns'fɜː(r)/	v.	转移
dynamics	/daɪ'næmɪks/	n.	动力学，动力
radical	/'rædɪkl/	adj.	重大的；彻底的

likewise	/ˈlaɪkwaɪz/	adv.	同样地
literacy	/ˈlɪtərəsi/	n.	读写能力
partisan	/ˌpɑːtɪˈzæn/	adj.	盲目拥护的
capitalize	/ˈkæpɪtəlaɪz/	v.	利用
tackle	/ˈtækl/	v.	处理，解决
imperative	/ɪmˈperətɪv/	adj.	命令式的，强制式的
essential	/ɪˈsenʃl/	adj.	基本的；重要的
sustainable	/səˈsteɪnəbl/	adj.	可持续的
encompass	/ɪnˈkʌmpəs/	v.	包含，包括
advocacy	/ˈædvəkəsi/	n.	拥护，提倡
propagation	/ˌprɒpəˈgeɪʃn/	n.	（观点、理论等的）传播
profound	/prəˈfaʊnd/	adj.	深刻的；极大的
migration	/maɪˈgreɪʃn/	n.	移民，迁徙
multiple	/ˈmʌltɪpl/	adj.	多个；多重的
disposition	/ˌdɪspəˈzɪʃn/	n.	性情
overlap	/ˌəʊvəˈlæp/	v.	重叠，与……重合

Task 1

Directions: *Please read the text and fill in the blanks below with a proper word.*

Understanding Global Competence
What is global competence?
● Global competence is a(n) (1) _____ capacity.
● Globally competent individuals can examine local, global, and (2) _____ issues, understand and appreciate the perspectives and world views of others, interact successfully and respectfully with others, and take responsible action toward (3) _____ and collective well-being.
Why do we need global competence?
● To live harmoniously in multicultural (4) _____;
● To thrive in a changing (5) _____ market;
● To use (6) _____ platforms effectively and responsibly;
● To support the (7) _____ development goals.

(Continued)

Understanding Global Competence
What does global competence include?
• **Dimension 1:** To examine issues of (8) _____, (9) _____, and (10) _____ significance;
• **Dimension 2:** Understand and appreciate the (11) _____ and (12) _____ of others;
• **Dimension 3:** (13) _____ in open, appropriate, and effective (14) _____ across cultures;
• **Dimension 4:** Take action for (15) _____ well-being and sustainable development.

Task 2

Directions: *Please read the text again and decide whether the following statements are true (T) or false (F) based on what you have learned from the text.*

_____ 1. Developing global competence is a one-time process that doesn't extend throughout an individual's life.

_____ 2. Global competence involves only specific skills that are applied in face-to-face interactions.

_____ 3. The definition of "competence" in the context of global competence includes skills in not only face-to-face but also virtual or mediated encounters.

_____ 4. Ethno-cultural conflicts have diminished since the end of the Cold War.

_____ 5. Young people's digital lives can lead them to disconnect from themselves and the world, potentially overlooking the impact of their actions on others.

_____ 6. Developing global competence is not linked to cultivating an understanding of human rights, gender equality, and global citizenship.

_____ 7. Individuals with a mature level of development demonstrate higher-order thinking skills by selecting and weighing appropriate evidence to reason about global developments.

_____ 8. Globally competent individuals, as highlighted in the text, primarily focus on their own perspectives without considering the viewpoints of others.

_____ 9. Individuals with global competence in Dimension 3 possess the ability to comprehend cultural norms, interactive styles, and levels of formality in intercultural contexts.

_____ 10. The four dimensions of global competence are independent of each other, and their interdependence does not justify the use of the singular term "global competence".

Task 3

Directions: *Please translate the following five sentences into English using the words or phrases in the parentheses.*

1. 这个国际合作项目需要我们集体的智慧和经验，以应对全球性挑战。（collective）
2. 在跨文化交流中，不同文化的习惯和价值观是相联系的。（interconnect）
3. 学生们的国际化体验可能会对他们未来的职业生涯产生深远的影响。（implication）
4. 在国际胜任力的养成中，培养一种开放、灵活的性情对于成功的跨文化交流至关重要。（disposition）
5. 在培养国际胜任力的过程中，我们需要审视各种文化之间的差异，以更好地促进全球理解和合作。（take stock of）

Task 4

Directions: *Please discuss the following questions in groups and role-play the following situation with your solution.*

> **Situation**
>
> Jo and Ai are collaborating on a school project with a student from another country, Mike. The students set up a video chat on a web platform to have a brainstorm, but at the convened time for the meeting, they find Mike online. When, a few hours later, the students manage to connect on the web platform, Jo complains that not showing up at the first meeting is not a good way to start, and gets angry when she receives no explanation at all from Mike, who remains silent on the other end of the line.
>
> ...

1. Which dimension of global competence does this story relate to?
2. Suppose you were the student Ai in this story, how would you solve this problem? Work out a solution with your group member and perform the entire situation.

Text B Developing Global Competence

Warm-up

Directions: *Look at the curriculum below and talk about which course you'd like to take to enhance your global competence. Give your opinions on your choices.*

Curriculum for College Students	
Course 1: World Cultures and Geography • Overview of the concept of global competence • Exploration of the importance of intercultural skills in today's world	**Course 6: Psychology and Sociology** • Introduction to basic concepts in psychology and sociology • Exploration of topics such as cognition, emotion, motivation, and behavior
Course 2: Fundamentals of Science and Mathematics • Core principles of science and mathematics • Developing analytical thinking and problem-solving skills	**Course 7: Introduction to Computer Science** • Basic concepts in computer science and technology • Understanding the binary system, data representation, and computer architecture
Course 3: Chinese Composition and Literature • Development of writing and analytical skills • Insights into the classical and contemporary Chinese literature	**Course 8: Global Economics and Trade** • Introduction to global economic systems and international trade • Understanding the impact of economic policies on different regions
Course 4: Language Communication in a Global Context • Introduction to the role of language in cross-cultural communication • Practical exercises to enhance language skills and intercultural communication	**Course 9: Cross-Cultural Experiences (Internship/Study Abroad)** • Practical application of global competence in a real-world setting • Reflection on experiences and challenges encountered during the internship or study abroad

(Continued)

Curriculum for College Students	
Course 5: Global Challenges and Sustainable Development • Analysis of major global challenges (e.g., climate change, poverty) • Exploration of sustainable development goals and initiatives	**Course 10: Capstone Project: Cultivating Global Competence** • Integrative project where students apply knowledge and skills gained • Presentation and reflection on personal growth in global competence

Developing Global Competence[1]

❶ What are universities actually doing to **instill** global competence in students, especially engineering students? In the U.S., a number of universities have developed international programs designed to prepare students to live and work in the global context of the 21st century, although most do not specifically mention global competence as a goal. These programs fall into four categories: co-majors or **dual** majors, **minors** or **certificates**, international internships or projects or study abroad. A number of these programs are open to students in any **discipline** but may be difficult for engineers to complete given the number of courses required outside the students' majors.

Co-majors or Dual Majors

❷ Students earn the **equivalent** of two bachelor's degrees, one in engineering and the other in liberal arts or international studies. The University of Rhode Island offers a five-year dual degree program in engineering and language (German, French or Spanish). In addition to meeting the requirements for the language and engineering degrees, students spend an academic year outside the U.S., either on an internship, studying at an exchange university or **undertaking** a combination of study and internship. Among all universities, the Rhode Island program provides the most **extensive** language study, the study of another culture (through advanced language courses), and the longest period of study overseas. However, this comprehensiveness comes at the cost of requiring an additional year of study. Moreover, there appears to be little **linkage** between the international study and the student's engineering major. The other co-majors (Penn State University and Iowa State University) involve taking ten courses outside of the

---

[1] The text was adapted from Lohmann, J., Rollins, H., & Hoey, J. 2006. Defining, developing and assessing global competence in engineers. *European Journal of Engineering Education*, *31*: 119–131.

major, including second language study and coursework in international studies. Penn State University requires minimal international experience (nine weeks), whereas Iowa State University requires none.

Minors or Certificates

❸ Two universities offer an international minor in engineering (the University of Illinois and the University of Michigan). Both programs require significant second language learning, two or three international courses, and a period of study or work (**minimum** six or eight weeks) outside the country. The University of Pittsburgh offers a global studies certificate designed to instill global competence through second language learning and international coursework, but with no international experience.

International Experience

❹ A number of universities place **exclusive** emphasis on international experience. Both Penn State University and Worcester Polytechnic Institute offer students well-developed international projects. In Penn State's Prestige **Consortium** students spend a semester overseas. They **collaborate** on a four-week design project with peers at European partner universities and then spend an additional four to eight weeks on internships. In the Global Perspective Program, Worcester Polytechnic Institute offers its engineering students a seven-week overseas project design course that **immerses** the students in the host country, designing solutions to local problems. Finally, the University of Minnesota has focused on integrating study abroad into engineering and other disciplines.

❺ All of these programs are commendable and represent pioneering efforts at international education for engineers. However, some of these programs omit one or more of the three components of global competency (language **proficiency**, international coursework and international experience) and others place differing emphases on the three elements. Some programs, especially the co-majors, may delay graduation for engineering students. Many of the programs require language learning and international coursework but do not tie these elements intentionally to the student's discipline.

❻ Georgia Institute of Technology also offers similar programs, however, it has recently launched a new **initiative**, called the International Plan, which is designed to go well beyond the traditional approaches to instill global competence. This program, designed for completion within four years, includes the three components **deemed** essential for global competence: coursework in international studies, language proficiency, and an **immersive** international experience. A **hallmark** of this program, and one that sets it apart from other programs, is that it is integrated into the student's disciplinary studies. Participants gain an appreciation for how cultural context affects the practice of the discipline. Successful participants receive a **designation** on their diploma and transcript **signifying** the depth and breadth of their global competence in the discipline (i.e. Bachelor of Science in Electrical Engineering: International Plan). Participating units then **tailor** their degree programs within this framework of requirements.

❼ Successful students must satisfy three requirements to earn the International Plan designation.

❽ First, students must complete four courses in international studies, choosing one course from each of the three general categories plus a **culminating** course. The three categories are international relations, global economics, and a course with an emphasis on a country or region. The three categories of courses provide both an academic foundation and a context to complement the international experience. The culminating course, which occurs either at the end of or after the international experience, integrates and brings to **closure** knowledge of the discipline and the international experience in a global context. The culminating course is offered by the student's major department or in **collaboration** with other departments.

❾ Second, participants must demonstrate second language proficiency. Students are expected to reach the proficiency level equivalent to two years of college-level language study. Proficiency is determined by an individually administered standardized test. Students who elect to study in a country whose primary language is not English will use the second language to study, work or conduct research and, therefore, are expected to meet a higher proficiency level in the second language.

❿ Finally, participants must engage in a significant international experience consisting of two terms (a minimum of 26 weeks) of international experience, which must be characterized by living among and immersed within the local academic, research or work **community**. The terms may consist of any combination of academic study, internship or research. Academic study may occur at one of Georgia Institute of Technology's overseas campuses, at an international partner institution or in a **faculty**-directed residential program.

⓫ Each academic discipline tailors the program to meet the specific needs of that discipline, such as the location and type of international experience and the nature of the culminating course. This approach not only makes the program particularly relevant to students in that discipline, it also enables the faculty in each discipline to take ownership of the International Plan and to feel comfortable recommending the plan to its majors.

(1,005 words)

Glossary

instill	/ɪnˈstɪl/	v.	逐渐灌输
dual	/ˈdjuːəl/	adj.	双重的
minor	/ˈmaɪnə(r)/	n.	辅修课程
certificate	/səˈtɪfɪkət/	n.	证明书；结业证书
discipline	/ˈdɪsəplɪn/	n.	（尤指大学的）学科，科目
equivalent	/ɪˈkwɪvələnt/	adj.	相同的；相等的
undertake	/ˌʌndəˈteɪk/	v.	从事；承担
extensive	/ɪkˈstensɪv/	adj.	广泛的
linkage	/ˈlɪŋkɪdʒ/	n.	联系
minimum	/ˈmɪnɪməm/	n.	最小量；最低限度
exclusive	/ɪkˈskluːsɪv/	adj.	专用的，专有的；独占的
consortium	/kənˈsɔːtiəm/	n.	联盟
collaborate	/kəˈlæbəreɪt/	v.	合作，协作
immerse	/ɪˈmɜːs/	v.	使专心于
proficiency	/prəˈfɪʃnsi/	n.	水平
initiative	/ɪˈnɪʃətɪv/	n.	倡议
deem	/diːm/	v.	认为；相信
immersive	/ɪˈmɜːsɪv/	adj.	拟真的；沉浸式的
hallmark	/ˈhɔːlmɑːk/	n.	标志；特征
designation	/ˌdezɪɡˈneɪʃn/	n.	名称；头衔
signify	/ˈsɪɡnɪfaɪ/	v.	表示；意味着
tailor	/ˈteɪlə(r)/	v.	定做；定制；使适应
culminate	/ˈkʌlmɪneɪt/	v.	以……告终；结果成为
closure	/ˈkləʊʒə(r)/	n.	结尾
collaboration	/kəˌlæbəˈreɪʃn/	n.	合作
community	/kəˈmjuːnəti/	n.	社区；社会；团体
faculty	/ˈfæklti/	n.	全体教员；（高等院校的）系，院

Unit 1 Global Competence

Task 1

Directions: *Please read the text and fill in the blanks in the summary.*

The article explores how universities, particularly in (1) _____, are addressing the instillation of global competence in students, with a focus on (2) _____ students. Various international programs are categorized into co-majors or (3) _____ majors, minors or (4) _____, international internships or projects, and study abroad. These (5) _____ aim to prepare students for the global context of the 21st century, emphasizing language (6) _____, international coursework, and experiences abroad. While commendable, the article highlights differences in program components and potential (7) _____ in graduation for engineering students. Notably, Georgia Institute of Technology's (8) _____ stands out for its integrated approach, requiring coursework in international studies, language proficiency, and a(n) (9) _____ international experience within disciplinary studies. Successful participants receive a(n) (10) _____ reflecting their global competence on their diploma and transcript.

Task 2

Directions: *Please read the text again and match the global competence approaches in Column B with universities in Column A. You may use one letter more than once.*

Column A

1. the University of Rhode Island
2. Penn State University
3. Iowa State University
4. the University of Illinois
5. the University of Michigan

Column B

a. Includes a period of study or work (minimum six or eight weeks) outside the country.

b. Offers a global studies certificate designed to instill global competence through second language learning and international coursework, but with no international experience.

c. Requires two or three international courses.

d. Co-majors involve taking ten courses outside the major, including second-language study and coursework in international studies.

e. Offers a seven-week overseas project design course.

6. the University of Pittsburgh	f. Involves co-majors requiring ten courses outside the major, including second-language study and international studies.
7. Worcester Polytechnic Institute	g. Offers the International Plan, designed for completion within four years.
8. the University of Minnesota	h. Offers a five-year dual degree in engineering and language (German, French or Spanish).
9. Georgia Institute of Technology	i. Focuses on integrating study abroad into engineering and other disciplines.

Task 3

***Directions**: Please translate the following paragraph into English using the words in the parentheses.*

在大学教育中，学校逐步教授给（instill）学生双重的（dual）知识体系，使他们能够从事（undertake）全球范围的合作与交流。学校认为，国际视野能够使学生在跨文化（cross-cultural）环境中具有更高的适应性，从而最终成长为具有卓越国际胜任力的优秀人才。

Task 4

***Directions**: Please debate on the following topic. You are encouraged to refer to other sources for the debate. You can use the following table to help you organize ideas.*

Topic: Should universities integrate global competence into the curriculum for their students?

Pros	Cons

Part II Drilling for GC Skills

How to Communicate Effectively in Cross-Cultural Contexts (I)

1. Importance of Cross-Cultural Communication

In today's interconnected world, the ability to communicate effectively across diverse cultural landscapes is not just a valuable skill; it is an essential competency. As global interactions become increasingly prevalent in **academic**, **professional**, and **personal** spheres, we find ourselves engaging with people from different backgrounds, beliefs, and communication styles. Cross-cultural communication is more than the mere exchange of words; it is a complex interplay of **languages**, **customs**, and **expectations** that shape the way we connect with others. The ability to bridge cultural gaps has become a hallmark of competence and success.

Example 1 Collaborating on academic projects

As an engineering student, I worked on a research project with peers from India, Brazil, and Japan. Our diverse backgrounds brought unique perspectives to the table. While discussing sustainable energy solutions, my Indian teammate's insights on solar innovations, the Brazilian perspective on bioenergy, and the Japanese approach to efficiency created a rich tapestry of ideas. Navigating cultural nuances in communication became integral to our success, fostering an environment where each voice contributed to a holistic and innovative research outcome.

Example 2 Navigating international business negotiations

As a business consultant, I led negotiations between a European technology firm and an Asian manufacturing company. Understanding cultural differences was paramount. While the European team favored a direct and assertive approach, the Asian counterparts valued harmony and indirect communication. By incorporating both styles, we fostered a collaborative atmosphere. Delicate topics were addressed tactfully, and compromises were reached through consensus-building.

Example 3 Fostering meaningful interpersonal relationships

As a student in an international exchange program, I forged deep connections with classmates from diverse backgrounds. Sharing meals, traditions, and personal stories allowed us to transcend cultural barriers. Our differences became sources of enrichment rather than obstacles. Through active listening and mutual respect, friendships blossomed, creating a supportive network that extended beyond the academic realm.

Task 1

Directions: *Please decide whether the following statements are true (T) or false (F).*

_____ 1. Cross-cultural communication involves only the exchange of words and does not encompass languages, customs, and expectations.

_____ 2. Effective communication across diverse cultural landscapes is considered a valuable skill but not an essential competency.

_____ 3. The complexity of cross-cultural communication lies solely in language differences and not in customs or expectations.

_____ 4. Global interactions are decreasing in prevalence in academic, professional, and personal spheres.

_____ 5. The capacity to connect across cultures is recognized as a key indicator of both competence and success.

Task 2

Directions: *Please reflect on the three examples and answer the questions below.*

Example 1: Have you ever worked on an academic project with peers from diverse backgrounds (for example, ethnic groups, another country or another province in China?) If so, how did cultural differences impact the collaboration?

_____
_____
_____

Example 2: Can you think of a scenario where you might need to navigate international business negotiations? How would you approach it?

_____
_____
_____

Example 3: What elements contributed to the creation of meaningful interpersonal relationships in the provided example?

_____

_____

_____

Task 3

Directions: *Please discuss the following two questions in pairs or groups. You may refer to resources outside the textbook.*

1. Why is effective cross-cultural communication considered an essential competency in today's globalized world?
2. In what ways does cross-cultural communication go beyond language proficiency?

2. Ways for Effective Cross-Cultural Communication

Cultural Sensitivity
• Being culturally sensitive involves understanding and respecting the nuances of different cultures. It requires awareness of cultural **norms**, **values**, and **customs**, enabling individuals to communicate with empathy and avoid unintentional misunderstandings.
Active Listening
• Actively listening to others involves not just hearing words but understanding the underlying **emotions**, **context**, and **cultural nuances**. It promotes a deeper connection and helps in grasping the complete message being conveyed.
Adaptability
• Successful cross-cultural communicators are adaptable. They are open to adjusting their communication **style**, **language**, and **behavior** to suit the cultural context, fostering smoother interactions.
Non-verbal Communication Awareness
• Non-verbal cues such as **gestures**, **facial expressions**, and **body language** vary across cultures. Being aware of these cues ensures that communication is not solely reliant on words, preventing misinterpretations.
Building Trust
• Trust is a foundation for effective communication. Building trust involves demonstrating **reliability**, **sincerity**, and a **genuine interest** in understanding others, creating a conducive environment for open dialogs.

(Continued)

Clarity and Simplicity

- Clear and simple communication is essential, especially when language differences exist. Avoiding jargon and using **straightforward language** enhances comprehension and reduces the risk of confusion.

Cultural Humility

- Cultural humility involves recognizing that one's cultural knowledge is limited and being open to continuous learning. It encourages a **humble** and **respectful** approach, fostering positive cross-cultural interactions.

Example 1

Liang, a Chinese exchange student in the United States, attended a casual gathering at a friend's house. Not familiar with the custom of bringing a small gift or dish to such events, Liang arrived empty-handed. Liang's hosts, though polite, noticed the absence of a gift and were surprised.

Example 2

In a global non-profit organization, Emily, a senior executive from a Western country, is overseeing a project with team members from various cultural backgrounds, including East Asian and African countries. In team meetings, Emily consistently disregards the input of her colleagues. She interrupts others frequently and makes the final decision all by herself.

Task 4

Directions: *Please read Example 1 and reflect on the impact of cultural norms in social situations. Answer the following questions.*

1. What is the cultural difference highlighted in this example?

___

___

2. What strategies can individuals like Liang employ to adapt to cultural norms in a new or unfamiliar social environment?

___

___

3. Do you know other norms around gift-giving across different cultures?

_____

_____

Task 5

Directions: *Please read Example 2 and analyze the cross-cultural challenges in this scenario.*

Working in a Multi-Cultural Team
Specific behavior of Emily   • _____   • _____   • _____
Potential cultural differences among the team   • _____   • _____
Consequences of Emily's behavior   • _____   • _____   • _____
Possible solutions   • _____   • _____

3. Zooming in

Hand Gestures Around the World[1]

The meanings of hand gestures and body language in various countries and cultures

---

1 This article was adapted from Crislip, K. 2022. Hand gestures in the world with more than one meaning. Retrieved from the Tripsavvy website.

may differ from your expectations. Check out the different meanings of the same hand and body gestures.

- **OK Sign**

For instance, an OK sign in the United States is a circle made with the thumb and the forefinger. In parts of Europe, it could mean that the person to whom you're making the gesture is a big fat zero. In Brazil, it could mean something really rude. And in some countries, the number three could be signified by a gesture that looks similar to the OK sign.

- **Pointing Finger**

In the early 2000s, a pointing finger came to be an affectionate gesture in the U.S.: sort of a "Yeah, you, you're cool." Previously, it had been perceived everywhere as a marginally rude gesture, though it was occasionally used to great effect in advertising (for example, "Uncle Sam Wants You"). It's not polite at all, to anyone in the Middle and the Far East (use an open hand to point when you're in that neighborhood). Which countries find it most offensive? China, Japan, Indonesia, and Latin America. And in many African countries, you should also only point at an inanimate object and never at humans.

- **Loser Sign**

Should you be lucky enough to travel to China, know that the vendor at that street stall is not telling you that you're a loser for playing it safe with the onion pancakes. No, the vendor's telling you what it costs... and it has to do with the number eight (two fingers up, and ten fingers minus eight fingers is two). From there, you're on your own—just don't feel offended by the gesture.

- **Thumbs Up**

Although we haven't personally had too much trouble with the thumbs up, we've got a friend who swears she supremely dissed a shopkeeper in West Africa with a thumbs-up sign. After asking around a bit, we learned that in some parts of the world, it means to sit on the thumb. And possibly spin. Again, better off with the enthusiastic smile to indicate that all is well. It's not just West Africa, though. The thumbs-up gesture is seen as offensive across large parts of the Middle East and South America, too. If you're in the habit of throwing a thumbs up at people to express your happiness, try to quash it for any trips to the regions mentioned above.

- **Crossed Fingers**

The crossed-fingers sign is most commonly used by Americans as a hopeful sign that beckons good luck. If one were wishing for something to happen, crossing your fingers would be the usual way to convey it. In Vietnam, however, the gesture means something very different. Crossed fingers are often construed as a rude way to refer to a part of the female anatomy. Using this gesture would be considered vulgar and disrespectful.

- **Peace Sign**

The peace sign seems so universal to us, but what is widely accepted in the U.S. can be seen as offensive in other countries around the world. The two fingers held aloft in a V are fine provided your palm is facing out, but in some countries—namely, Australia, New Zealand, and the United Kingdom—it's an insult of the first order if you make the same gesture but with your palm facing inward. In other words, you don't order two beers in an English pub by holding up two fingers with your palm facing you unless you want to get in a bit of a brawl. In fairness, it's not likely to offend many people these days, but could be taken the wrong way, so it is best to use carefully and not at all if possible. And to some (mostly to older generations), two fingers held up with the palm facing out means V for victory—hard to insult anyone with that sentiment, but you may find yourself rather misunderstood.

Task 5

Directions: *Please decide whether the following statements are true (T) or false (F).*

_____ 1. The OK sign made with the thumb and forefinger has the same meaning across all countries.

_____ 2. In parts of Europe, the OK sign could mean that the person is a big fat zero.

_____ 3. Pointing with a finger is considered a polite gesture in Middle Eastern and Far Eastern cultures.

_____ 4. The loser sign in China indicates that someone is considered a failure.

_____ 5. Thumbs up is universally accepted as a positive gesture.

_____ 6. The thumbs-up gesture is universally accepted as positive in West Africa.

_____ 7. Crossing fingers is universally understood as a hopeful sign.

_____ 8. The peace sign made with the palm facing inward is considered an insult in Australia, New Zealand, and the United Kingdom.

Task 6

Directions: *Please look at the following hand gestures and summarize their meanings in different regions. For places not specified in the introduction above, you may refer to resources outside the textbook.*

Hand Gestures	East Asia	Middle and Far East	America	Europe	Australia and New Zealand

Task 7

Directions: *Please discuss the following questions in groups. You are encouraged to refer to other sources for the discussion.*

1. How might a simple gesture like the thumbs up be perceived differently in various regions, and what challenges could this pose in cross-cultural communication?

2. How would you adapt your non-verbal communication, specifically hand gestures, to ensure respectful and effective communication? What steps could you take to avoid unintentionally causing offense?

Part III Notes from China

Ancient Chinese Philosophy and Global Competence[1]

One of the major things I notice as I visit and work with world language programs all around the country is how important it is that schools actively recognize the vital link between language learning and a broader agenda of global competence for students.

I see a lot of language programs that essentially exist as a class within a school building, and not much more outside of that classroom. I also see programs—the most successful and dynamic programs—that consistently make connections for students between what they are doing as second language learners and what they are doing in their courses of other subject areas, and in their life beyond school. We often think of making these connections—understanding multiple perspectives and negotiating meaning and understanding across different languages and cultures—as core parts of global competence. For many educators, this is a new paradigm. For others, it resonates with what they have been doing in their entire careers. And for some, there may be faint echoes of earlier traditions of thought and practice.

For me, having spent a good bit of my graduate school years studying ancient East and South Asian texts, the concept of global competence is in some ways a very Confucian notion. One of the texts that forms an important part of the Confucian tradition in East Asia is *The Great Learning* (《大学》), one of "The Four Books" ("四书") that forms part of the Song Dynasty Confucian canon, and was the basis for education in imperial China. In grad school, I remember having to recite and write from memory a famous passage from the text that talks about the root of a well-ordered society being the cultivation (and education) of the individual. I would like to revive this passage for a new generation as a Confucian counterpart to the profile of a globally competent learner.

The text reads as follows:

古之欲明明德于天下者，先治其国；

---

[1] This article was adapted from Livaccari, C. 2024. Is global competence a new idea? Retrieved from the Asiasociety website.

欲治其国，先齐其家；
欲齐其家，先修其身；
欲修其身者，先正其心；
欲正其心者，先诚其意；
欲诚其意者，先致其知；
致知在格物。

Just as our current definition of global competence, the basis for self-cultivation here lies in one's investigation of the world.

Of course, the Confucians did not understand a "global" world in the exact same sense that we do today. But their call to investigate the world was uttered in the same spirit as our own to students today. What we might call "recognizing the perspectives of others" might well relate to the Confucian value of making one's intentions sincere. Communication and action are inherent in this paradigm, as the connection is made explicitly between self-cultivation and managing households and states.

Just like global competence for our students today, this Confucian text presents the individual's self-cultivation through investigating the world as the basis for a harmonious and productive society. And while our current definition of global competence may not sing with the elegant terseness of classical Chinese, I think it's a notion that Confucius, Mencius, Zhu Xi, and all the other famous Confucian thinkers throughout history would clearly have recognized.

(565 words)

Directions: *Please read the text and share your thoughts on global competence and Chinese philosophy. The following tips may help you.*

My Thoughts on Global Competence
Tip 1: Please find out the translated version of the Confucian text cited in this article. Or you can try to give your own version of translation.
Tip 2: Do you agree that the idea of global competence is closely related to Chinese philosophy?
Tip 3: Can you think of or find out other Chinese traditional texts that encompass the elements of global competence? What are they? You can share them with your classmates.

Global Peace and the UN

Part I Reading for GC Knowledge

Text A The United Nations and Its Duties

Warm-up

Self-Assessment of Common Knowledge of the UN

Directions: *Please rate yourself on a scale of 1 to 5, where 1 = Strongly Disagree; 2 = Disagree; 3 = Neutral; 4 = Agree; 5 = Strongly Agree. Then discuss the questions that follow.*

Self-Assessment Questionnaire	Scale				
Cultural Awareness					
I know completely about the UN's nature and goals.	1	2	3	4	5
I know well about how much effort the UN has taken to resolve the global issues.	1	2	3	4	5
I am aware of the activities the UN has undertaken to solve some specific issues.	1	2	3	4	5
Africa Issue					
I know what major challenges Africa is facing.	1	2	3	4	5
I know what the UN has done to alleviate the problems striking Africa.	1	2	3	4	5
I know what China has done to help the development of Africa.	1	2	3	4	5
Aging Issue					
I am aware of the population aging problems in the world.	1	2	3	4	5
I am aware of the population aging problems in China.	1	2	3	4	5
I know what actions the UN has taken to handle the global population aging problems.	1	2	3	4	5
Atomic Energy Issue					
I am knowledgeable about the atomic energy issue.	1	2	3	4	5

(Continued)

Self-Assessment Questionnaire	Scale				
I know the International Atomic Energy Agency's role in securing peaceful development of nuclear energy	1	2	3	4	5
I know what China has done to develop safe atomic energy.	1	2	3	4	5

1. Based on your self-assessment, what is the most significant role the UN plays in international affairs?

2. Considering your score, would you say that you possess a relatively comprehensive knowledge of the UN?

3. Do you know any Chinese people who worked or are currently working in the UN system?

The United Nations and Its Duties

❶ As the world's only truly **universal** global organization, the United Nations has become the foremost **forum** to address issues that **transcend** national boundaries and cannot be resolved by any one country acting alone.

❷ To its initial goals of safeguarding peace, protecting human rights, establishing the framework for international **justice** and promoting economic and social progress, in the seven decades since its creation, the United Nations has added on new challenges, such as AIDS, big data, and climate change.

❸ While conflict resolution and peacekeeping continue to be among its most visible efforts, the UN, along with its specialized agencies, is also engaged in a wide **array** of activities to improve people's lives around the world—from disaster **relief**, through education and advancement of women, to peaceful uses of atomic energy.

❹ Through its unique capacities as the world's premier vehicle for international cooperation, the UN system plays a crucial role in **coordinating** assistance of all kinds—to help Africa help itself. From promoting the development of democratic institutions, to establishing peace between warring nations, the UN is present on the ground supporting economic and social development.

❺ In this effort, the UN works closely with Africa's regional cooperation **mechanisms** and has five active peacekeeping operations at present. UN peacekeepers serve in the Central African Republic (MINUSCA), the Democratic Republic of the Congo

(MONUSCO), Western Sahara (MINURSO), South Sudan (UNMISS), and in the disputed Abyei area (UNISFA). To advance its support for Africa even further, the United Nations Office of the Special Adviser on Africa was established in 2003 to enhance international support for African development and security and to improve the **coordination** of UN system support. It also works to **facilitate** global deliberations on Africa, particularly with respect to the New **Partnership** for Africa's Development (NEPAD)—a strategic framework adopted by African leaders in 2001. In 2018, NEPAD's **mandate** was reformed and transformed into the African Union Development Agency-NEPAD (AUDA-NEPAD). It is now serving as the first development agency of the African Union.

❻ Africa Day is an annual commemoration of the establishment of the Organization of African Unity (OAU) on May 25, 1963. On that day, 32 independent African states signed the founding charter in Addis Ababa, Ethiopia. In 2002, the OAU became the African Union. Africa Day is celebrated around the world.

Aging Problems

❼ The world's population is aging. Virtually every country in the world is experiencing growth in the number and proportion of older persons in their population.

❽ Population aging is poised to become one of the most significant social **transformations** of the 21st century, with implications for nearly all sectors of society, including labor and financial markets, the demand for goods and services, such as housing, transportation, and social protection, as well as family structures and intergenerational ties.

❾ Older people are increasingly seen as **contributors** to development, whose abilities to act for the betterment of themselves and their societies should be woven into policies and programs at all levels. In the coming decades, many countries are likely to face fiscal and political pressures in relation to public systems of healthcare, **pensions**, and social protections for a growing older population.

❿ According to the World Population Prospects 2022, the population above the age of 65 is growing more rapidly than the population below that age.

⓫ The proportion of people aged 65 and above is increasing at a faster rate than those below that age. This means that the percentage of the global population aged 65 and above is expected to rise from 10% in 2022 to 16% in 2050. It is projected that by 2050, the number of individuals aged 65 years or above across the world will be twice the number of children under age five and almost equivalent to the number of children under 12 years old.

⓬ To begin addressing these issues, the General Assembly convened the first World

Assembly on Aging in 1982, which produced a 62-point Vienna International Plan of Action on Aging. It called for specific action on such issues as health and **nutrition**, protecting elderly consumers, housing and environment, family, social welfare, income security and employment, education, and the collection and analysis of research data.

⑬ In 1991, the General Assembly adopted the United Nations Principles for Older Persons, enumerating 18 entitlements for older persons—relating to independence, participation, care, self-fulfillment, and dignity. The following year, the International Conference on Aging met to follow up on the Plan of Action, adopting a **Proclamation** on Aging. Following the Conference's recommendation, the UN General Assembly declared 1999 the International Year of Older Persons. The International Day of Older Persons is celebrated on the 1st of October every year.

⑭ Action on behalf of the aging continued in 2002 when the Second World Assembly on Aging was held in Madrid. Aiming to design international policy on aging for the 21st century, it adopted a Political Declaration and the Madrid International Plan of Action on Aging. The Plan of Action called for changes in attitudes, policies, and practices at all levels to fulfill the enormous potential of aging in the 21st century. Its specific recommendations for action give **priority** to older persons and development, advancing health and well-being into old age, and ensuring enabling and supportive environments.

Nuclear Issues

⑮ The UN and the nuclear age were born almost **simultaneously**. The horror of the Second World War, culminating in the nuclear blasts in Hiroshima and Nagasaki, brought home the need to address the nuclear issue. By its first resolution, the General Assembly established the UN Atomic Energy Commission to deal with the problems raised by the discovery of atomic energy. And a landmark address by the United States President Dwight D. Eisenhower in 1953, "Atoms for Peace", led to the establishment in 1957 of the International Atomic Energy Agency (IAEA).

⑯ The International Atomic Energy Agency works with its member states and multiple partners worldwide to promote the safe, secure, and peaceful use of nuclear technologies. The IAEA's relationship with the United Nations is guided by an agreement signed in 1957. It **stipulates** that: "The Agency undertakes to conduct its activities in accordance with the Purposes and Principles of the United Nations Charter to promote peace and international cooperation, and in **conformity** with policies of the United Nations furthering the establishment of safeguarded worldwide disarmament and in conformity with any international agreements entered into **pursuant** to such policies."

⑰ As of 2023, 32 countries worldwide are operating 413 nuclear reactors for electricity generation and 58 new nuclear plants are under construction. By the end of 2022, 12 countries relied on nuclear energy to supply at least one-quarter of their total electricity. In France and Slovakia, nuclear power even makes up more than half of the total electricity production.

⑱ Nuclear safety is the responsibility of every nation that utilizes nuclear technology. The IAEA, through the Department of Nuclear Safety and Security, works to provide a strong, sustainable, and visible global nuclear safety and security framework for the protection of people, society, and the environment. This framework provides for the harmonized development and application of safety and security standards, guidelines and requirements, but it does not have the mandate to enforce the application of safety standards within a country.

(1,187 words)

 Glossary

universal	/ˌjuːnɪˈvɜːsl/	adj.	全体的，普遍的
forum	/ˈfɔːrəm/	n.	论坛，讨论会
transcend	/trænˈsend/	v.	超越，超过
justice	/ˈdʒʌstɪs/	n.	正义，公正
array	/əˈreɪ/	n.	一长列（物品）
relief	/rɪˈliːf/	n.	救济；解救，解围
coordinate	/kəʊˈɔːdɪneɪt/	v.	使协调，使调和
mechanism	/ˈmekənɪzəm/	n.	机制；方法
coordination	/kəʊˌɔːdɪˈneɪʃn/	n.	协作；协调；配合
facilitate	/fəˈsɪlɪteɪt/	v.	促进；使便利；促使
partnership	/ˈpɑːtnəʃɪp/	n.	伙伴；合伙公司
mandate	/ˈmændeɪt/	n.	授权；强制执行；委托办理
transformation	/ˌtrænsfəˈmeɪʃn/	n.	（彻底的）变化，转变
contributor	/kənˈtrɪbjətə(r)/	n.	做出贡献者
pension	/ˈpenʃn/	n.	养老金，退休金
nutrition	/njuˈtrɪʃn/	n.	营养；滋养
proclamation	/ˌprɒkləˈmeɪʃn/	n.	宣言；公告；声明
priority	/praɪˈɒrəti/	n.	优先事项，首要事情
simultaneously	/ˌsɪmlˈteɪniəsli/	adv.	同时；联立

stipulate	/ˈstɪpjuleɪt/	v.	规定；明确要求
conformity	/kənˈfɔːməti/	n.	一致性；（对社会规则的）遵守
pursuant	/pəˈsjuːənt/	adj./adv.	依照（的），按照（尤指规则或法律）（的）

Task 1

Directions: *Please read the text and fill in the blanks in the summary.*

> This article introduces the UN as a truly (1) _____ global organization, which plays a significant role in solving the problems of Africa, handling the challenges of population aging and dealing with atomic energy problems. The UN, along with its specialized (2) _____, makes full efforts to improve the people's lives around the world. With Africa in particular, the UN established the UN Office of the Special Adviser on Africa to (3) _____ international support for African development and security, as well as to improve (4) _____ of UN system support. Population aging is poised to be one of the most important social (5) _____ of the 21st century, affecting all sectors of society. Faced with the increasing percentage of global population aged 65 and above, the UN called for (6) _____ actions on issues concerning health and nutrition to protect elderly people. The UN and nuclear age were born (7) _____. To (8) _____ the peaceful and safe use of atomic energy, UN Atomic Energy Commission and the International Atomic Energy Agency (IAEA) were established. IAEA, together with its member states and multiple (9) _____, secures the peaceful use of atomic energy. So far, there is more demand for nuclear reactors for electricity generation. Therefore, nuclear safety is the responsibility of all nations (10) _____ nuclear technology.

Task 2

Directions: *Please read the text again and decide whether the following statements are true (T) or false (F) based on what you have learned from the text.*

_____ 1. The UN, as the major coordinator of multiple special agencies, mainly assists international efforts to improve people's lives around the world.

_____ 2. The UN, as a leading entity of international cooperation, urges African countries to take the initiative to solve their own problems.

_____ 3. With the establishment of specific agencies in Africa, the problems of African development and security can be effectively solved.

_____ 4. Population aging is regarded as a positive contributor to the progress of all sectors of society.

_____ 5. The faster growth of aging population number has set alarm to issues like health, nutrition, protecting elderly consumers, housing and environment, family, social welfare, income security, employment, education, etc.

_____ 6. The International Day of Older Persons is to highlight the problems facing an aging population.

_____ 7. Older people have enormous potential to be fulfilled which calls for changes of attitudes, policies and practices at all levels.

_____ 8. The UN takes the primary responsibility for the safe use of atomic energy, which necessitates a strong, substantial, and visible global nuclear safety and security framework.

_____ 9. The International Atomic Energy Agency takes the leading role in promoting the safe, secure, and peaceful use of nuclear technologies.

_____ 10. As the Atomic Energy framework provides authoritative guidelines and requirements for harmonized development and safe application of atomic energy, all the countries worldwide must abide by it unconditionally.

Task 3

Directions: *Please translate the following five sentences into English using the words or phrases in the parentheses.*

1. 联合国致力于维护世界公正，解决国际冲突，这一宗旨自成立以来从未改变。（justice）

2. 世界老龄人口的持续增加导致了社会结构的转型及一系列相关问题的产生。（transformation）

3. 这一国际化论坛的举办对于各国讨论和平利用核能促进全球经济发展大有裨益。（forum）

4. 减轻非洲贫困的问题必须依靠联合国协调下的相关国际组织和国家建立伙伴关系，共同努力。（coordination）

5. 世界各国在发展利用核能的同时，必须遵从联合国指定的核能安全框架以确保对人民、社会和环境的保护。（simultaneously）

Unit 2 Global Peace and the UN

Task 4

Directions: *Please discuss the following questions in groups and role-play the following situation with your solution.*

> **Situation**
>
> With the development of the economy, the longevity of some developing countries has been lengthened unprecedentedly. However, though the economy of these countries is witnessing a rising trend, its capacity to deal with the aging problem is still limited. With more people getting retired yearly, the pension burden on the government budget is becoming more serious. Meanwhile, medication for senior people also poses a profound challenge.

1. _____
2. _____

Task 5

If you were the UN Standby Advisory Council member, work out a scheme to help mitigate the aging problem facing developing countries. Your scheme is supposed to cover at least three perspectives.

Task 6

Directions: *Please debate on the following topic. You are encouraged to refer to other sources for the debate. You may use the following table to help you organize ideas.*

The UN has been making constant efforts to advance the peaceful development of atomic energy in the world. However, there are different voices questioning the use of atomic energy. Students can join the team of supporters or the team of opponents to have a debate on atomic energy use. The supporters are supposed to list all the pros of atomic energy and defend yourself. The opponents are supposed to list all the cons of atomic energy and question the supporters.

Pros	Cons

Text B The UN and the Maintenance of Global Security and Peace

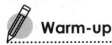
Warm-up

Directions: *Read the passage in the box and discuss the questions below.*

> **Observing the Ceasefire in Jammu and Kashmir**
>
> The first group of United Nations military observers arrived in the mission area on 24 January 1949 to supervise the ceasefire between India and Pakistan in the State of Jammu and Kashmir. These observers, under the command of the Military Adviser appointed by the UN Secretary-General, formed the nucleus of the United Nations Military Observer Group in India and Pakistan (UNMOGIP).
>
> Following renewed hostilities of 1971, UNMOGIP has remained in the area to observe developments pertaining to the strict observance of the ceasefire of 17 December 1971 and report thereon to the Secretary-General.

1. What is the typical way for the UN to secure peace in the world?
2. Apart from UNMOGIP, do you know any other military observing actions from the UN? Do you know the UN's response to the conflict in the Gaza Strip?

The UN and the Maintenance of Global Security and Peace[1]

❶ The United Nations was created in 1945, following the devastation of the Second World War, with one central **mission**: the maintenance of international peace and security. The UN accomplishes this by working to prevent conflict, helping parties in conflict make peace, **deploying** peacekeepers, and creating the conditions to allow peace to hold and **flourish**. These activities often overlap and should reinforce one another, to be effective.

Security Council

❷ The UN Security **Council** has the primary responsibility for international peace and security. The General Assembly and the Secretary-General play major, important, and complementary roles, along with other UN offices and bodies.

❸ The Security Council takes the lead in determining the existence of a threat to the peace or an act of aggression. It calls upon the parties to a dispute to settle it by peaceful

---
[1] The text was adapted from the UN official website.

means and recommends methods of adjustment or terms of settlement. Under Chapter VII of the UN Charter, the Security Council can take enforcement measures to maintain or restore international peace and security. Such measures range from economic **sanctions** to international military action. The Council also establishes UN Peacekeeping Operations and Special Political Missions.

General Assembly

❹ The General Assembly is the main deliberative, policy-making, and **representative** organ of the UN. Through regular meetings, the General Assembly provides a forum for member states to express their views to the entire membership and find **consensus** on difficult issues. It makes recommendations in the form of General Assembly resolutions. Decisions on important questions, such as those on peace and security, admission of new members and **budgetary** matters, require a two-thirds majority, but other questions are decided by a simple majority.

How Does the UN Maintain International Peace and Security?

(1) Preventive Diplomacy

❺ The Secretary-General's vision for centering the organization's work on peace and security around prevention and through a surge in **diplomacy** for peace reaffirms the United Nations' founding mission.

❻ Preventive diplomacy refers to diplomatic action taken to prevent disputes from escalating into conflicts and to limit the spread of conflicts when they occur. While it is conducted in different forms and fora, both public and private, the most common expression of preventive diplomacy is found in the work of **envoys** dispatched to crisis areas to encourage dialog, **compromise**, and the peaceful resolution of tensions. Preventive diplomacy can also encompass the involvement of the Security Council, the Secretary-General, and other actors to discourage the use of violence at critical moments.

❼ The Secretary-General provides his "good offices" to parties in conflict both personally and through the diplomatic envoys he/she dispatches to areas of tension around the world. The Department of Political and Peacebuilding Affairs (DPPA) is the principal support structure for those efforts, providing conflict analysis, planning and support to the work of peace envoys, and overseeing more than a dozen field-based political missions that serve as key platforms for preventive diplomacy. Of these missions, regional offices covering Central Africa, West Africa, and Central Asia have explicit mandates for preventive diplomacy and strengthening the capacity of states and regional actors to manage sources of tension peacefully. Preventive diplomacy is also carried out frequently within the context of peacekeeping missions.

❽ The Security Council, as the UN organ with the primary responsibility for peace and security, also has a critical role to play in supporting preventive action. Recent years have seen increased Council engagement and **flexibility** in addressing emerging threats before they come on the Council's formal agenda. Through its actions, the Council can send important signals that help discourage violence and open space for preventive action including by the Secretary-General.

❾ The work of the United Nations in conflict prevention extends well beyond traditional preventive diplomacy to involve a broad **constellation** of United Nations entities operating across a wide range of relevant disciplines—poverty **eradication** and development, human rights and the rule of law, elections and the building of democratic institutions, the control of small arms, to name just a few.

(2) Mediation

❿ Since its **inception**, the United Nations has played a crucial role in helping mediate inter- and intra-state conflicts at all stages: before they **escalate** into armed conflict, after the outbreak of violence, and during **implementation** of peace agreements. The Secretary-General and its representatives carry out good offices and mediation efforts at the request of parties to disputes, on the Secretary General's initiative, or in response to a request from the Security Council or the General Assembly. The Department of Political Affairs (DPA) was established in 1992 to assist in this work and in 2019, DPA joined forces with the Peacebuilding Support Office (PBSO) to form the new DPPA.

⓫ Successful conflict mediation requires an adequate support system to provide envoys with the proper staff assistance and advice, and to ensure that talks have the needed **logistical** and financial resources. The United Nations, led by DPPA, has moved over the past several years to sharpen its ability to provide such support to its own mediation efforts as well as to those of partner organizations.

⓬ DPPA's Mediation Support Unit (MSU), established in 2006, works closely with the Department's regional divisions to plan and support mediation efforts in the field. Among its functions, MSU provides **advisory**, financial, and logistical support to peace processes; works to strengthen the mediation capacity of regional and sub-regional organizations; and serves as a **repository** of mediation knowledge, policy and guidance, lessons learned, and best practices.

⓭ The Department manages the United Nations Standby Team of Mediation Experts— an "on-call" group of experts established in 2008 that can be deployed to assist mediators in the field. Team members have provided support in dozens of negotiations, and hold **expertise** on issues including power-sharing, natural resources and conflict, constitution-making, cease-fires and other security arrangements, and gender issues as they relate to conflict. In addition, all Standby Team experts are expected to mainstream gender considerations in all of their deployments. Standby team members have the flexibility to deploy on short notice to assist UN or non-UN mediators globally, or to provide analysis and advice remotely. Starting in 2020, the practice of remote or virtual deployments of the Standby Team was substantially expanded so as to meet the evolving needs of mediation actors. With support from donors, the Department has also established a rapid response fund to start up mediation processes at short notice. Advance planning and ready resources are a key to effective early mediation when crises are brewing.

⑭ DPPA provides backing to the High-Level Advisory Board (HLAB) on Mediation, established by Secretary-General António Guterres in September 2017. The 18 members of the HLAB—current and former global leaders, senior officials and renowned experts—back specific mediation efforts around the world with their **unparalleled** range of experience, skills, knowledge, and contacts.

⑮ DPPA also developed and maintains the online mediation support tool UN Peacemaker. Intended for peacemaking professionals, it includes an extensive database of close to 800 peace agreements, guidance material, and information on the UN's mediation support services.

(3) Peacemaking

⑯ UN peacemaking flourished in the decade following the end of the Cold War, as many longstanding armed conflicts were brought to an end through political negotiated settlements.

⑰ The organization continues to play a **preeminent** role in peacemaking, working increasingly in partnership with regional organizations in order to bring ongoing conflicts to an end, and to prevent new crises from emerging or escalating.

⑱ DPPA anchors the UN's peacemaking efforts, monitoring global political developments and advising the Secretary-General on the prevention and management of crises, including through the use of his diplomatic "good offices" to help parties in conflict settle disputes peacefully. The department provides support to numerous envoys of the Secretary-General engaged in peace talks or crisis diplomacy, while overseeing field-based United Nations special political missions with mandates to help countries and regions resolve conflicts and tensions peacefully.

(1,282 words)

Glossary

mission	/ˈmɪʃn/	n.	使命；任务
deploy	/dɪˈplɔɪ/	v.	部署，调动
flourish	/ˈflʌrɪʃ/	v.	繁荣；兴旺
council	/ˈkaʊnsl/	n.	委员会，理事会，顾问委员会
sanction	/ˈsæŋkʃn/	n.	制裁；惩罚
representative	/ˌreprɪˈzentətɪv/	n.	典型人物；代表他人者
consensus	/kənˈsensəs/	n.	共识；一致的意见
budgetary	/ˈbʌdʒɪtəri/	adj.	预算的
diplomacy	/dɪˈpləʊməsi/	n.	外交；外交手段
envoy	/ˈenvɔɪ/	n.	特使，使节
compromise	/ˈkɒmprəmaɪz/	v.	妥协，折中，和解
flexibility	/ˌfleksəˈbɪləti/	n.	灵活性，弹性，适应性
constellation	/ˌkɒnstəˈleɪʃn/	n.	一系列（相关的想法、事物）
eradication	/ɪˌrædɪˈkeɪʃn/	n.	根除
mediation	/ˌmiːdiˈeɪʃn/	n.	调解；仲裁
inception	/ɪnˈsepʃn/	n.	（机构、组织等的）开端，创始
escalate	/ˈeskəleɪt/	v.	加剧，逐步升级
implementation	/ˌɪmplɪmenˈteɪʃn/	n.	实施；执行；完成；贯彻
logistical	/ləˈdʒɪstɪkl/	adj.	物流的；后勤的；组织管理的
advisory	/ədˈvaɪzəri/	adj.	咨询的；顾问的
repository	/rɪˈpɒzətri/	n.	仓库；存放处；贮藏室；智囊
expertise	/ˌekspɜːˈtiːz/	n.	专业知识；专门技能
unparalleled	/ʌnˈpærəleld/	adj.	无与伦比的；空前的
preeminent	/priˈemɪnənt/	adj.	卓越的；优秀的

Task 1

Directions: *Please read the text and fill in the blanks below with a proper word.*

The UN and Global Security and Peace
What are the key contents of maintaining international peace and security?
• The prevention of (1) _____, helping parties in conflict make (2) _____,

(Continued)

The UN and Global Security and Peace
the deployment of (3) _____, and the creation of the conditions to (4) _____ peace.
What are the major functions of the UN Security Council?
• To determine the existing (5) _____ to peace or act of (6) _____;   • To call upon parties to dispute to solve it with (7) _____ means.   • To take enforcement measures to (8) _____ or (9) _____ international peace and security;   • To establish UN peacekeeping (10) _____ and special political mission.
What are the major functions of the General Assembly?
• To provide a(n) (11) _____ for member states to express their views and find (12) _____ on difficult issues;   • To decide upon important questions like peace and (13) _____, (14) _____ of new members and (15) _____ matters by two-thirds majority and other issues by simple majority.

Task 2

Directions: *Please read the text again and decide whether the following statements are true (T) or false (F) based on what you have learned from the text.*

_____ 1. It is impossible to solve regional or international disputes without sending envoys to the crisis area.

_____ 2. Preventive diplomacy emphasizes the peaceful solving of crises.

_____ 3. The Department of Political and Peacebuilding Affairs (DPPA) provides conflict analysis, planning, and support to the governments of countries in the crisis area to help them solve their problems.

_____ 4. The Security Council is not authorized to get engaged in a regional or international conflicts in solving emerging threat if it is not on the Council's formal agenda.

_____ 5. More UN entities are getting involved in solving problems of a wide range of disciplines, like poverty eradication, human rights and rules of law, election and building of democratic institutions, etc.

_____ 6. The UN's mediation role is most effective in the prevention of armed conflicts of intra- as well as inter-states.

_____ 7. Successful mediation requires not only staff assistance and support, but also money and transportation guarantee.

_____ 8. Stand Team of Mediation Experts plays a key role in solving diverse international conflicts.

_____ 9. With special budget allotment, the UN has established a rapid response fund to start mediation process at short notice.

_____ 10. UN peacemaking is mainly achieved through political negotiated settlement.

Task 3

Directions: *Please translate the following five sentences into English using the words or phrases in the parentheses.*

1. 在确保区域和平稳定，维系国家关系和谐方面，预防性外交是避免冲突升级和扩散的有效手段。（preventive diplomacy）
2. 向冲突地区派出使团有利于冲突各方达成妥协并以和平的方式解决紧张关系。（envoy）
3. 自联合国肇始，它就在斡旋国内与国际冲突方面起着关键作用。（inception）
4. 联合国常设调停专家组就与冲突相关的诸如分权、制宪、自然资源、停火以及性别方面的事务提出专业建议。（expertise）
5. 联合国在创造和平方面，通过不断加强与区域组织的合作，在终止冲突、预防冲突发生与升级方面扮演着至关重要的角色。（preeminent）

Task 4

Directions: *Please discuss the following questions in groups and role-play the following situation with your solution.*

> ***Situation***
>
> Country A is faced with poor educational facilities and low literacy rates, with many children lacking the opportunity to receive basic education. Meanwhile, due to the low technical level, the local agriculture heavily relies on manual labor. With children asa helping hand in the crop field, many local families are reluctant to send their children to school.

(Continued)

> ...
> If you are the envoy dispatched by the UN to this area, what actions will you take? Please work out a blueprint with the perspectives to focus on, strategies to take, the stages of the scheme execution, the fund source from which you get budgetary support, and your reaction to potential resistance to your scheme.

1. _____
2. _____

Part II Drilling for GC Skills

How to Communicate Effectively in Cross-Cultural Contexts (II)

1. Cultural Stereotypes and Bias

Cultural stereotypes and bias are central to understanding and navigating cross-cultural communication effectively. A cultural stereotype is a widely held but simplified and generalized belief about a particular group of people or culture. These stereotypes are often based on oversimplifications and can be positive, negative, or neutral, but they tend to lack nuance and do not reflect the complex realities of individuals within these groups. Cultural bias, on the other hand, is the inclination or prejudice for or against one person or group, especially in a way considered to be unfair. It stems from an individual's background, cultural environment, and personal experiences, influencing judgment and behaviors unconsciously.

Example 1   All Asians are good at math.

This stereotype assumes that individuals of Asian descent inherently possess superior mathematical skills. While seemingly positive, it places undue pressure on Asian individuals and overlooks their diverse talents and interests outside of mathematics. It also makes the diverse cultures of Asia seem all the same.

Example 2   Latin Americans are always late.

Known as the "mañana" stereotype, it suggests that people from Latin American cultures are not punctual. This stereotype can lead to misunderstandings and unfair expectations in professional and social contexts, disregarding individual differences and the varied cultural attitudes towards time across different societies.

Example 3** **Africans live in rural villages.

This stereotype paints a single image of Africa as a continent without cities and modern life, ignoring the existence of major metropolitan areas and the diversity of lifestyles within African countries. It reduces a rich, diverse continent to a single image, overshadowing the achievements and realities of urbanized areas in Africa.

Task 1

Directions: *Please decide whether the following statements are true (T) or false (F).*

_____ 1. Cultural stereotypes always reflect the complex realities of individuals within a group.

_____ 2. Cultural bias can influence an individual's judgment and behavior unconsciously.

_____ 3. The stereotype that "All Asians are good at math" acknowledges the diverse talents and interests of Asian individuals.

_____ 4. The "mañana" stereotype about Latin Americans considers individual differences and the varied cultural attitudes towards time.

_____ 5. Recognizing and addressing cultural stereotypes and bias is important for effective cross-cultural communication.

Task 2

Directions: *Please reflect on the three examples and answer the questions below.*

Example 1: Why might the stereotype that "All Asians are good at math" be considered a form of oversimplification? How can positive stereotypes like this one negatively impact individuals or groups?

_____

_____

_____

Example 2: What assumptions does the stereotype "Latin Americans are always late" make about time management and cultural values? How do cultural norms about punctuality vary around the world? Why is it important to understand these differences in a globalized society?

___

___

___

Example 3: What does the stereotype "Africans live in rural villages" imply about the diversity and modernity of the African continent? How might this stereotype influence people's perception of African countries and their development?

___

___

___

Task 3

Directions: *Please discuss the following two questions in pairs or groups. You may refer to resources outside the textbook.*

1. Can you think of other examples where a group is stereotyped for having a specific skill or characteristic?
2. What strategies can be employed to challenge and change the cultural stereotypes and bias?

2. Technology and Intercultural Communication

Technology, particularly social media, video conferencing, and virtual reality (VR), plays a pivotal role in facilitating cross-cultural communication, breaking down geographical barriers and enabling real-time interaction across the globe. Social media platforms serve as dynamic spaces for cultural exchange, allowing users to share and explore diverse cultural content, from traditional recipes to holiday celebrations; thereby, enhancing mutual understanding and appreciation. Video conferencing tools, such as Zoom and Tencent meeting, have transformed personal and professional communication, making it possible to hold face-to-face meetings without the need for physical travel; thus, fostering collaboration and relationship-building among individuals from different cultural backgrounds. Virtual reality offers an immersive experience, providing a unique opportunity to "visit" and explore foreign environments and cultural practices without leaving one's home. This immersive technology can enhance empathy and understanding by providing vivid, first-hand experiences of other cultures. Together, these technologies make intercultural communication more accessible and effective than ever before.

While technology has significantly enhanced the ease and scope of cross-cultural communication, it also introduces unique challenges that need careful navigation. Misunderstandings, loss of nuance, and the potential for digital divides can hinder the effectiveness of these technological bridges, necessitating a thoughtful approach to their use.

Example 1

Lei, based in China, collaborates with Raj, from India, on a software development project via video conferencing and social media tools. They share coding resources, troubleshoot problems in real-time, and occasionally, explore each other's cultures through virtual reality tours of local landmarks.

Example 2

John from the United States schedules a virtual reality meeting to discuss a new marketing strategy with his team in Japan. Despite the innovative approach, the team encounters several issues: Time zone differences lead to scheduling conflicts, and subtle non-verbal cues crucial in Japanese communication are lost in the virtual environment. Furthermore, the reliance on English disadvantages some team members less fluent in the language, inadvertently creating a communication hierarchy.

Task 4

Directions: *Please read Example 1 and reflect on the impact of cultural norms in social situations. Answer the following questions.*

1. How did Lei and Raj use technology to overcome the physical distance between China and India, and what specific tools do you think they can utilize to enhance their collaboration?

   _____
   _____
   _____

2. In what ways did the use of virtual reality tours contribute to their understanding of each other's cultures?

3. Can technology fully substitute for face-to-face interactions in building cross-cultural relationships? Why or why not?

_____

_____

_____

Task 5

Directions: *Please read Example 2 and analyze the challenges of technology in this scenario.*

Challenges of Technology in Cross-Cultural Communication
Specific obstacles   • _____   • _____   • _____
Potential consequences   • _____   • _____   • _____
Possible solutions   • _____   • _____   • _____

3. Zooming in

Decoding the Dress Code in Global Events[1]

It is often challenging to decipher the dress code when it comes to events. Many events create inventive dress codes which can confuse people more, but always look for the key words, be it formal, cocktail, casual, lunch or dinner.

A good guideline is, when in doubt, to go with elegance and simplicity. Take advice from the one and only Coco Chanel:

"Before you leave the house, look in the mirror and take one thing off."

"Dress shabbily and they remember the dress; dress impeccably and they remember the woman."

- **Black Tie**

Ladies, for black tie events, prepare to wear a long gown, be it a simple piece or filled with intricate details if you please. This is the occasion to dress up and be fancy. If you have no time to find a long gown, a formal cocktail dress will work, but try your very best to wear a long gown. In any case, be sure to accessorize with beautiful jewelry pieces.

For the men, black tie means wearing a full tuxedo (black or white coat). If you do not have a full tuxedo, go with the bow tie and a formal suit to match. It is less common nowadays, but the most formal of all dress codes is the white tie, where men don a black-tailed tuxedo jacket with a white tie and white vest. Women come in long gowns, their best jewelry and even white gloves.

- **Formal**

A long gown, a pantsuit, separates and skirts or dresses that rise to the occasion are welcome. There is more room to play around here. But, short outfits are not part of the code. For men, bring your blazers. A full suit is preferred, and a pocket square, if possible.

- **Semi-formal**

Here, shorter ensembles can come out to play. Semi-formal events allow for shorter ensembles. Women may opt for a little black dress or other playful combinations that retain a dressy appearance. Men may choose between a full suit or a blazer and tie, paired with other pants or jeans.

---

1 This text was adapted from Francisco, I. M. 2016. Decode the dress code. Retrieved from the Taterasia website.

- **Cocktail**

    Many people tack on formal or chic or casual or festive words to help guests dress for cocktails, so pay attention to the descriptors. Generally, for cocktails, women can feel more playful. Wear whimsical things, mix and match, wear patterns or heels or you go in a little black dress. Average cocktail attire is not too formal; it is more of (around knee length) dresses, mix and match pants or skirts with tops or jumpsuits. But if you are unsure, always over dress up a little bit. For men, wear jeans and a sports coat or a blazer.

- **Business Formal**

    Ladies should choose something less party-oriented and a little more conservative. Lots of jewelry is not recommended. Wear a suit, a pantsuit, a skirt set, pencil skirts or a muted dress. For men, a suit is recommended if this actually is a business event, if not something pantsuit semi-formal works too. Wear dress shoes.

- **Business Casual**

    Women can dress more relaxed with business casual. Wearing lighter colors and daywear is OK but remain slightly conservative. More patterns can be used here and mixing and matching is welcome. Men can choose to wear a sports coat, a blazer and match it with a button down to a polo. A tie can be worn if you please. Wear loafers or dress shoes.

- **Dressy Casual**

    Girls can be a lot less made up. Wear what makes you comfortable, from shorts to a sundress, to cotton clothing. Stylize it with bags and accessories. Guys can wear jeans and a short sleeve polo or shirts that are not too casual, perhaps a cotton long sleeve, or a button down.

- **Casual**

    This is perfect for a day or night in with friends, a day at the beach, in the park, at a barbeque and lunches. Shorts and T-shirts, sleeveless tops, and flip flops are welcome.

Task 6

Directions: *Please decide whether the following statements are true (T) or false (F).*

_____ 1. For black tie events, it is acceptable for women to wear short cocktail dresses if they cannot find a long gown.

_____ 2. Men attending a black tie event can opt for a colorful tuxedo instead of the traditional black or white one.

_____ 3. A pantsuit is not considered appropriate attire for a formal event.

_____ 4. Semi-formal attire allows for shorter ensembles and is less restrictive than formal attire.

_____ 5. For cocktail attire, it is recommended that men wear jeans and a sports coat or a blazer.

_____ 6. Business formal attire for women suggests wearing lots of jewelry.

_____ 7. In a business casual setting, men are discouraged from wearing loafers.

_____ 8. Dressy casual attire permits girls to wear shorts and stylize their outfit with accessories.

Task 7

Directions: *Please match the correct pictures in Column B with the events in Column A.*

Column A	Column B
1. Black tie	a.
2. Formal	b.
3. Semi-formal	c.

4. Cocktail

5. Business formal

6. Business casual

7. Dressy casual

8. Causal

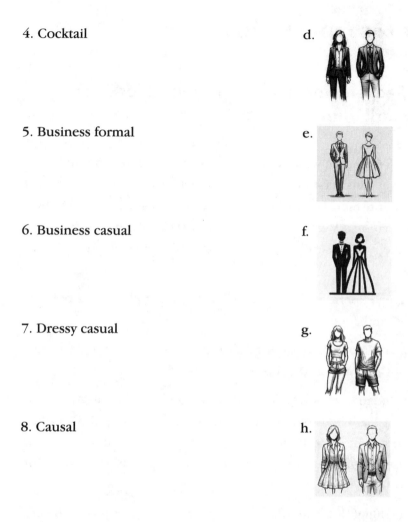

Task 8

Directions: *Please discuss the following questions in groups. You are encouraged to refer to other resources for the discussion.*

1. How do cultural interpretations of dress codes at global events reflect broader societal values and norms, and what challenges might arise when these interpretations vary significantly across different cultures?

2. In an increasingly globalized world, how can event organizers effectively communicate dress code expectations to a diverse international audience to ensure cultural sensitivity while maintaining the intended formality or informality of the event?

Part III   Notes from China

UNMISS Peacekeepers from China Recognized for Their Contributions in South Sudan[1]

For Blue Helmets serving for peace with the United Nations Mission in South Sudan (UNMISS), personal reward remains second to helping conflict-affected populations feel safe. 332 dedicated women and men from China deployed as engineers and medical peacekeepers to this young nation's Western Bahr El Ghazal state recently received the prestigious UN medal for their unceasing efforts to improve the lives of communities there.

It has been a life-changing experience revealed by Major Guang Zhiyong, a political instructor to Chinese troops, and a medal recipient.

"This is my first UN peacekeeping mission and to be honest, it may be the only chance I get to do my bit for the cause of world peace," he stated.

"As our time in South Sudan comes to an end, I speak on behalf of all my fellow peacekeepers from China—it has been immensely fulfilling to help people who need our support. The UN medal will have pride of place in our homes and future rotations will continue to support this country in its quest for a lasting peace," added Major Guang.

And speakers at the meaningful ceremony lauded Chinese peacekeepers. "Chinese engineers and medical peacekeepers have provided exceptional support to communities, humanitarian partners, and the mission. Their work in Western Bahr El Ghazal has been excellent and we are grateful for their contributions to peace, stability, and development," said Brigadier General Kweku Dankwa Hagan, UNMISS Sector Commander in the state.

Recognition also came from state authorities. "It is hard to find the right words to express gratitude to the Chinese engineers who have rendered immense services to our people by ensuring that the state capital, Wau, remains connected to counties by building and maintaining top-notch roads and bridges," averred Sarah Cleto Hassan, state Governor.

Through their work in rehabilitating major supply routes, including four key bridges as well as consistent airport maintenance, these engineers have also shored up

---

1 The text was adapted from the UNMISSIONS website.

travel possibilities to neighboring Warrap and Unity states, thereby boosting trade as well as helping communities convene and connect.

What's more, these dedicated peacekeepers won the hearts and minds of host communities through numerous cultural exchanges; helped bolster food security by building agricultural capacities among local interlocutors; and provided encouragement to students by handing over school supplies.

"Our Chinese peacekeepers have braved tough terrain and adverse conditions to make sure that the people we are on the ground to serve have their needs met. They have earned the community's admiration and goodwill," said Sam Muhumure, Head of the UNMISS Field Office in the state.

His words are borne out by Major Cheng Jun, the Chief Operations Officer for the Chinese Horizontal Engineering Company who recounts the challenges in repairing a major bridge.

"We drove 452 kilometers, stayed seven days in makeshift shelters at the location and used eight specialized personnel to repair damages to Billy Bridge without any large equipment. It was enormously challenging but the positive impact on local populations made every effort worth it," revealed the Major with a smile.

The last word came from Lieutenant-Colonel Li Hui, Commanding Officer of the Chinese contingent.

"The Chinese army emphasizes high standards and strict commitment, and I have ensured that the contingent takes every job seriously. I am heartened to see that our work has made a tangible difference," he concluded with quiet pride.

(545 words)

Directions: *Please answer the following questions based on the passage above.*

1. What are the major working fields of Chinese peacekeepers in United Nations Mission in South Sudan?
2. Please make an investigation and figure out a timeline of China's participation in UN peacekeeping operations.
3. Please work with your partners, choose one event from China's participation in UN peacekeeping operations and tell one peacekeeping story. Your story is supposed to include the event, the participants, unforgettable stories in the mission, contributions to the area, etc.

Global Development and APEC

Part I Reading for GC Knowledge

Text A An Introduction to APEC

Warm-up

Self-Assessment of APEC Commitment

Directions: *Please rate yourself on a scale of 1 to 5, where 1 = Strongly Disagree; 2 = Disagree; 3 = Neutral; 4 = Agree; 5 = Strongly Agree. Then discuss the questions that follow.*

Self-Assessment Questionnaire	Scale				
I think the establishment of APEC marked the integration of the Asian market.	1	2	3	4	5
I think the 21 member economies in APEC are of different roles in their influences in the unified market in the Asia Pacific region.	1	2	3	4	5
I think the annual APEC Leader Declaration heralds the trend of Asia Pacific Common Market development in the future.	1	2	3	4	5
I agree that what the specific committees and working groups do lays the foundation for further Asia Pacific Economic Policy formation.	1	2	3	4	5
I think the role of APEC Business Advisory Council (ABAC) is to provide high-quality professional guidance for development in specialized business areas.	1	2	3	4	5
I think the three pillars of APEC—Trade and Investment Liberalization, Business Facilitation, and ECO-tech (Economic and Technical Cooperation)—are conducive to the economic development of all APEC member economies.	1	2	3	4	5
I don't think it is necessary for APEC to discuss the economic issue of one specific member economy since this organization is concerned about the whole region's development.	1	2	3	4	5

(Continued)

Self-Assessment Questionnaire	Scale				
I think the realization of the Free Trade Area of the Asia Pacific (FTAAP) is more beneficial to the developed member economies rather than to the developing or underdeveloped member economies.	1	2	3	4	5
I think the involvement of gender in the projects of all areas is necessary since females' empowerment is an important index to evaluate the advancement level of a member economy.	1	2	3	4	5
I think collaboration and communication among APEC members can help eradicate the barrier of competition.	1	2	3	4	5

1. Based on your common knowledge, what do you think is the most significant role of APEC?

2. Based on your self-assessment, would you say that you have a comprehensive understanding of APEC?

3. How can China enlarge its role in APEC and make more contributions to the development of the APEC region?

An Introduction to APEC

1. A General Introduction

❶ The Asia-Pacific Economic Cooperation (APEC) is a regional economic forum established in 1989 to **leverage** the growing interdependence of the Asia Pacific. APEC's 21 members aim to create greater **prosperity** for the people of the region by promoting balanced, inclusive, sustainable, innovative, and secure growth and by **accelerating** regional economic **integration**. In November 1991, the People's Republic of China officially joined APEC, along with Chinese Taipei and Hong Kong, China.

❷ APEC works to help all residents of the Asia Pacific participate in the growing **economy**, to promote economic interdependence among member economies. The forum adapts to allow members to deal with important new challenges to the region's economic well-being, to strengthen the open **multilateral** trading system, and to reduce regional trade and investment barriers.

❸ APEC's 21 member economies are Australia, Brunei Darussalam, Canada, Chile, People's Republic of China, Hong Kong, China, Indonesia, Japan, Republic of Korea, Malaysia, Mexico, New Zealand, Papua New Guinea, Peru, The Philippines, The Russian Federation, Singapore, Chinese Taipei, Thailand, United States of America, and Vietnam. In addition, APEC has three official observers: ASEAN, the Pacific Economic Cooperation Council, and the Pacific Islands Forum.

❹ Among these members, Hong Kong, China and Chinese Taipei joined as regions. Therefore, APEC uses the term member economies instead of member countries to refer to its members.

2. Structure of APEC

❺ The highest level of APEC meetings is the Economic Leaders' Meeting, which is held **annually** with one member economy as the host, and the leaders of all APEC economies issue the leader's declaration of the year.

❻ The second level is the **Ministerial** Meeting, which includes the Ministerial Meeting and the **Sectoral** Ministerial Meeting. The Ministerial Meeting is also called the "Double Ministers" Meeting, with foreign ministers and trade ministers attending. APEC holds the Sectoral Ministerial Meeting regularly, which addresses the problems and challenges posed to specific areas, and discusses strategic cooperations and **blueprints** or roadmaps for the development of specific sectors in the future. The Sectoral Minister Meetings are the Trade Ministers Meeting, Finance Ministers Meeting, Small and Medium **Enterprise** Ministers Meeting, Energy Ministers Meeting, Ocean Ministers Meeting, Mining Ministers Meeting, Telecommunications Ministers Meeting, Tourism Ministers Meeting, Ministerial Meeting on Food Security, Ministerial Meeting on Structural Reform, Transport Ministers Meeting, Human Resources Ministers Meeting, Education Ministers Meeting, Women and Economic Meeting, etc.

❼ The third level is the Senior Officials' Meeting (SOM). Working under the direction of APEC Ministers, Senior Officials guide the activities of the **committees**, working groups, and task forces. Senior Officials develop recommendations for APEC Ministers and APEC Economic Leaders. Senior Officials' Meetings are held three to four times a year with the chair from the host economy.

❽ The fourth level is committees and working groups. There are four committees under the Senior Officials' Meeting: Committee on Trade and Investment (CTI), Economic Committee (EC), Senior Official **Steering** Committee on ECOTECH (SCE), and Budget and Management Committee (BMC). CTI coordinates APEC's work on the **liberalization** and facilitation of trade and investment; EC studies regional economic development trends and coordinates structural reforms; SCE instructs and coordinates economic and technological cooperation; BMC is responsible for budget management and **administration**. In addition, there are also working groups under the Senior Officials' Meeting to carry out specific work and cooperation.

⑨ The fifth level is the APEC **Secretariat**, which is based in Singapore and operates as the core support mechanism for the APEC process. It provides coordination, technical, and advisory support as well as information management, communications, and public **outreach** services.

3. Three Pillars of APEC

⑩ The three pillars of APEC are Trade and Investment Liberalization, Business Facilitation, and Economic and Technical Cooperation (ECO-Tech).

⑪ With the development of the world economy, APEC members not only cooperate on "the three pillars", but also extend cooperation into many other fields, such as regional economic integration, interconnection, economic structural reform and innovative development, global multilateral trading system, economic and technical cooperation, capacity building, etc.

⑫ These fields include education, energy, environment, finance, **sanitation**, human resources development, mining, ocean, technology, small and medium-sized enterprises, sustainable development, telecommunication information, tourism, trade, traffic, women, etc. All the cooperations in these fields are coordinated and guided by the different committees and working groups of APEC which are in charge of different **domains**. The committees and working groups are usually made of experienced staffs of professional backgrounds and skills. And experts and scholars in different fields are invited to join the thinking tank. The working groups regularly organize forums and seminars which these experts, scholars, and **entrepreneurs** attend and discuss the major problems and challenges existing in a certain field, and work out the strategic development blueprints with specified timelines for member economies to fulfill the development goal stage by stage. Member economies can also submit project proposals concerning specific problems in some fields to the committees to evaluate. If the proposal is admitted, the committees would advance the project among member economies to facilitate its execution.

4. Cooperation Pattern and ABAC

⑬ APEC adopts a non-binding, voluntary cooperation mechanism. Consensus must be reached by all members before decisions are made. The meeting documents are not legally binding, but members are politically and morally responsible for their implementation.

⑭ To strengthen the ties with the business community, the APEC Business Advisory Council (ABAC) was established in 1995, with three representatives from each economy. ABAC is responsible for offering policy suggestions, according to their individual industry development, to APEC Leaders over trade and investment liberalization, and economic and technical cooperation to create a favorable business environment. ABAC is the main channel for business fields to join the cooperation in APEC. The council holds four meetings every year. The secretariat is in Manila, the Philippines.

5. Free Trade Agreement and Regional Trade Agreement

⑮ Since the establishment of APEC, the number of regional trade agreements (RTAs) and free trade agreements (FTAs) that have been completed or are under negotiation among member economies has been steadily increasing. The overlapping and conflicting of these agreements lead to a serious tendency of trade diversion, which has damaged the welfare of the region and the world to a certain extent, and has adverse consequences on APEC process. Against this background, academics and business people have proposed to integrate the increasing number of regional trade agreements and free trade agreements in the APEC region and to establish a free trade zone under the APEC framework, the Free Trade Area of the Asia Pacific (FTAAP). In 2005, APEC Leaders included the promotion of high-quality RTAs and FTAs as an element of the Busan Roadmap towards the Bogor Goals and Committed APEC to develop model measures for commonly accepted FTA chapters.

⑯ In November 2014, APEC Leaders endorsed the Beijing Roadmap for APEC's Contribution to the Realization of the Free Trade Area of the Asia Pacific (FTAAP) to translate the vision of the FTAAP into reality. The Roadmap provides for a Collective Strategic Study on Issues related to the Realization of the FTAAP to be concluded by the end of 2016, as well as enhanced information sharing and capacity building.

(1,165 words)

 Glossary

leverage	/ˈliːvərɪdʒ/	v.	充分利用
prosperity	/prɒˈsperəti/	n.	繁荣；成功；兴旺；昌盛
accelerate	/əkˈseləreɪt/	v.	加速；（使）加速；加快

integration	/ˌɪntɪˈɡreɪʃn/	n.	整合；一体化；融合
economy	/ɪˈkɒnəmi/	n.	经济体
multilateral	/ˌmʌltiˈlætərl/	adj.	多边的；多国的
annually	/ˈænjuəli/	adv.	一年一次地
ministerial	/ˌmɪnɪˈstɪəriəl/	adj.	部长的；大臣的
sectoral	/ˈsektərl/	adj.	不同行业的；某一经济部门的
blueprint	/ˈbluːprɪnt/	n.	计划蓝图；行动方案
enterprise	/ˈentəpraɪz/	n.	企业；公司
committee	/kəˈmɪti/	n.	委员会
steering	/ˈstɪərɪŋ/	adj.	操控的；控制的
liberalization	/ˌlɪbrəlaɪˈzeɪʃn/	n.	自由主义化；自由化
administration	/ədˌmɪnɪˈstreɪʃn/	n.	行政；政府；行政部门；管理部门
secretariat	/ˌsekrəˈteəriət/	n.	（大型国际组织、政治组织的）秘书处，书记处
outreach	/ˈaʊtriːtʃ/	n.	伸出，展开；能达到的范围
pillar	/ˈpɪlə(r)/	n.	支柱；核心，基础
sanitation	/ˌsænɪˈteɪʃn/	n.	卫生；卫生设施体系
domain	/dəˈmeɪn/	n.	（知识、活动的）领域，范围，范畴
entrepreneur	/ˌɒntrəprəˈnɜː(r)/	n.	企业家

Task 1

Directions: *Please read the text and fill in the blanks in the summary.*

> APEC is a regional economic (1) _____ established in 1989. Its aim is to (2) _____ balanced, inclusive, sustainable, innovative, and secure economic growth and (3) _____ economic integration in the Asia Pacific region. The organization is committed to providing a forum for all the member economies to deal with economic (4) _____, to help build up and strengthen an open (5) _____ trading system, and reduce regional trade and investment barriers. APEC has three pillars, which serve as the fundamental (6) _____ to guide all APEC meetings and actions, and also lay the foundation for all APEC policies, initiatives, blueprints, and roadmaps. The three pillars are Trade and Investment Liberalization, Business Facilitation, and Economic and Technical Cooperation. Beyond that, APEC also advocates the enhancement of regional economic (7) _____, strengthening interconnection, pushing forward economic

(Continued)

> structural (8) _____ and innovative development, and constructing a global multilateral trading system, etc. In 1995, to strengthen the ties with the business (9) _____, APEC Business Advisory Council (ABAC) was founded. ABAC offers (10) _____ suggestions to APEC leaders regarding trade and investment liberalization, economic and technical cooperation, etc.

Task 2

Directions: *Please read the text again and decide whether the following statements are true (T) or false (F) based on what you have learned from the text.*

_____ 1. China is one of the initiators of APEC.

_____ 2. Regional integration and interdependence among APEC member economies may hamper the independence of individual member's economic policy-making.

_____ 3. APEC is an important forum for member economies to discuss strategies and solutions to deal with the economic challenges facing the Asia Pacific region.

_____ 4. Chinese Taipei and Hong Kong, China are addressed as member economies because they are not independent political entities, but part of China.

_____ 5. Among the five levels of APEC Meetings, the lower the level of the meeting is, the more specific detailed issues will be researched and analyzed in depth.

_____ 6. The "Double Minister" Meeting is held because both foreign ministers and sectoral ministers attend the meeting to discuss cooperative issues in specific sectors.

_____ 7. APEC members' cooperations are based on, but not limited to the three pillars of Trade and Investment Liberalization, Business Facilitation, and ECO-Tech.

_____ 8. APEC, as its name shows, always prioritizes economic growth and resilience in all its policy-making decisions.

_____ 9. Since APEC is the authoritative economic organization in the Asia Pacific region, its decisions and policies must be abided by and carried out by all members.

_____ 10. ABAC offers policy suggestions applicable to APEC members according to their specific situations so as to help each member economy create a favorable business environment.

Task 3

Directions: *Please translate the following five sentences into English using the words in the parentheses.*

1. 亚太经济合作组织是一个调节亚太地区不断增长的相互依赖关系的经济论坛。(leverage)
2. 亚太经济合作组织致力于为该区域人民创造更大的经济繁荣,提升该地区平衡、包容、可持续、具有创新性和安全性的发展前景。(prosperity)
3. 亚太专门部长会议每年定期召开,探讨该地区所面临的经济挑战,制定某一特定领域的战略合作与发展蓝图。(blueprint)
4. 经济委员会负责研究亚太地区的经济发展趋势并协调该地区的经济结构改革过程。(coordinate)
5. APEC 商务顾问委员会代表根据各成员经济体的具体经济情况提出政策建议,并为相关领导人就贸易与投资自由化,经济与技术合作建言献策。(liberalization)

Task 4

Directions: *Please discuss the following questions in groups and role-play the following situation with your solution.*

> ***Situation***
>
> China, as an important member of APEC, is playing more and more important roles in Asia Pacific's economic development and prosperity. Discuss with your team members and work out a development blueprint to boost the development of a specific sector in the next five years, which can benefit both China and other APEC members. You can take the following sample for reference.
>
> ***Sample***
>
> To achieve carbon neutrality and zero emission of greenhouse gases, many countries in the world are faced with the challenge of abandoning environmental polluting techniques and equipment and upgrading neo-environmental techniques. Among all the pollutant emission sources, the automobile is a typical one. It is urgent for automobile enterprises to produce new-energy vehicles. However, there is a devoid of innovative power in many developing countries. Therefore, it is of significant necessity to enhance the cooperation of new-energy technical innovation and accelerate the pace of the automobile industry transformation from fossil-fuel based to new-energy oriented.

> ***The key points of discussion***
>
> 1. Persuade governments of different countries to set up special environmental technique innovation funds;
>
> 2. Persuade governments of different countries to pass favorable policies to encourage the innovation and application of new-energy techniques;
>
> 3. Persuade governments of different countries to pass favorable investment and taxation policies to the new-energy projects of enterprises;
>
> 4. Coordinate the cooperation between governments/international organizations (such as APEC or specific science committees, etc.) and new-energy research institutes to facilitate the transformation of new-energy techniques into productivity;
>
> 5. Set up an international standard to evaluate the exhaust gas emission;
>
> 6. Set up a time table for the transition of energy from fossil fuel to hybrid power to total clean energy

Text B APEC, Creating a Resilient and Sustainable Future for All

 Warm-up

Self-Assessment of APEC Commitment

Directions: *Please rate yourself on a scale of 1 to 5, where 1 = Strongly Disagree; 2 = Disagree; 3 = Neutral; 4 = Agree; 5 = Strongly Agree.*

Self-Assessment Questionnaire	Scale				
I think APEC's role in facilitating cooperation and development of economy in the Asia Pacific region is important.	1	2	3	4	5
I think the environmental and climatic challenges are of different degrees to different economies in the Asia Pacific region.	1	2	3	4	5
I think developed APEC economies should make more efforts to build a free, open, fair, non-discriminatory, transparent, inclusive, and predictable trade and investment environment.	1	2	3	4	5

(Continued)

Self-Assessment Questionnaire	Scale				
I agree that the Free Trade Area of the Asia Pacific can strengthen the integration of APEC economies rather than catalyze their competition.	1	2	3	4	5
I think physical connectivity, institutional connectivity, and people-to-people connectivity are of equal importance.	1	2	3	4	5
I agree net-zero greenhouse gas emissions or carbon neutrality is the only valid way to deal with climate challenge.	1	2	3	4	5
I don't think it is necessary for all economies to reach net-zero greenhouse gas emissions and carbon neutrality at the same pace.	1	2	3	4	5
I think the sustainable resource management of agriculture, forestry, and marine resources and fisheries can help make our agri-food systems more resilient, productive, innovative, and sustainable.	1	2	3	4	5
I think the purpose of creating pathways for MSMEs (micro, small, and medium-sized enterprises) and start-ups to grow is to counterbalance giant enterprises' manipulation of the market.	1	2	3	4	5
I think the APEC Internet and Digital Economy Roadmap (AIDER) shows us that digitalization is the trend of both domestic and international economic development.	1	2	3	4	5

APEC, Creating a Resilient and Sustainable Future for All

❶ The economic leaders of APEC met in San Francisco, California, on November 16–17, 2023. The APEC economic leaders emphasized that effective policies require, above all, **responsiveness** to all the people and economies.

❷ Today, all the APEC economies face a different and **dynamic** set of economic challenges. All the APEC members must **harness** technological and economic progress to continue to **unleash** the enormous potential and tremendous dynamism across the APEC region, **spur** economic growth, as well as to address all environmental challenges, including climate change. All efforts will be made to move the region towards new ways of bringing **resiliency**, sustainability, interconnection, **innovation** and **inclusion** to respond to the most pressing economic challenges.

❸   APEC members reaffirm their determination to deliver a free, open, fair, non-discriminatory, **transparent**, **inclusive**, and predictable trade and investment environment. They also reaffirm the importance of the rules-based multilateral trading system, with the World Trade Organization (WTO) at its core, which continues to **catalyze** our region's extraordinary growth. They are committed to the necessary reform of the WTO to improve all of its functions, including conducting discussions with a view to having a full and well-functioning dispute settlement system **accessible** to all members by 2024.

❹   All APEC members underscore their commitment to advancing economic integration in the region in a manner that is market-driven, including through the work on the Free Trade Area of the Asia Pacific **Agenda**. To this end, they will enhance their capacity-building and technical-cooperation efforts in support of economies' readiness to participate in high-quality and comprehensive regional undertakings.

❺   APEC reaffirms its commitment to keep markets open and address supply chain **disruptions**, including by working to support our businesses in building secure, effective, resilient, sustainable, and open supply chains that create a predictable, competitive, and digitally interconnected Asia Pacific region. By recognizing the unique needs and interests of all **stakeholders**, APEC economies can work towards more inclusive and sustainable policies that ensure trade and investment equitably benefit all the people and economies. APEC remains committed to implementing the APEC **Connectivity** Blueprint (2015–2025) by strengthening physical, institutional, and people-to-people connectivity. All member economies will **intensify** efforts to promote regional, sub-regional, and remote area connectivity. In this regard, the importance of quality **infrastructure** development and investment is reaffirmed.

❻   The world continues to confront profound challenges posed by the impacts of climate change. More intensive efforts are needed for economies to accelerate their clean, sustainable, just, affordable, and inclusive energy **transitions** through various pathways, consistent with the goal of net-zero greenhouse gas emissions or carbon neutrality by or around mid-21st century, while taking into account the latest scientific developments and different domestic circumstances. APEC recalls its commitment to **rationalize** and phase out inefficient fossil fuel **subsidies** that encourage wasteful consumption while recognizing the importance of providing those in need with essential energy services.

❼   APEC will pursue and encourage efforts to triple renewable energy capacity globally through existing targets and policies as well as demonstrate similar ambition with respect to other low- and zero-emissions technologies including **abatement** and removal technologies in line with domestic circumstances by 2030. To spur the transition to and investment in low- and zero-emissions transportation in the region through various pathways, efforts will be made to accelerate the transition towards low- and zero-emissions vehicles, sustainable aviation fuels, and low- and zero-emissions maritime shipping and port de-carbonization.

❽ APEC commits to fully implementing the Food Security Roadmap Towards 2030 as a pathway to make our agri-food systems more resilient, productive, innovative, and sustainable while recognizing there is a "no-one-size-fits-all" approach to agricultural sustainability. APEC also reaffirms its commitment to work towards the sustainable resource management of agriculture, forestry and marine resources and fisheries, including combatting illegal, unreported, and unregulated fishing, and emphasizes the relationship between open, undistorted agri-food systems, climate change, and food security and nutrition. APEC reaffirm the importance of agricultural productivity, international trade, and prevention and reduction of food loss and waste in achieving food security, and will increase efforts to ensure food security and nutrition.

❾ APEC emphasizes the importance of creating pathways for MSMEs and start-ups to grow, including through opportunities to become more competitive, specialized, and innovative. APEC will support MSMEs to expand into regional and global markets, including by integrating into global value chains, through collaboration with large enterprises, and through the use of digital tools and technologies. APEC encourages the development of easy-to-use and **cost-effective** products and solutions that help MSMEs accelerate their digital transformation. APEC recognizes the importance of access to finance to **facilitate** growth. APEC reaffirms the importance of building an enabling environment for MSMEs, as well as supporting the transition of economic actors from the informal to the formal economy.

❿ We, as economies of APEC, reaffirm our commitment to create an enabling, inclusive, open, fair and non-discriminatory digital ecosystem for businesses and consumers. We commit to implementing the APEC Internet and Digital Economy Roadmap (AIDER) to foster an inclusive digital economy for all. All economies are to accelerate efforts to implement AIDER, including in the areas of data privacy, cloud computing, telecommunications networks, promoting **interoperability**, ICT security, and digital trade and **e-commerce**, emerging technologies, and promoting innovation and adoption of enabling technologies and services. To unlock the full potential of digital technology, equitably share its benefits, and **mitigate** risks, APEC will explore a **concerted** and collaborative policy response, promote international cooperation on digital technology, and welcome a continued international discussion on **governance** for digital technology. APEC will strengthen digital infrastructure, facilitate access to information and communication technology goods and services, and ensure that no one is left behind by equipping all people with the necessary skills needed to **thrive** in the digital economy. We will accelerate digital transformation and cooperate on facilitating the flow of data and strengthening business and consumer trust in digital **transactions**, including through cooperation on regulatory approaches regarding the Internet and digital economy, as well as consumer protection and data privacy in the digital environment.

(976 words)

 Glossary

responsiveness	/rɪˈspɒnsɪvnəs/	n.	响应性；响应度
dynamic	/daɪˈnæmɪk/	adj.	充满活力的；发展变化的
harness	/ˈhɑːnɪs/	n.	控制
unleash	/ʌnˈliːʃ/	v.	发泄；突然释放；使爆发
spur	/spɜː(r)/	v.	刺激；促进，加速
resiliency	/rɪˈzɪliənsi/	n.	弹性；跳回
innovation	/ˌɪnəˈveɪʃn/	n.	创新；改革
inclusion	/ɪnˈkluːʒn/	n.	包含；被包括的人（或事物）
transparent	/trænsˈpærənt/	adj.	透明的；显而易见的
inclusive	/ɪnˈkluːsɪv/	adj.	兼收并蓄的
committed	/kəˈmɪtɪd/	adj.	尽心尽力的；坚信的；坚定的
catalyze	/ˈkætəlaɪz/	v.	催化；使起催化作用
accessible	/əkˈsesəbl/	adj.	可使用的；可接近的；可到达的
agenda	/əˈdʒendə/	n.	议题，议事日程
disruption	/dɪsˈrʌpʃn/	n.	中断；扰乱；混乱
stakeholder	/ˈsteɪkhəʊldə(r)/	n.	股东；利益相关者
connectivity	/ˌkɒnekˈtɪvɪti/	n.	互联互通
intensify	/ɪnˈtensɪfaɪ/	v.	（使）增强，加剧；强化
infrastructure	/ˈɪnfrəstrʌktʃə(r)/	n.	基础设施，基础建设
transition	/trænˈzɪʃn/	n.	过渡；转变；变革；变迁
rationalize	/ˈræʃnəlaɪz/	v.	合理化；进行合理化改革
subsidy	/ˈsʌbsədi/	n.	补贴；津贴

Unit 3 Global Development and APEC

abatement	/əˈbeɪtmənt/	n.	减少；减轻；减弱
cost-effective	/ˌkɒstɪˈfektɪv/	adj.	成本效益好的
interoperability	/ˌɪntərɒpərəˈbɪləti/	n.	互操作性；互用性
e-commerce	/ˌiːˈkɒmɜːs/	n.	电子商务
mitigate	/ˈmɪtɪgeɪt/	v.	减轻；缓和
concerted	/kənˈsɜːtɪd/	adj.	一致的
governance	/ˈgʌvənəns/	n.	管理方式
thrive	/θraɪv/	v.	繁荣；蓬勃发展
transaction	/trænˈzækʃn/	n.	交易；处理；业务；买卖

Task 1

Directions: *Please read the text and fill in the blanks below with a proper word.*

APEC's regional economic development
• To unleash the maximal potential and great dynamism across the APEC region, and to (1) _____ economic growth, technical and economic progress need to be (2) _____ by all APEC economies.
• A free, open, fair, non-discriminatory, transparent, inclusive, and predictable (3) _____ and (4) _____ environment is very important to the achievement of economic prosperity in the APEC region.
• The building of secure, effective, resilient, sustainable, and open (5) _____ can serve as a robust support to the infusion of vitality in APEC economies.
• APEC economies can work towards more (6) _____ and (7) _____ policies that ensure trade and investment equitably benefit all the people and economies.
APEC's commitment to carbon neutrality and food security
• To achieve net zero (8) _____ and (9) _____ by the mid-21st century, APEC economies should intensify their efforts to use clean, sustainable, just, affordable, and inclusive energy.
• To spur the transition to and investment in low- and zero-emissions transportation in the APEC region, efforts will be made to accelerate the transition towards low- and zero-emissions (10) _____, sustainable (11) _____ aviation fuels, and low- and zero-emissions maritime shipping and port (12) _____.

(Continued)

• To fully implement the (13) _____ Towards 2030 as a pathway to make our agri-food systems more resilient, productive, innovative, and sustainable, APEC is committed to working towards the sustainable (14) _____ of agriculture, forestry, and marine resources and fisheries.
The development of MSMEs
• APEC encourages the development of easy-to-use and cost-effective products and solutions that help MSMEs accelerate their digital (15) _____ .

Task 2

Directions*: Please read the text again and decide whether the following statements are true (T) or false (F) based on what you have learned from the text.*

_____ 1. Technical and economic innovation are important to the maintenance of regional economic resiliency and sustainability.

_____ 2. Economic challenges can only be met when technical innovation is controlled by APEC economies.

_____ 3. The rules of the APEC multilateral trading system are in parallel with those of the WTO.

_____ 4. APEC economies are endeavored to enlarge the predictability of their investment and trade environment.

_____ 5. Market integration of APEC economies must be realized in accordance with the APEC Free Trade Area of the Asia Pacific Agenda.

_____ 6. Secure, effective, resilient, sustainable, and open supply chains are conducive to the prosperity of the economy in the Asia Pacific region.

_____ 7. All APEC economies must make intensified efforts to achieve net-zero greenhouse gas emissions or carbon neutrality according to the unified standard.

_____ 8. The establishment of a resilient, productive, innovative, and sustainable agri-food system requires all APEC economies to work out a standardized approach that is accessible to each member.

_____ 9. The integration of MSMEs into the global value chain doesn't expel their collaboration with big enterprises.

_____ 10. The acceleration of digital transformation and the facilitation of data flow indicates that digital transactions will be the future trend of international trade.

Task 3

Directions: *Please translate the following five sentences into English using the words or phrase in the parentheses.*

1. APEC 各经济体致力于打造一个自由、开放、透明、包容和具有可预测性的贸易与投资环境。(inclusive)

2. APEC 各经济体致力于以市场为驱动力，推动区域经贸融合，建立亚太地区自由贸易区。(integration)

3. APEC 各经济体致力于通过打造安全、有效、有弹性、可持续且开放的供应链，建立一个具有预测性、竞争力和数字互联的亚太地区市场。(resilient)

4. APEC 各经济体必须共同努力加速完成清洁、可持续、经济性新能源过渡工作，以达到 21 世纪中期温室气体零排放和碳中和的目标。(carbon neutrality)

5. APEC 成员承诺致力于对农业、渔业、海洋资源的可持续资源管理。(sustainable)

Task 4

Directions: *Please discuss the following questions in groups and role-play the following situation with your solution.*

> **Situation**
>
> Suppose your group were a Model APEC Business Advisory Council. There are many MSMEs that lack basic information, technology, and access to the international market. In the era of the digital economy, how can the MSMEs grasp the opportunity to participate in the global value chain? You are supposed to discuss the question to work out a strategy for MSMEs' development with at least five specific points.

Part II Drilling for GC Skills

How to Write a Report (I)

1. What Is a Report?

A report is a formal document that is structured and presented in an organized manner, with the aim of conveying information, analyzing data, and providing recommendations. It is often used to communicate findings and outcomes to a specific audience. Reports can vary in length and format, but they usually contain a clear introduction, body, and conclusion.

2. The Importance of a Report

A report allows individuals to effectively communicate their findings, ideas, and recommendations on global issues. It enables them to present complex information in a clear and concise manner, making it easier for others to understand and engage with the topic. Also, a report requires thorough research and analysis, encouraging individuals to delve deep into global issues. This process enhances their understanding of various perspectives, challenges, and potential solutions. In addition, creating a report fosters critical thinking skills by encouraging individuals to analyze and evaluate information from diverse sources. It helps develop the ability to discern reliable information, identify biases, and form evidence-based conclusions. Finally, a report often requires collaboration with others, promoting teamwork and intercultural understanding. Working with individuals from different backgrounds enhances global competence by exposing individuals to diverse perspectives and fostering cross-cultural communication skills.

Example 1   Communication

A report on the impact of climate change in vulnerable coastal communities can effectively communicate the urgency of the issue and propose strategies for adaptation and mitigation.

Example 2   Research and analysis

A report on the socio-economic effects of globalization can involve extensive research, including case studies, statistical analysis, and expert opinions, to provide a comprehensive overview of the topic.

Example 3   Critical thinking

A report on the ethical implications of global supply chains would involve critically examining labor practices, environmental impacts, and corporate responsibility to present a balanced and informed perspective.

Example 4   Collaboration

A collaborative report on the impact of migration on local communities could involve input from researchers, policy-makers, and representatives from migrant communities, ensuring a comprehensive and inclusive analysis.

Task 1

Directions: *Please decide whether the following statements are true (T) or false (F).*

_____ 1. A report allows individuals to communicate their findings, ideas, and recommendations on global issues.

_____ 2. A report only presents simple information and does not require analysis.

_____ 3. Creating a report does not contribute to the development of critical thinking skills.

_____ 4. Collaboration is not necessary when creating a report.

_____ 5. Working with individuals from different backgrounds does not enhance global competence.

3. Major Types of Reports

By understanding the different types of reports, individuals can select the appropriate format and structure to effectively communicate information and achieve their objectives. However, which type of report will be used depends on its purpose, audience, and context.

Informational reports: These reports provide information about a topic, such as a product, service, or process.

Analytical reports: These reports present data or information in a structured and organized manner, often with charts, graphs, or tables, to help the reader understand trends, patterns, or relationships.

Progress reports: These reports provide updates on a project or initiative, detailing the progress made and any challenges or obstacles encountered.

Technical reports: These reports provide technical information, such as specifications, designs, or performance data, often aimed at a technical audience.

Research reports: These reports present the findings of research conducted on a particular topic or issue, often including a literature review, data analysis, and conclusions.

Feasibility reports: A feasibility report assesses the likelihood of achieving success for a suggested project or initiative.

Business reports: These reports are used in a business setting to communicate information about a company's performance, operations, or strategies. Different types of business reports include financial statements, marketing reports, and annual reports.

Task 2

Directions: *Please match the corresponding features in Column B with the reports in Column A.*

Column A	Column B
1. Informational reports	a. present the findings of research conducted on a particular topic or issue, often including a literature review, data analysis, and conclusions.
2. Analytical reports	b. assess the likelihood of achieving success for a suggested project or initiative.
3. Progress reports	c. are used in a business setting to communicate information about a company's performance, operations, or strategies. Different types of business reports include financial statements, marketing reports, and annual reports.
4. Technical reports	d. provide technical information, such as specifications, designs, or performance data, often aimed at a technical audience.
5. Research reports	e. provide updates on a project or initiative, detailing the progress made and any challenges or obstacles encountered.
6. Feasibility reports	f. present data or information in a structured and organized manner, often with charts, graphs, or tables, to help the reader understand trends, patterns, or relationships.

7. Business reports   g. provide information about a topic, such as a product, service, or process.

4. The Structure of a Report

The structure of a report refers to its overall organization and layout, including the sections and subsections that make up the report, their order, and their relationships to each other. The following is a typical structure of a report.

Preliminary Parts:

- Title
- Date
- Acknowledgments (Preface or Foreword)
- Table of contents
- List of tables and illustrations

Main Text:

- Introduction
- Statement of findings and recommendations
- Results
- Implications of the results
- Conclusion

End Matter:

- Appendices
- Bibliography of sources consulted

This structure provides a clear and organized framework for presenting a research report, ensuring that all important information is included and presented in a logical and easy-to-follow manner.

Task 3

Directions: *Please read the report below and fill in the blanks with the elements of a report.*

(1) _____ APEC: Fostering Economic Cooperation and Integration

(2) _____: The Asia-Pacific Economic Cooperation (APEC) is a regional forum comprising 21 member economies from the Asia Pacific region. This report provides a brief overview of APEC's objectives, initiatives, and impact on regional economic development.

(3) _____: APEC has played a significant role in promoting economic cooperation and integration in the Asia Pacific region. Through its commitment to trade liberalization, connectivity, and inclusive growth, APEC has achieved notable progress. However, there are areas that require further attention and action:

1. Trade and Investment Liberalization: APEC has made substantial strides towards trade and investment liberalization. To further enhance this process, member economies should expedite the implementation of existing commitments and work towards resolving outstanding issues. Continued efforts to reduce trade barriers, harmonize regulations, and simplify customs procedures will foster a more conducive environment for businesses.

2. Regional Economic Integration: APEC's initiatives towards regional economic integration, such as the Free Trade Area of the Asia Pacific (FTAAP), hold immense potential. It is crucial for member economies to intensify their efforts to negotiate and conclude high-standard trade agreements. APEC should also focus on bridging the development gap among member economies to ensure inclusive growth and equitable benefits.

3. Connectivity and Infrastructure Development: APEC recognizes the pivotal role of connectivity and infrastructure development in promoting economic growth. To maximize its impact, APEC should facilitate greater public-private partnerships, encourage technology transfer, and provide technical assistance to address infrastructure gaps. Collaboration in developing digital infrastructure and promoting e-commerce will further strengthen regional connectivity.

4. Inclusive and Sustainable Growth: APEC's emphasis on inclusive and sustainable growth is commendable. However, member economies should prioritize policies that promote gender equality, support SMEs, enhance skills development, and address environmental challenges. APEC should continue to facilitate knowledge-

(Continued)

sharing platforms and capacity-building programs to ensure the benefits of growth are widely distributed.

(4) _____: APEC has emerged as a vital platform for economic cooperation and regional integration in the Asia Pacific region. Its commitment to trade liberalization, connectivity, and inclusive growth has yielded positive results. To sustain and amplify these achievements, member economies must work together to accelerate trade and investment liberalization, deepen regional economic integration, enhance connectivity and infrastructure, and promote inclusive and sustainable growth. APEC's continued efforts will contribute to the prosperity and resilience of the Asia Pacific region as it navigates evolving global challenges and opportunities.

5. The Format of Report Writing

The format of report writing refers to the structure of a formal document that provides information on a particular topic or issue, which typically includes eight essential elements. The title is the first thing that readers will see, and it should be clear and concise. The title should include the report's subject or topic and the author's name, date of writing, or who the report is for. The title should be brief and informative, avoiding vague or ambiguous language. The following is an example of the title page.

"2023 APEC Economic Policy Report: Structural Reform and an Enabling Environment for Businesses"

Author: APEC Economic Committee

Date: November, 2023

Company: Asia-Pacific Economic Cooperation

Department: Strategy and Planning

In this example, the title page includes the name of the report, "2023 APEC Economic Policy Report: Structural Reform and an Enabling Environment for Businesses", the author's name, "APEC Economic Committee", the submission date, "November, 2023", and other details such as the name of the organization, "Asia-Pacific Economic Cooperation".

Table of Contents

The table of contents provides an overview of the report's contents. It should list all sections and subsections with clear headings. It is essential to make the table of contents organized and easy to read, allowing readers to locate specific information quickly. The following example of the table of contents is from "2023 APEC Economic Policy Report: Structural Reform and an Enabling Environment for Businesses".

TABLE OF CONTENTS

Preface i

List of figures iii

List of tables iii

List of boxes iv

Key abbreviations v

Key messages vi

1. Introduction 1

What is structural reform and why is it helpful? 1

Elements of structural reform 3

Structural reform to advance broader societal goals 4

APEC's structural reform efforts 5

Outline of the report 6

2. Structural reform and good regulatory practice (GRP) 8

What are GRPs? 9

Foundational principles of GRPs 11

Key regulatory management tools 12

Benefits of GRP 19

How GRPs improve the quality and sustainability of business environments 21

3. Structural reform and an enabling business environment 23

Structural reform and business dynamics 24

Role of SMEs 50

Concluding remarks 57

(Continued)

4. Structural reform, innovation, inclusion and sustainability..........59
Promoting sustainability 59
Promoting inclusion..67
Promoting resilience 74
Promoting innovation 82
Concluding remarks...85
5. Sustainability performance of structural reforms..........................86
Measuring structural reforms and sustainability 86
Corporate reporting on sustainability 93
Concluding remarks...105
6. Summary and policy recommendations..106
Policy recommendations..109
Appendices..115
Appendix A   Measuring structural reforms and sustainability 116
Appendix B   Guidance and requirements for ESG disclosure.......148
References 153

Introduction

This part introduces the report's topic and informs readers what they can expect to find in the report. The introduction should capture readers' attention and provide relevant background information. It should be clear and concise, including why the report was written and its objectives. The following example of elements included in the Introduction is from "2023 APEC Economic Policy Report: Structural Reform and an Enabling Environment for Businesses".

1. Introduction..1
What is structural reform and why is it helpful?...............................1
Elements of structural reform...3

(Continued)

Structural reform to advance broader societal goals 4
APEC's structural reform efforts 5
Outline of the report.. 6

Body

The body is the longest section and includes all the information, data, and analysis. It should present information in an organized manner, often using subheadings and bullet points. The body should include all relevant research findings and data, often accompanied by visuals such as graphs and tables. It is essential to cite all sources correctly and remain objective, avoiding personal opinions or biases. The following example of elements included in the body is from "2023 APEC Economic Policy Report: Structural Reform and an Enabling Environment for Businesses".

2. Structural reform and good regulatory practice (GRP) 8
What are GRPs?... 9
Foundational principles of GRPs 11
Key regulatory management tools 12
Benefits of GRP 19
How GRPs improve the quality and sustainability of business environments 21
3. Structural reform and an enabling business environment 23
Structural reform and business dynamics 24
Role of SMEs... 50
Concluding remarks... 57
4. Structural reform, innovation, inclusion and sustainability 59
Promoting sustainability 59
Promoting inclusion... 67
Promoting resilience 74
Promoting.. 82

(Continued)
Concluding remarks..85
5. Sustainability performance of structural reforms............................86
Measuring structural reforms and sustainability 86
Corporate reporting on sustainability 93
Concluding remarks..105

Conclusion

The conclusion summarizes the findings and conclusions of the report. It should wrap up all the essential information presented in each part of the body and make recommendations based on corresponding findings. The conclusion must be brief and clear, avoiding the introduction of any new information not previously presented in the body.

Summary

The summary or executive summary provides a brief overview of the entire report. It should summarize the report's main points, including findings, objectives, and recommendations. The summary should be written after the entire report is completed, and it should be concise and summarized. The following example of summary is from "2023 APEC Economic Policy Report: Structural Reform and an Enabling Environment for Businesses".

> 1. Structural reforms are a key element for achieving innovation, inclusion, and sustainability through the incentives they create for firms.
>
> 2. Good regulatory practice can provide a predictable and enabling business environment for firms, particularly SMEs.
>
> 3. Structural reforms shape a dynamic business environment. Complementary policies can help address market failures and barriers.
>
> 4. Firms are increasingly reporting on their sustainability performance.
>
> 5. Monitoring of structural reforms should be expanded to the issues of inclusion, resilience and sustainability, especially at the firm level and for SMEs.

Recommendations

The recommendation section should provide suggested goals or steps based on the report's information. It should be realistic and achievable, providing well-crafted solutions. It is often included in the conclusion section. The following example of recommendations is from "2023 APEC Economic Policy Report: Structural Reform and an Enabling Environment for Businesses".

> 1. Where markets work: Let markets work.
> 2. Where markets fail: Rectify, regulate, and realign.
> 3. Tracking progress: Measure, monitor, and modify.
> 4. Synergizing efforts: Cooperate across borders.

Appendices

The appendices section includes additional technical information or supporting materials, such as research questionnaires or survey data. It should provide supplementary information to the report without disrupting its main content.

It is important to use clear headings and subheadings and to label tables and figures. Also, proofreading and fact-checking are critical before submitting the report. A well-crafted report is concise, informative, and free of personal bias or opinions.

Part III Notes from China

China Contributes to APEC Sub-Fund to Combat COVID-19 Pandemic[1]

China has contributed USD 1 million toward the establishment of a new APEC sub-fund on combating COVID-19 and economic recovery (CCER), aiming to support initiatives that strengthen member economies' capacity to address and manage impacts from the pandemic and fast-track recovery.

A memorandum of understanding on China's contribution to the sub-fund was signed virtually by Lu Mei, China APEC Senior Official and Dr. Rebecca Sta Maria, Executive Director of the APEC Secretariat.

---

[1] The text was adapted from the APEC website.

"The COVID-19 pandemic has posed an unprecedented challenge to APEC members that requires a collective and inclusive response," said Lu. "APEC economies have strengthened cooperation to respond to COVID-19. The establishment of the sub-fund is part of these varied and continuous efforts as well as the contribution of additional resources across APEC to combat the pandemic," said Lu.

"We hope that this sub-fund will assist APEC in combatting current and future pandemics, safeguarding the health and well-being of people, accelerating economic recovery and harnessing new opportunities of the digital economy, which also contributes to the implementation of the APEC Putrajaya Vision," Lu added.

APEC is responding to COVID-19 with numerous policy measures and tools that address different pain points caused by the health and economic crisis. These initiatives range from high-level commitments to expert analyses and recommendations as well as innovative tools and practical projects.

The CCER sub-fund will be directed to support projects and initiatives to help member economies in their efforts to address and manage the economic impacts of COVID-19, strengthen public health systems and capacity building, expedite economic recovery and build resiliency against future large-scale economic disruptions.

The sub-fund also aims to facilitate APEC economies to better adapt to available and innovative digital tools such as telemedicine, online education, and teleworking to boost economic recovery and growth.

Member economies can also tap into the sub-fund for activities that support capacity building for micro, small, and medium-sized enterprises and vulnerable groups to recover and build resiliency to economic disruptions caused by COVID-19.

"As we keep our focus on recovery, we see opportunities for member economies to deepen cooperation and work together for the prosperity of all our people," said Dr. Rebecca Sta Maria. "This sub-fund will support initiatives focused on recovery in APEC, ensuring that we remain the world's most dynamic and interconnected region."

Projects are a vital part of the APEC process. They help translate the policy directions of APEC Economic Leaders and Ministers into actions and help create tangible benefits for people living in the Asia Pacific region. APEC provides funding for over 100 projects each year, with around USD 17.7 million available in 2021.

(433 words)

Directions: *Based on your understanding of the passage, answer the following questions.*

1. Why was CCER established?

2. From the example mentioned in the passage, what role do you think China plays in APEC causes?

3. Please work with your partners and tell another story about China's contribution to APEC as well as regional development.

Global Health and the WHO

Part I Reading for GC Knowledge

Text A Global Health—Key Concepts and Misperceptions

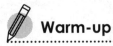
Warm-up

Self-Assessment of Global Health

Directions: Check your understanding of global health by choosing the best answer to the following assessment. Then discuss the questions that follow.

Global Health Assessment
Question 1: What is the leading cause of death globally? A. HIV/AIDS. B. Tuberculosis. C. Malaria. D. Cardiovascular disease.
Question 2: Approximately how many people worldwide lack access to clean drinking water? A. 100 million. B. 500 million. C. 1 billion. D. 2 billion.
Question 3: Which of the following factors contributes most significantly to health disparities between high-income and low-income countries? A. Access to healthcare. B. Genetic differences. C. Climate change. D. Education level.

(Continued)

Global Health Assessment
Question 4: Which infectious disease is the leading cause of death in children under five years old in low-income countries? A. Malaria. B. Diarrheal diseases. C. Measles. D. Pneumonia.
Question 5: Which organization leads global efforts to eradicate polio (小儿麻痹症)? A. World Health Organization (WHO). B. United Nations Children's Fund (UNICEF). C. Centers for Disease Control and Prevention (CDC). D. Rotary International.

1. Based on your answers to the self-assessment, what do you think are the biggest health challenges facing the world today?
2. What factors contribute to these challenges?

Global Health—Key Concepts and Misperceptions[1]

A Brief History

❶ Our current understanding of the concept of global health is based on information in the **literature** in the past seven to eight decades. Global health as a scientific term first appeared in the literature in the 1940s. It was **subsequently** used by the World Health Organization (WHO) as guidance and theoretical foundation. Few scholars discussed the concept of global health until the 1990s and the number of papers on this topic rose rapidly in the subsequent decade when global health was promoted under the Global Health Initiative—a global health plan signed by the U.S. President Barack

---

1 The text was adapted from Chen, X., Li, H., Lucero-Prisno, D. E., Abdullah, A. S., Huang, J., Laurence, C., ... & Zou, Y. 2020. What is global health? Key concepts and clarification of misperceptions: Report of the 2019 GHRP editorial meeting. *Global Health Research and Policy, 5*(14):1–8.

Obama. As a key part of the national strategy in economic globalization, security and international policies, global health in the United States has promoted collaborations across countries to deal with challenging medical and health issues through federal funding, development aids, capacity building, education, scientific research, policy-making, and implementation.

❷ Developmentally and historically, we have learned and will continue to learn global health from the WHO. WHO's projects are often ambitious, involving multiple countries, or even global in scope. Through research and action projects, the WHO has established a solid knowledge base, relevant theories, models, methodologies, valuable data, and lots of experiences that can be directly used in developing global health. Typical examples include WHO's efforts for global HIV/AIDS control and the primary healthcare programs to promote health for all.

The Definition of Global Health

❸ From published studies in the international literature and our experiences in research, training, teaching and practice, our meeting reached a consensus—global health is a newly established branch of health sciences, growing out from medicine, public health and international health, with much input from the WHO. What makes global health different from them is that (1) global health deals with only medical and health issues with global impact; (2) the main task of global health is to seek global solutions to the issues with global health impact; and (3) the **ultimate** goal is to use the power of academic research and science to promote health for all, and to improve health **equity** and reduce health **disparities**.

❹ Therefore, global health targets populations in all countries and involves all sectors beyond medical and health systems, although global health research and practice can be conducted locally.

The Concept of Global Impact

❺ Global impact is a key concept for global health. Different from other public health and medical disciplines, global health can address any issue that has a global impact on the health of humankind, including health system problems that have already affected or will affect a large number of people or countries across the globe. **Illustrative** examples are (1) the SARS **epidemic** that occurred in several areas in Hong Kong, China could spread globally in a short period to cause many medical and public health challenges; (2) the global epidemic of HIV/AIDS; and (3) the COVID-19 epidemic that first broke out in December 2019 in Wuhan and quickly spread to many countries in the world.

❻ Along with rapid and **unevenly** paced globalization, economic growth, and technological development, more and more medical and health issues with global impact emerge. Typical examples include growing health disparities, migration-related medical and health issues, issues related to Internet abuse, the spread of **sedentary** lifestyles and lack of physical activity, obesity, increasing rates of substance abuse, depression, suicide, and many other emerging mental health issues.

The Concept of Global Solution

❼ Another concept parallel to global impact is global solution. What do we mean by global solutions? Different from the conventional understanding of public health and medicine, global health selectively targets issues with global impact. Such issues often can only be effectively solved at the macro level through cross-cultural, international, and/or even global collaboration and cooperation among different **entities** and stakeholders. Furthermore, as long as the problem is solved, it will benefit a large number of the population. We identify this type of **intervention** as a global solution. For example, the measures used to end the SARS epidemic are global solutions; and the ongoing measures to control influenza and **malaria** and the measures taken by China, WHO, and many countries in the world to control the COVID-19 epidemic started in China are also great examples of global solutions. Global solutions are also needed for many emerging health problems, including cardiovascular diseases, sedentary lifestyle, obesity, Internet abuse, drug abuse, tobacco smoking, suicide, and other problems. As described earlier, global solutions are not often a medical intervention or a procedure for individual patients but frameworks, policies, strategies, laws, and regulations. Using social media to deliver interventions represents a promising approach in establishment of global solutions, given its power to penetrate physical barriers and can reach a large body of audience quickly.

Global Health, International Health, and Public Health

❽ As previously discussed, global health has been linked to several other related disciplines, particularly public health, international health, and medicine. To our understanding, global health can be considered as an application of medical and public health sciences together with other disciplines in tackling those issues with global impact and in the effort to seek global solutions.

❾ Thus, global health treats public health sciences and medicine as their foundations, and will selectively use theories, knowledge, techniques, **therapeutics**, and prevention measures from public health, medicine, and other disciplines to understand and solve global health problems.

⑩ There are also clear boundaries between global health, public health and medicine with regard to the target population. Medicine targets patient populations, public health targets health populations in general, while global health targets the global population. We have to admit that there are obvious overlaps between global health, public health and medicine, particularly between global health and international health. It is worth noting that global health can be considered as an **extension** of international health with regard to its scope and purposes.

⑪ International health focuses on the health of participating countries with the intention to affect non-participating countries, while global health directly states that its goal is to promote health and prevent and treat diseases for all people in all countries across the globe. Thus, global health can be considered as developed from, and **eventually** replace international health.

(1,028 words)

 Glossary

literature	/ˈlɪtrətʃə(r)/	n.	文献
subsequently	/ˈsʌbsɪkwəntli/	adv.	随后，后来，之后；接着
ultimate	/ˈʌltɪmət/	adj.	最终的，终极的
equity	/ˈekwəti/	n.	公平，公正
disparity	/dɪˈspærəti/	n.	明显差异
illustrative	/ˈɪləstrətɪv/	adj.	说明性的；解说性的
epidemic	/ˌepɪˈdemɪk/	n.	（疾病的）流行
unevenly	/ʌnˈiːvnli/	adv.	不均衡地
sedentary	/ˈsedntri/	adj.	需要久坐的
entity	/ˈentəti/	n.	实体
intervention	/ˌɪntəˈvenʃn/	n.	干涉
malaria	/məˈleəriə/	n.	疟疾
therapeutics	/ˌθerəˈpjuːtɪks/	n.	治疗学
extension	/ɪkˈstenʃn/	n.	延伸，延展
eventually	/ɪˈventʃuəli/	adv.	终于；最终

Task 1

Directions: Please read the text and fill in the blanks below with a proper word.

Global Health	Examples
A brief history	
• Introduction of global health as a term in (1) _____. • Importance underlined by the WHO and increased (2) _____, especially after the 1990s.	• Global Health Initiative by Barack Obama. • WHO's ambitious projects like (3) _____.
Definition	
• Outline global health as a branch evolved from (4) _____, public health, and international health, influenced significantly by the WHO. • Key differences: global impact focus, global solutions seeking, and goal of promoting (5) _____.	• Target populations globally, transcends local research and practice.
The concept of global impact	
• Discusses the significance of issues with a worldwide impact on health. • Highlight the broader scope compared with other health disciplines.	• Examples include SARS, HIV/AIDS, and (6) _____. • Mention of emerging global health issues due to (7) _____ and lifestyle changes.
The concept of global solution	
• Introduce global solutions as responses to globally impactful health issues. • Emphasize cross-cultural, (8) _____ for macro-level solutions.	• SARS and COVID-19 control measures. • Non-medical interventions like (9) _____ for health promotion.

Global Health	Examples
Comparison with related disciplines	
• Place global health in context with public health, international health, and medicine. • Explore the foundations, overlaps, and distinctions among these fields.	• Medicine vs. public health vs. global health target populations. • Global health as (10) _____ and eventual replacement of international health.

Task 2

Directions: *Please read the text again and decide whether the following statements are true (T) or false (F) based on what you have learned from the text.*

_____ 1. The term "global health" was first used in the 1960s.

_____ 2. The World Health Organization (WHO) has had a minor role in the development of global health.

_____ 3. Global health emerged solely as an extension of public health without contributions from other fields.

_____ 4. One of the main tasks of global health is to find global solutions for issues that have a worldwide impact on health.

_____ 5. Global health research and practice are strictly conducted on an international level, without any local interventions.

_____ 6. The SARS epidemic is an example of a health issue that had a global impact.

_____ 7. Global solutions to health problems are typically medical interventions aimed at individual patients.

_____ 8. Public health, international health, and global health all target the same populations.

_____ 9. Global health is distinguished from international health by its broader scope and inclusive goals that aim to promote health for all people across the globe.

_____ 10. Economic globalization and technological development have only negative impacts on global health.

Task 3

Directions: *Please translate the following five sentences into English using the words or phrases in the parentheses.*

1. 随着全球化的快速发展，健康不平等和健康差异成为全球卫生研究的重要话题。（disparity）
2. 全球公共卫生的倡议需要跨文化合作和全球合作来寻找有效的解决方案。（collaboration）
3. 过度使用互联网和久坐等生活方式的传播加剧了全球范围内的医疗和健康问题。（sedentary lifestyle）
4. 世界卫生组织在推动全球健康方面发挥了关键作用，通过其雄心勃勃的项目和国际合作改善了全球健康状况。（ambitious）
5. 全球卫生的终极目标是利用学术研究和科学的力量促进全民健康，改善健康公平，减少健康差异。（ultimate goal）

Task 4

Directions: *Work in groups and research a global health initiative not mentioned in the text that has been implemented in the last decade. Describe the initiative and its goals and outcomes. Discuss how it aligns with the concept of global health as outlined in the passage.*

Text B The Way Forward: WHO's Five Strategic Directions

 Warm-up

Directions: *Familiarize yourself with the WHO and its key functions. Find out basic facts of the WHO and share your answers with your classmates.*

WHO Fact Hunt	
Fact 1: When was the WHO founded?	**Fact 2:** Where is its headquarters located?
Fact 3: What is its primary mission?	**Fact 4:** Name three major global health issues that the WHO focuses on addressing.

(Continued)

WHO Fact Hunt	
Fact 5: What are the WHO's key initiatives or campaigns?	**Fact 6:** How does the WHO respond to global health emergencies?
Fact 7: Name one current project or program led by the WHO in China.	**Fact 8:** Who is the current Director-General of the WHO?

The Way Forward: WHO's Five Strategic Directions[1]

❶ To meet the **fundamental** challenges faced by today's health systems, the strategy proposes five interdependent strategic directions that need to be adopted in order for health service delivery to become more people-centered and **integrated**.

- The five strategic directions are:
- **Empowering** and engaging people;
- Strengthening governance and **accountability**;
- **Reorienting** the model of care;
- **Coordinating** services;
- Creating an enabling environment.

❷ Action on each of these strategic directions is intended to have an influence at different levels—from the way services are delivered to people, families and communities, to changes in the way organizations, care systems, and policy-making operate. Put together, the five strategic directions represent an interconnected set of actions that seeks to transform health systems to provide services that are more people-centered and integrated.

❸ The five strategic directions should be regarded as interdependent, which means that achieving success requires their **simultaneous** adoption. The **cumulative** benefit of the five strategic directions is necessary to help build more effective health systems. This means that a lack of progress in one area has the potential to **undermine** progress

---

1 The text was adapted from "WHO Global Strategy on People-Centered and Integrated Health Services: Interim Report", 2015. Retrieved from the World Health Organization website.

made in other areas.

❹ What the evidence strongly suggests is that the development of interventions in specific country contexts needs to be locally developed and negotiated. In each specific context, the exact mix of strategies to be used will need to be designed and developed taking account of the local context, values, and preferences.

Strategic Direction 1: Empowering and Engaging People

❺ Empowering and engaging people is about providing the opportunity, skills, and resources that people need to be **articulate** and empowered users of health services. The purpose of this strategic direction is to unlock community and individual resources for action at all levels. It seeks to empower individuals to make effective decisions about their own health, becoming articulate and empowered co-producers of health services. Communities are enabled to become actively engaged in co-producing healthy environments, providing care services in partnership with the health sector and contributing to healthy public policy. Special attention is given to engaging and supporting the voices of **minorities**.

❻ Involving individuals, families, and communities in healthcare has long been considered an essential component of healthcare services and systems. For example, since 2005, the WHO has led global efforts on family and patient engagement through establishing Patients for Patient Safety, a network of patient advocates that serves as a platform to bring the patient's voice to healthcare. Most recently, the WHO has sought to establish a framework for action on patients and family engagement in the knowledge that this can support improved care experiences and outcomes while reducing healthcare costs.

Strategic Direction 2: Strengthening Governance and Accountability

❼ Strengthening governance and accountability involves promoting **transparency** in decision-making and generating **robust** systems for the collective accountability of health providers and health system managers through **aligning** governance, accountability, and **incentives**. Governance and accountability mechanisms are needed to improve policy dialogs on national health policies, strategies, and plans with citizens and communities. These are too often dominated by health financing and macroeconomic policies, disease-specific rather than population-oriented programs of care and the priorities and frameworks of development agencies and donors. Robust governance and accountability mechanisms are required to achieve a coherent and integrated approach in healthcare policy and planning.

Strategic Direction 3: Reorienting the Model of Care

❽ Reorienting the model of care means ensuring that efficient and effective healthcare services are purchased and provided through models of care that **prioritize** primary and community care services and the co-production of health. This encompasses the shift from inpatient to **ambulatory** and **outpatient** care and the need for a fully integrated and effective **referral** system. It requires clear investment in **holistic** care, including health promotion and ill-health prevention strategies that support people's health and well-being. Reorienting models of care will also create new opportunities for inter-sectoral action at a community level to address the social **determinants** of health and make the best use of scarce resources. The role of multiple sectors in an integrated manner is particularly critical for risk management for health.

Strategic Direction 4: Coordinating Services

❾ Coordinating services involve coordinating care around the needs of people at every level of care, as well as promoting activities to integrate different healthcare providers and create effective networks between health and other sectors. The core purpose of this strategic direction is to overcome the **fragmentations** in care delivery that can undermine the ability of health systems to provide safe, accessible, high quality, and cost-effective care in order to improve care experiences and outcomes for people. It **entails** the integration of key public health functions including surveillance, early detection, and rapid emergency response capacity into the health service delivery system to address emergencies due to any hazard faced by the system.

Strategic Direction 5: Creating an Enabling Environment

❿ In order for the four previous strategies to become an operational reality, there is a need to create an enabling environment that brings together the different stakeholders to undertake transformational change. **Inevitably**, this is a complex task involving a diverse set of processes to bring about the necessary changes in **legislative** frameworks, financial arrangements and incentives, and the reorientation of the workforce and public policy-making. Such fundamental changes are challenging, whatever the country context, and many care systems have yet to reap significant benefits from their efforts.

⓫ The aim of this strategic direction is to create an enabling environment for change that promotes population health in a **participatory** and inclusive manner. This can be done through adopting and managing strategic approaches that facilitate the large-scale, transformational changes that are needed to support people-centered and integrated health services for all.

(1,012 words)

 Glossary

fundamental	/ˌfʌndəˈmentl/	adj.	基本的，根本的
integrated	/ˈɪntɪgreɪtɪd/	adj.	融合的，各部分密切协调的
empower	/ɪmˈpaʊə(r)/	v.	使能够
accountability	/əˌkaʊntəˈbɪləti/	n.	责任，责任心
reorient	/ˌriːˈɔːrient/	v.	重定，再调整
simultaneous	/ˌsɪmlˈteɪniəs/	adj.	同时的
cumulative	/ˈkjuːmjələtɪv/	adj.	累积的
undermine	/ˌʌndəˈmaɪn/	v.	逐渐削弱
articulate	/ɑːˈtɪkjələt/	adj.	善于表达的
minority	/maɪˈnɒrəti/	n.	少数
transparency	/trænsˈpærənsi/	n.	透明性
robust	/rəʊˈbʌst/	adj.	强劲的；富有活力的
align	/əˈlaɪn/	v.	使一致
incentive	/ɪnˈsentɪv/	n.	激励，刺激
prioritize	/praɪˈɒrɪtaɪz/	v.	优先处理
ambulatory	/ˈæmbjələtəri/	adj.	非固定的，可移动的
outpatient	/ˈaʊtpeɪʃnt/	n.	门诊病人
referral	/rɪˈfɜːrəl/	n.	移交，送交
holistic	/həʊˈlɪstɪk/	adj.	整体的；全面的
determinant	/dɪˈtɜːmɪnənt/	n.	决定因素；决定条件
fragmentation	/ˌfrægmenˈteɪʃn/	n.	破碎；分裂
entail	/ɪnˈteɪl/	v.	牵连；导致
inevitablely	/ɪnˈevɪtəbli/	adv.	必然发生地
legislative	/ˈledʒɪslətɪv/	adj.	立法的
participatory	/pɑːˌtɪsɪˈpeɪtəri/	adj.	参与的

Task 1

Directions: *Please read the text and fill in the blanks in the summary.*

The World Health Organization (WHO) has outlined five (1) _____ directions to address fundamental challenges in health systems, aiming to make them more (2) _____ and integrated. These strategies include empowering and engaging individuals and (3) _____, enhancing governance and accountability, (4) _____ care models to prioritize primary and community services, coordinating services to overcome care (5) _____, and creating an enabling environment for systematic transformation. Each strategic direction is interdependent, suggesting that (6) _____ adoption is crucial for effective health system reform. Emphasizing the need for local context in (7) _____ development, the WHO advocates for strategies to be tailored to specific country contexts, respecting local values and (8) _____. Special attention is given to involving (9) _____ and ensuring that health services are co-produced with communities. Furthermore, improving governance and accountability is highlighted as (10) _____ for transparent decision-making. Overall, these strategic directions aim to facilitate transformational change, promoting health inclusively and participatorily.

Task 2

Directions: *Please read the text again and match each strategic direction in Column A with its corresponding goal or main action in Column B.*

Column A

1. Empowering and engaging people

2. Strengthening governance and accountability

3. Reorienting the model of care

Column B

a. involves promoting transparency in decision-making and establishing robust systems for collective accountability of health providers and system managers.

b. prioritizes primary and community care services, promoting health and well-being through integrated care models.

c. aims to overcome care fragmentation by coordinating care around the needs of people and integrating healthcare providers across sectors.

4. Coordinating services

d. seeks to unlock community and individual resources, making people to be articulate and empowered co-producers of health services.

5. Creating an enabling environment

e. brings together stakeholders for transformational change, involving changes in legislative frameworks, financial arrangements, and public policy-making.

Task 3

Directions: *Please translate the following paragraph into Chinese.*

In the quest to strengthen global health systems, empowering communities and enhancing governance are essential steps toward achieving accountability and transparency in healthcare delivery. A reorientation of the model of care is crucial, prioritizing holistic approaches that encompass both preventative strategies and ambulatory services. By coordinating health services, we can address fragmentation and ensure that interventions are not only robust and articulated but also culturally inclusive, catering to the needs of minorities and the wider population alike. The cumulative effect of these interdependent strategies, supported by simultaneous and aligned efforts, can significantly undermine health disparities, laying the foundation for a more inclusive, effective, and empowered health system worldwide.

Task 4

Directions: *Work in groups and choose one of the five strategic directions. Develop a brief outline of a hypothetical health initiative that could be implemented in a local community. The initiative should include the following details:*

- Name of the initiative;
- Strategic direction chosen;
- Goals of the initiative;
- Key activities;
- Expected outcomes;
- How it addresses local context, values, and preferences.

Part II Drilling for GC Skills

How to Write a Report (II)

There are usually seven steps to write a report.

1. Choose a Topic Based on the Assignment

Before you start writing, you need to choose the topic of your report. Usually, the topic is assigned to you, as with most business reports, or predetermined by the nature of your work, as with scientific reports. If that's the case, you can ignore this step and move on. If you're in charge of choosing your own topic, as with a lot of academic reports, then this is one of the most important steps in the whole writing process. Try to choose a topic that fits these two criteria:

- There's adequate information: Choose a topic that's not too general but not too specific, with enough information to fill your report without padding, but not too much that you can't cover everything.

- It's something you're interested in: Although this isn't a strict requirement, it does help the quality of a report if you're engaged by the subject matter.

Task 1

Directions: *Please read the topics below and choose one as the topic of your report and share the reason why you choose this topic.*

(1) Maternal and Child Health

(2) Infectious Disease Outbreaks

(3) The Impact of Climate Change on Global Health

(4) The Global Burden of Non-communicable Diseases (NCDs)

(5) Access to Healthcare in Low- and Middle-Income Countries

2. Conduct Research

With business and scientific reports, the research is usually your own or provided by the company—although there's still plenty of digging for external sources in both. For academic papers, you're largely on your own for research, unless you're required to use class materials. That's one of the reasons why choosing the right topic is so crucial; you won't go far if the topic you picked doesn't have enough available research. The key is to search only for reputable sources: official documents, other reports, research papers, case studies, books from respected authors, etc. You can use research cited in other similar reports. You can often find a lot of information online through search engines, but a quick trip to the library can also help in a pinch.

Task 2

Directions: *Please read the skills below and share which one you usually use to make sure the resources are reputable when you are doing your research.*

- Evaluate the credibility of the author or organization.
- Assess the publication or website.
- Check for references and citations.
- Consider objectivity and bias.
- Review the publication date.
- Cross-reference with multiple sources.
- Consider the target audience and purpose.

3. Write a Thesis Statement

Before you go any further, write a thesis statement to help you conceptualize the main theme of your report. Just like the topic sentence of a paragraph, the thesis statement summarizes the main point of your report. Once you've collected enough research, you should notice some trends and patterns in the information. If these patterns all infer or lead up to a bigger, overarching point, that's your thesis statement. For example, if you were writing a report on the wages of fast-food employees, your thesis might be something like, "Although wages used to be commensurate with living expenses, after years of stagnation they are no longer adequate." From there, the rest of your report will elaborate on that thesis, with ample evidence and supporting arguments. It's good to include your thesis statement in both the executive summary and introduction of your report, but you still want to figure it out early so you know which direction to go when you work on your outline next. The following example is from "The Global Burden of Non-communicable Diseases (NCDs)".

> The global burden of non-communicable diseases (NCDs) poses a significant challenge to public health systems worldwide, necessitating comprehensive strategies to prevent, manage, and mitigate the impact of NCDs on individuals and society.

Task 3

Directions: *Please try to write a thesis statement for the report topic you have chosen in Task 1.*

4. Prepare an Outline

Writing an outline is recommended for all kinds of writing, but it's especially useful for reports given their emphasis on organization. Because reports are often separated by headings and subheadings, a solid outline makes sure you stay on track while writing without missing anything. You should start thinking about your outline during the research phase when you start to notice patterns and trends. If you're stuck, try making a list of all the key points, details, and evidence you want to mention. See if you can fit them into general and specific categories, which you can turn into headings and subheadings respectively. The following example is from "The Global Burden of Non-communicable Diseases (NCDs)".

---

1. **Introduction**

    Definition and scope of non-communicable diseases (NCDs)

    Importance and impact of NCDs on global health

2. **Overview of Non-communicable Diseases**

    Common types of NCDs

    Prevalence and trends of NCDs globally

3. **Risk Factors and Determinants of NCDs**

    Behavioral risk factors

    Environmental risk factors

    Socioeconomic determinants

4. **Global Burden of NCDs**

    Mortality rates and causes of death related to NCDs

(Continued)

> Disability-adjusted life years (DALYs) associated with NCDs
>
> Regional variations in NCD burden
>
> **5. Economic Impact of NCDs**
>
> Direct healthcare costs of NCD treatment and management
>
> Indirect costs, including productivity losses and economic burden
>
> Implications for healthcare systems and national economies
>
> **6. Global Initiatives and Policies**
>
> World Health Organization's Global Action Plan for the Prevention and Control of NCDs
>
> United Nations Sustainable Development Goals (SDGs) related to NCDs
>
> National policies and strategies to address NCDs
>
> **7. Prevention and Control Strategies**
>
> Health promotion and education campaigns
>
> Public health interventions for NCD prevention
>
> Access to diagnosis, treatment, and care for NCDs
>
> **8. Challenges and Barriers**
>
> Lack of awareness and understanding of NCDs
>
> Inadequate healthcare infrastructure and workforce
>
> Socioeconomic inequalities in access to prevention and treatment
>
> **9. Innovations and Best Practices**
>
> Technological advancements in NCD prevention and management
>
> Successful interventions and programs in different countries
>
> Community engagement and partnerships for NCD control
>
> **10. Conclusion**
>
> Recap of key findings on the global burden of NCDs
>
> Importance of addressing NCDs for global health and development
>
> Recommendations for future actions and research

5. Write a Rough Draft

Actually writing the rough draft, or first draft, is usually the most time-consuming step. Here's where you take all the information from your research and put it into words. To avoid getting overwhelmed, simply follow your outline step by step to make sure you don't accidentally leave out anything. Don't be afraid to make mistakes; that's the number one rule for writing a rough draft. Expecting your first draft to be perfect adds a lot of pressure. Instead, write in a natural and relaxed way, and worry about the specific details like word choice and correcting mistakes later. That's what the last two steps are for.

6. Revise and Edit Your Report

Once your rough draft is finished, it's time to go back and start fixing the mistakes you ignored the first time around. First, re-read your report for any major issues, such as cutting or moving around entire sentences and paragraphs. Sometimes you'll find your data doesn't line up, or that you misinterpreted a key piece of evidence. This is the right time to fix the "big picture" mistakes and rewrite any longer sections as needed. If you're unfamiliar with what to look for when editing, you can read our previous guide with some more advanced self-editing tips. For example:

> × Austen's style is frequently humorous, her characters are often described as "witty". Although this is less true of *Mansfield Park*.
>
> √ Austen's style is frequently humorous. Her characters are often described as "witty", although this is less true of *Mansfield Park*.

7. Proofread and Check for Mistakes

Last, it pays to go over your report one final time, just to optimize your wording and check for grammatical or spelling mistakes. In the previous step you checked for "big picture" mistakes, but here you're looking for specific, even nitpicky problems. For example:

> × Mary Crawfords character is a complicate one and her relationships with Fanny and Edmund undergoes several transformations through out the novel.
>
> √ Mary Crawford's character is a complicated one, and her relationships with both Fanny and Edmund undergo several transformations throughout the novel.

Task 4

Directions: *Based on the steps and examples above, please work in groups and write a report on one of the topics below. The report is supposed to be no less than 1,000 words.*

(1) Maternal and Child Health

(2) Infectious Disease Outbreaks

(3) The Impact of Climate Change on Global Health

(4) The Global Burden of Non-communicable Diseases (NCDs)

(5) Access to Healthcare in Low- and Middle-Income Countries

Part III Notes from China

The Globalization of Chinese Medicine[1]

Traditional Chinese Medicine (TCM) is a national treasure and a fully institutionalized and government-supported part of the Chinese healthcare system. Besides almost 3,000 dedicated hospitals, over 95% of Western medical hospitals also have fully-fledged Chinese-medicine wards and outpatient departments.

Officially, there are three distinct methods by which TCM is integrated into China's healthcare system. The first is the use of TCM drugs or treatment techniques by biomedical physicians to enhance the effectiveness of biomedical treatment to treat its side effects. The second is the use of TCM as a medical system in its own right; and the third consists of the integration of Chinese and Western medicine. In practice, the boundary between the three methods is difficult to draw. Biomedical ideas and concepts have been assimilated into Chinese medicine, biomedical drugs are routinely prescribed in Chinese-medicine wards and outpatient departments.

Given its commitment to modernization and the development of science and technology, the Chinese government is pressing hard for the systematization of TCM disease categories, diagnostic standards, and therapeutic techniques, and to enforce a more stringent evaluation of therapeutic outcomes. At the same time, however, the scientific status of TCM is decreed as a fact a priori rather than defined through inter-

---

1 This article was adapted from Scheid, V. 2000. The globalization of Chinese medicine. *The Lancet*, 354.

professional struggles. TCM is thus developing as a complex hybrid at the interface of tradition, modernity, and post-modernity, and cannot be reduced to one single system of practice.

Public support for Chinese medicine in China remains impressive. Exercises such as *qigong* and *taijiquan* are practiced daily by millions of Chinese people. TCM is now practiced in one form or another by more than 300,000 practitioners in over 140 countries. The first hospital for Chinese medicine in Europe was opened in Germany in 1990. British general practitioners are increasingly contracting out for acupuncture services, public health insurance companies in Germany routinely refund part of the costs of acupuncture treatment provided by trained doctors, and in France, acupuncture is a widely accepted part of healthcare provision. Degree programs in Chinese medicine are now offered at several British universities, and courses in TCM are established at European medical schools. Tongrentang, Beijing's oldest pharmacy founded in the 17th century, opened a branch in central London in 1995.

Given the worldwide hegemony of biomedicine throughout most of this century, the global emergence of TCM is a monumental event. Indeed, proponents speak of the 21st century as the "century of TCM". More likely is a continued integration of TCM into existing healthcare systems worldwide. TCM may be institutionalized along the Chinese model with similar long-term outcomes. Or TCM may develop into a heterogeneous, vibrant tradition for the sake of clinical efficacy, grounded in personal experience and modern research.

Directions: *Please read the text and share your thoughts on global health and China's contributions. The following tips may help you.*

My Thoughts on China's Contributions to Global Health
Tip 1: How has traditional Chinese medicine (TCM) contributed to global health practices, and what unique insights or approaches does it offer compared with Western medicine?
Tip 2: What are the possible challenges and opportunities associated with integrating TCM into mainstream global healthcare systems?
Tip 3: In what ways can China enhance global health diplomacy and cooperation, and how might these efforts contribute to broader global health goals and initiatives?

Unit 5

Global Ecology and the World Bank

Part I Reading for GC Knowledge

Text A Economy-Wide and Enabling Policies for Carbon Neutrality

Warm-up

Self-Assessment of Global Competence

Directions: *Please rate yourself on a scale of 1 to 5, where 1 = Strongly Disagree; 2 = Disagree; 3 = Neutral; 4 = Agree; 5 = Strongly Agree. Then discuss the questions that follow.*

Self-Assessment Questionnaire	Scale				
I am familiar with the concept of economy-wide policies.	1	2	3	4	5
I am familiar with the concept of enabling policies.	1	2	3	4	5
I am familiar with the concept of carbon neutrality.	1	2	3	4	5
I understand the relationship between economy-wide policies and ecological concerns.	1	2	3	4	5
I can well explain that economy-wide policies contribute to environmental sustainability.	1	2	3	4	5
I can well explain that enabling policies can promote ecological conservation.	1	2	3	4	5
I am aware of the potential conflicts between economy-wide policies and ecological concerns.	1	2	3	4	5
I understand the need to balance economic growth and environmental protection.	1	2	3	4	5
I can explain well the role of enabling policies in achieving sustainable development.	1	2	3	4	5
I am quite confident in discussing the relationship between economy-wide policies and ecology.	1	2	3	4	5

1. Based on your self-assessment, what do you think of the relationship between economic development and ecological preservation?
2. Considering your score, would you say that you have a good understanding of sustainable development? How much do you know about China's ecological civilization?

Economy-Wide and Enabling Policies for Carbon Neutrality[1]

❶ A growth-friendly and inclusive **decarbonization** strategy requires carefully designed economy-wide policies to complement sectoral climate policy actions. Economy-wide climate policies are necessary to **internalize** both the negative externality of carbon emissions and the positive externalities from innovation that result in the underprovision of low-carbon technologies. However, achieving carbon neutrality will require more than low-carbon policies alone. How quickly and smoothly the economy adjusts to a change in relative prices depends in large measure on how flexible and efficient factor and product markets are. Broader structural reforms to promote a more decisive role of market forces in guiding the **allocation** of capital, labor, and **R&D investment** are hence critical to enable the economy to adapt more efficiently to changing price signals and regulations, thereby lowering adjustment costs. Adopting climate actions within such a comprehensive policy framework would help ease the inevitable **trade-offs** and maximize the potential **synergies** between China's climate and development objectives. This section will explore the options for economy-wide policies that can facilitate the transition—macroeconomic and structural policies, green finance, and the just transition.

1. Macroeconomic and Structural Policies: Carbon Pricing, Competition, Trade, and Innovation

(1) Expand the Role of Carbon Pricing

❷ Carbon pricing is widely seen as one of the most efficient ways to drive economy-wide abatement. Unlike administrative measures, carbon pricing does not require policy-makers to make detailed centralized decisions on the most cost-effective abatement investments. Instead, carbon pricing signals the costs of emissions, allowing decentralized market participants to discover cost-effective abatement options, reallocate resources, and dynamically drive innovation. However, there are several **prerequisites** for carbon pricing to be effective; foremost, functioning markets where price signals

---
[1] This text was adapted from "Chapter Three of China: Country Climate and Development Report", 2022. Retrieved from the World Bank Group website.

drive the behavior of both producers and consumers. In heavily regulated or state-owned monopoly market structures, however, the effects of price signals are often **muted**.

(2) Foster Decarbonization Through SOE Reforms and Competition

❸ **State-owned enterprises (SOEs)** continue to play a **dominant** role in China's economy, especially in carbon-intensive sectors. SOEs are estimated to account for around 25%–40% of GDP and around 40% of employment. SOEs control value chains for sectors responsible, directly or indirectly, for the majority of China's emissions: coal, electricity, oil, gas, steel, and cement. It is estimated that SOEs **generate** about half of the country's total greenhouse gas emissions. Addressing emissions generated by SOEs will therefore form a key component of reaching China's goal of carbon neutrality before 2060.

(3) Level Trade Costs for Low-Carbon Production

❹ Like elsewhere in the world, there are implicit trade policy distortions that favor trade in high-carbon products. Analysis for this report demonstrates that China's Non-Tariff Barriers (NTBs) and import tariffs are on average higher on lower-carbon products. This is estimated to result in an implicit subsidy on imports of high-carbon products equivalent to around \$68 per ton of CO_2. This pattern of incentives that favor high-carbon products has started to change over the past decade. Since the announcement of the 30–60 targets, there has also been an increased discussion about changing the export and import tariff structure. In April 2021, the Customs Tariff Commission declared that it would **scrap** import tariffs on certain steel products and raw materials, increase export tariffs for iron and other products, and remove export **rebates** for certain steel products. This has been accompanied by further planned import tariff reforms in 2022. The country has also introduced eco-efficient industrial parks and green special economic zones in an attempt to **boost** low-carbon production. However, fewer than 5 percent of industrial parks were green-certified in 2019.

(4) Strengthen Low-Carbon Innovation Policy

❺ Innovation policy will also play a critical role in the low-carbon transition by resolving market failures that can lead to underinvestment in low-carbon technologies. These market failures include knowledge **spillovers** from innovation that are not taken into account by private firms; path dependency of research, which gives established technologies an advantage and creates entry barriers due to economies of scale; sunk costs; and network effects. They also include difficulties in accessing financing for emerging technologies due to high uncertainty/risk, a long lag until innovation pays off, and a lack of knowledge and information among investors. Global evidence suggests that targeted innovation policies such as **feed-in tariffs** for low-carbon products have more significant impacts on low-carbon innovation than rising energy and carbon prices, which tend to have more **incremental** impacts within existing firms.

2. Green Finance

❻   China has a large financial system that holds great potential to support its decarbonization goals. With a high domestic savings rate and a large financial system equivalent to over four times its GDP, China can mobilize a **substantial** amount of commercial capital and reorient it toward sectors that are most in need. Financing from domestic policy financial institutions can help unlock further commercial capital, while insurance can increase household and business **resilience** against climate-related risks.

3. Ensuring a Just Transition

❼   The low-carbon transition will have distributional implications. Households will be affected through several channels. Rising energy prices—either because of explicit carbon pricing or regulations—will affect household consumption, with poorer households often less able to adjust to lower-carbon alternatives. Households will also be affected by changes in the labor market, with some experiencing job losses and transitions, and positive or negative impacts on their wages and other sources of income. The specific policies adopted also matter. As discussed in Section 1, carbon revenues could be recycled to mitigate some of these impacts through compensation to households through transfers, with an expanded social safety net that is able to effectively cover **vulnerable** households. China can play an important role in steering global climate coordination. There is no viable path for the world to stay within the 1.5℃ (2.7℉) warming limit without decarbonization in China. In addition to direct contributions to emissions reduction, the actions of large emitters, like China, can also strategically influence the decisions of other countries, by altering expectations over potential positive future climate outcomes and optimal choices for other countries. This strategic importance of China's decisions was demonstrated by China's carbon-neutrality pledge in September 2020. China's pledge was followed by a wave of new pledges in other countries, with the share of global greenhouse gas emissions covered by a net-zero pledge reaching almost half of the global total.

(1,072 words)

Glossary

decarbonization	/ˌdiːkɑːbənaɪˈzeɪʃn/	n.	脱碳（作用）
internalize	/ɪnˈtɜːnəlaɪz/	v.	使……内在化
allocation	/ˌæləˈkeɪʃn/	n.	分配
synergy	/ˈsɪnədʒi/	n.	协同作用
prerequisite	/ˌpriːˈrekwəzɪt/	n.	先决条件，前提
muted	/ˈmjuːtɪd/	adj.	（声音）压低的，减弱的
dominant	/ˈdɒmɪnənt/	adj.	占支配地位的
generate	/ˈdʒenəreɪt/	v.	产生，引起
scrap	/skræp/	v.	放弃，抛弃（计划、体系）
rebate	/ˈriːbeɪt/	n.	退还款
boost	/buːst/	v.	推动，使增长
spillover	/ˈspɪləʊvə(r)/	n.	溢出
incremental	/ˌɪŋkrəˈmentl/	adj.	增加的，递增的
substantial	/səbˈstænʃl/	adj.	大量的
resilience	/rɪˈzɪliəns/	n.	恢复力，复原力
vulnerable	/ˈvʌlnərəbl/	adj.	脆弱的，易受伤害的；易患病的

 Useful Expressions

economy-wide	全经济范围的，整个经济的
carbon neutrality	碳中和
R&D investment	研发投入
trade-offs	权衡
GHG emissions	温室气体排放
feed-in tariffs	上网电价

Task 1

Directions: *Please read the text and fill in the blanks below with a proper word.*

> **Economy-Wide and Enabling Policies for Carbon Neutrality**
>
> Macroeconomic and structural policies: carbon pricing, competition, trade, and innovation

(Continued)

Economy-Wide and Enabling Policies for Carbon Neutrality
• Carbon pricing is widely seen as one of the most efficient ways to drive economy-wide (1) _____. However, there are several (2) _____ for carbon pricing to be effective. In heavily regulated or state-owned monopoly market structures, the effects of price signals are often (3) _____.
• State-owned enterprises (SOEs) continue to play a(n) (4) _____ role in China's economy, especially in carbon-intensive sectors. It is estimated that SOEs (5) _____ about half of the country's total greenhouse gas emissions.
• This is estimated to result in an implicit (6) _____ on imports of high-carbon products. This pattern of (7) _____ that favors high-carbon products has started to change over the past decade. In April 2021, the Customs Tariff Commission declared that it would (8) _____ import tariffs on certain steel products and raw materials, increase export tariffs for iron and other products, and remove export (9) _____ for certain steel products.
• These market failures include knowledge (10) _____ from innovation that are not taken into account by private firms. Global evidence suggests that targeted innovation policies such as feed-in tariffs for low-carbon products have more significant impacts on low-carbon innovation than rising energy and carbon prices, which tend to have more (11) _____ impacts within existing firms.
Green finance
• China can mobilize a(n) (12) _____ amount of commercial capital and (13) _____ it toward sectors that are most in need.
Ensuring a just transition
• Rising energy prices will affect household consumption, with poorer households often less able to adjust and (14) _____ to lower-carbon alternatives.
• Carbon revenues could be recycled to (15) _____ some of these impacts through compensation to households through transfers.

Task 2

Directions: *Please read the text again and decide whether the following statements are true (T) or false (F) based on what you have learned from the text.*

_____ 1. Carbon pricing requires policy-makers to make detailed centralized decisions on the most cost-effective abatement investments.

_____ 2. Carbon pricing allows decentralized market participants to discover cost-effective abatement options.

_____ 3. In heavily regulated or state-owned monopoly market structures, the effects of price signals are often amplified.

_____ 4. State-owned enterprises (SOEs) account for a small percentage of China's GDP.

_____ 5. SOEs are responsible for the majority of China's emissions in sectors such as coal, electricity, oil, gas, steel, and cement.

_____ 6. China's Non-Tariff Barriers (NTBs) and import tariffs are lower on lower-carbon products.

_____ 7. The implicit subsidy on imports of high-carbon products in China is equivalent to \$68 per ton of CO_2.

_____ 8. Targeted innovation policies such as feed-in tariffs have a more significant impact on low-carbon innovation than rising energy and carbon prices.

_____ 9. China's large financial system is equivalent to over four times its GDP.

_____ 10. Rising energy prices due to carbon pricing or regulations will affect household consumption, with poorer households often easier to adjust to lower-carbon alternatives.

Task 3

Directions: *Please translate the following five sentences into English using the words in the parentheses.*

1. 各缔约方须继续推进这一模式，探求有利于应对其他环境挑战特别是气候变化的协同增效。（synergy）
2. 环境保护和生态平衡的努力至关重要，减少污染、森林砍伐和栖息地破坏对确保我们星球的可持续未来至关重要。（abatement）
3. 可再生能源产生清洁和可持续的电力，减少我们对化石燃料的依赖，减轻气候变化的影响。（generate）
4. 欧盟还将逐步减少传统的补贴和生产配额，最终取消那种让农场主为了防止生产过剩而让10%的土地休耕的做法。（subsidy）
5. 我们必须通过可再生能源、减排、可持续实践、生态系统保护、气候适应型基础设施、社区教育和全球合作来减缓气候变化，以实现可持续的未来。（mitigate）

Task 4

Directions: Please discuss the following questions in groups and role-play the following situation with your solution.

> **Situation**
>
> John had dedicated years of his life to working in a high-carbon industry, unaware of the impending changes that would shake his world. As the world shifted towards sustainability, his industry faced a decline, leaving him jobless and uncertain about his future. Amidst John's struggles, an environmentalist Mark recognized the challenges faced by those in high-carbon industries and was determined to make a difference. He reached out to John, offering his support and guidance.

1. What is John's difficulty in this story?
2. Suppose you were Mark in this story, how would you help John solve this problem? Work out a solution with your group member and perform the whole situation.

Text B Further Global Cooperation on Biodiversity Conservation

Warm-up

Directions: Look at the options below and talk about which measure you'd like to take to maintain global biodiversity. Give your opinions on your choices.

1. **Cross-border conservation agreements:** Establish cross-border conservation agreements with neighboring countries to coordinate efforts and ensure the protection of shared ecosystems and species. This can include joint management plans, information sharing, and collaborative conservation projects.

2. **Regional biodiversity networks:** Join regional biodiversity networks or initiatives that bring together multiple countries to exchange knowledge, share best practices, and collaborate on conservation strategies. This can help in identifying common conservation priorities and implementing coordinated actions.

3. **Transnational conservation corridors:** Work with other countries to establish transnational conservation corridors that connect protected areas and habitats across borders. This facilitates the movement of species, enhances genetic diversity, and promotes ecosystem resilience.

4. **Sustainable resource management:** Collaborate with other countries to develop and implement sustainable resource management practices. This can include sharing expertise on sustainable agriculture, fisheries, forestry, and other natural resource sectors to minimize negative impacts on biodiversity.

5. **Ecotourism partnerships:** Foster partnerships with other countries to promote responsible and sustainable ecotourism practices. This can involve joint marketing campaigns, sharing tourism revenue, and developing ecotourism guidelines that prioritize biodiversity conservation and benefit local communities.

Further Global Cooperation on Biodiversity Conservation[1]

❶ Facing the global challenge of biodiversity loss, all countries form a community of shared future. China firmly practices **multilateralism** and actively carries out international cooperation on **biodiversity** conservation through extensive consultations to build consensus. It is contributing solutions to global biodiversity conservation and working together with the international community to build a shared future for humanity.

1. Actively Implementing International Conventions

❷ By actively implementing the Convention on Biological Diversity and related **protocols**, with a strong sense of responsibility as a major country, China has worked to enhance synergies among biodiversity-related conventions and played an important role in global biodiversity conservation and governance.

❸ Actively implementing the Convention on Biological Diversity and related protocols. China firmly supports the multilateral governance system for biodiversity and has adopted strong policies and measures to fulfill its obligations under the Convention since 1992. As an important signing party of the Convention and its protocols China has submitted high-quality national reports on a regular basis. In July 2019, China submitted its Sixth National Report to the Convention on Biological Diversity and in October the Fourth National Report to the Cartagena Protocol on Biosafety. Since 2019, China has been the largest contributor to the core budget of the Convention and its protocols and has strongly supported its operation and implementation. In recent years, China has continued to increase its contributions to the Global Environment Facility (GEF) and has become the largest developing country contributor to the GEF, lending strong support

---

1 This text was adapted from Chapter Three of China: Country Climate and Development Report, World Bank Group, 2022.

to global biodiversity conservation.

❹ Enhancing synergies among biodiversity-related conventions. Biodiversity is closely related to other eco-environmental issues. China supports collaborative efforts in building a stronger global ecological security barrier and an ecosystem that respects nature and is ready to work with all the parties to push for a joint role for the Convention and other international conventions. China takes an active part in implementing the Convention on International Trade in Endangered Species of Wild Fauna and Flora, the United Nations Framework Convention on Climate Change, the United Nations Convention to Combat Desertification, the Convention on Wetlands of International Importance Especially as Waterfowl Habitat, and the documents of the UN Forum on Forests. In cooperation with relevant international organizations, China has established the International Desertification Control Knowledge Management Center. China and New Zealand jointly led the efforts on Nature-based Solutions (NBS) projects, making NBS a synergistic solution in combating climate change and biodiversity loss. In September 2020, China announced that it would strive to **peak** carbon emissions by 2030 and achieve carbon neutrality by 2060, contributing its share to the global response to climate change mitigation.

❺ Achieving remarkable results in fulfilling obligations. China has made a positive contribution to the 2020 global biodiversity targets (the Aichi targets) and the United Nations 2030 Sustainable Development Goals. In 2010, the China National Biodiversity Conservation Strategy and Action Plan (2011–2030) was published. Since then, China has been working for a better eco-environment by improving the legal system and other mechanisms, strengthening in-situ and ex-situ conservation, increasing public participation and boosting international cooperation and exchanges on biodiversity. China has over-fulfilled three of the Aichi targets—establishing terrestrial nature **reserves**, restoring and ensuring important ecosystem services, and increasing ecosystem resilience and carbon storage—and made progress in 13 targets, including **mainstreaming** biodiversity, sustainable management of agriculture, forestry and fishery, and sustainable production and consumption.

2. Strengthening International Exchanges and Cooperation

❻ China is an **advocate** of multilateralism. It engages in extensive cooperation and exchanges, **pooling** global forces in biodiversity conservation and governance. With the help of multi lateral cooperation mechanisms such as the Belt and Road Initiative (BRI) and South-South Cooperation, China has provided support for biodiversity conservation in developing countries and is striving to build a shared future for all life on Earth.

❼ Establishing multi lateral cooperation mechanisms for green development under the BRI. China regards cooperation in eco-civilization as a key component of the BRI and has adopted a series of green measures in infrastructure, energy, and finance to support participating countries with funds, technology, and capacity building. These measures are helping them transform faster to green, low-carbon growth to the benefit of the people. China has established the Belt and Road Initiative International Green Development Coalition, with international partners from over 40 countries. The Coalition facilitates cooperation on biodiversity conservation, global climate change governance, and green transformation. The BRI Environment Big Data Platform is in the making. The platform aims to collect biodiversity data from over 100 countries and provides data in support of the initiative's green development. A Green Silk Road Envoy program has been launched to jointly build environmental protection capacity with other developing countries. Under the program, China has helped relevant countries, through training and other project cooperation, to implement the United Nations 2030 Agenda for Sustainable Development.

❽ Stepping up South-South Cooperation. China has provided support for more than 80 developing countries in biodiversity conservation under the framework of South-South Cooperation. China has established a center for the Lancang-Mekong environmental cooperation and hosted regular roundtable meetings with a focus on ecosystem management and biodiversity conservation. It has set up the China-ASEAN Environmental Cooperation Center and launched and implemented with ASEAN member states a number of cooperation initiatives, including the China-ASEAN Cooperation Plan on Biodiversity and Ecological Conservation, and the Core Environment Program and Biodiversity Conservation Corridors Initiative in the Greater Mekong Subregion. Fruitful results have been achieved in biodiversity conservation, **corridor** planning and management, and community livelihood improvement. The Southeast Asia Biodiversity Research Institute of the Chinese Academy of Sciences (CAS-SEABRI) was **unveiled** in 2015 to carry out joint field studies, major scientific research, policy consultation, and personnel training. The China-Africa Environment Cooperation Center has been established for cooperation on environmental technology and for sharing green development opportunities.

❾ Carrying out extensive **bilateral** and multilateral cooperation. Following the principles of extensive consultation, joint contribution, and shared benefits, China has constantly expanded biodiversity cooperation. It has taken an active part in international conferences and activities, including the United Nations Summit on Biodiversity and the Leaders' Summit on Climate, giving **impetus** to biodiversity conservation and sustainable development. In 2020, China organized an online ministerial roundtable "Biodiversity Beyond 2020: Building a Shared Future for All Life on Earth" to discuss global biodiversity governance after 2020. China and France jointly issued the Beijing Call for Biodiversity Conservation and Climate Change in 2019. China carries out long-term cooperation on migratory bird protection with Russia, Japan, and other countries. China has worked with Russia, Mongolia, Laos, Vietnam and other countries in establishing transboundary PAs and ecological corridors. The number of species in the China-Russia transboundary nature reserve continues to grow and wild Siberian tigers are beginning to migrate freely between PAs in Russia and China. The China-Laos transboundary biodiversity reserve, with an area of 200,000 hectares, effectively protects rare and endangered species such as Asian elephants and their habitats. China has established bilateral cooperation mechanisms with Germany, the United Kingdom, South Africa, and some other countries, through which extensive cooperation and exchanges on biodiversity and ecosystem services, climate change, and **biosecurity** have been carried out. It has established a mechanism of tripartite policy dialog on biodiversity with Japan and the ROK.

(1,192 words)

 Glossary

multilateralism	/ˌmʌltiˈlætərəlɪzəm/	n.	多边主义
biodiversity	/ˌbaɪəʊdaɪˈvɜːsəti/	n.	生物多样性
protocol	/ˈprəʊtəkɒl/	n.	国际议定书；协议
peak	/piːk/	v.	达到高峰，达到最大值
reserve	/rɪˈzɜːv/	n.	保护区
mainstream	/ˈmeɪnstriːm/	v.	使主流化，使成为主流
advocate	/ˈædvəkeɪt/	n.	拥护者，提倡者
pool	/puːl/	v.	集中（资源、钱财等）以备共用
corridor	/ˈkɒrɪdɔː(r)/	n.	走廊
unveil	/ˌʌnˈveɪl/	v.	为……揭幕；推出
bilateral	/ˌbaɪˈlætərəl/	adj.	双边的
impetus	/ˈɪmpɪtəs/	n.	动力，促进
biosecurity	/ˌbaɪəʊsɪˈkjʊərəti/	n.	生物安全性

Task 1

Directions: *Please read the text and fill in the blanks in the summary.*

> The article outlines the solutions China (1) _____ to global biodiversity conservation. As a(n) (2) _____ of (3) _____, China actively carries out international cooperation on biodiversity conservation, implements the Convention on Biological Diversity and related (4) _____, and has established relevant institutions and projects. China announced that it would strive to (5) _____ carbon emissions by 2030 and achieve carbon neutrality by 2060, contributing its share to the global response to climate change (6) _____. Moreover, it (7) _____ global forces in biodiversity conservation and governance and establishes multilateral cooperation (8) _____ for green development under the BRI. China has established the Belt and Road Initiative International Green Development Coalition to (9) _____ cooperation on biodiversity conservation, global climate change governance, and green transformation. Following the principles of extensive consultation, (10) _____ contribution and shared benefits, China has constantly expanded biodiversity cooperation.

Task 2

Directions: *Please read the text again and match the functions in Column B with various cooperations in Column A. You may use one letter more than once.*

Column A	Column B
1. Belt and Road Initiative International Green Development Coalition	a. unveiled in 2015 to carry out joint field studies, major scientific research, policy consultation, and personnel training
2. The BRI Environment Big Data Platform	b. aiming to collect biodiversity data from over 100 countries and provide data in support of the initiative's green development
3. A Green Silk Road Envoy program	c. established for cooperation on environmental technology and for sharing green development opportunities

4. The Southeast Asia Biodiversity Research Institute of the Chinese Academy of Sciences

5. The China-Africa Environment Cooperation Center

d. facilitating cooperation on biodiversity conservation, global climate change governance, and green transformation

e. launched to jointly build environmental protection capacity with other developing countries

Task 3

Directions: *Please translate the following paragraph into English.*

多边主义（multilateralism）在应对生态和环境保护的复杂挑战方面发挥着至关重要的作用。事实证明，没有一个国家能够单独且有效地解决生物多样性（biodiversity）丧失和气候变化等问题。多边主义通过国际合作和分担责任，促进（facilitate）了旨在保护地球自然资源的议定书（protocol）的制定和执行（implementation）。

Task 4

Directions: *Please debate on the following topic. You are encouraged to refer to other sources for the debate. You may use the following table to help you organize ideas.*

Should governments prioritize economic development over biodiversity conservation, or should they strike a balance between the two? Discuss the potential implications of each approach and provide evidence to support your argument.

Pros	Cons

Part II Drilling for GC Skills

How to Write a Project Proposal (I)

Proposal writing is very important because a good proposal can effectively present a clear prospect of a project/program to the readers. Since the purpose of a proposal is to convince readers of the necessity, urgency, and value of a scheme/project/business, the structure must be logical and clear, and the language applied must be rational and persuasive.

There are usually three typical types of proposals—research proposal, business proposal, and project proposal. As a part of global competence development, it is important to cultivate young people's ability to study and analyze problems that are of common international concern and importance. Meanwhile, it is also equally important to develop their ability to work out a project to solve the problem. Since the problem addressed is of international concern, the proposal is usually submitted to an international organization responsible for the field. Therefore, in this chapter we focus on the project proposal.

A project proposal usually comprises the sections of Project Summary, Project Objective, Outputs and Outcomes of the Project, Beneficiaries, Dissemination, Project Effectiveness and Budget. All the sections will be introduced as follows. And the instruction of the same sections is to be assisted by the corresponding sections of a sample proposal entitled "APEC Women Amidst Fourth Industrial Revolution 2.0"

Section 1: Project Summary

The first part of the proposal starts with the proposal title/topic, and a brief summary of the proposal. The summary is supposed to be brief and concise, giving a condensed and precise description of what issue you will address or examine, and outlining the key things that your project will do, in terms of what, where, when, and with whom. The summary of the project helps the readers get an overall knowledge of it, which can facilitate their further reading of the following sectors.

Sample of summary:

The project we will propose is "APEC Women Amidst Fourth Industrial Revolution 2.0". It aims to offer an information-sharing and achievement-recording platform for the tertiary education receivers of STEM and ICT fields to trigger their potential for further internship, employment, and even the start of an enterprise and meanwhile help build females, especially the indigenous women and women in remote and rural areas, technology-enabled skills and access to e-commerce. We are planning to implement a mentoring program and a database for tertiary education receivers and launch an assistance plan for females. The project seeks the cooperation of all APEC economies and is expected to be completed in five years.

Task 1

Directions: *Discuss with your team members to decide on a topic for a proposal. The topic must be an issue concerning the development, transformation, reform, or innovation of some sectors, which has international significance. The following is an example.*

Sustainable development is a typical contemporary topic of international concern. With more attention paid to healthy economic development and more concern about the environment, the sustainable development of agriculture, energy, tourism, eco-city construction, etc., are common topics that involve people's well-being not only locally, but also globally. You can choose one area of sustainable development as a topic, and search relevant materials, information, policy, and data at the official websites of some international organizations. After deciding on the topic, each team is required to give a presentation to introduce the proposal outline.

Task 2

Directions: *Work with your partners and discuss how to write a summary of a project proposal.*

After the topic has been decided, each student is supposed to write a proposal summary. The summary should cover the specific issue, the duration, areas, and the participants and beneficiaries, the project funding, and how the capacity of the beneficiaries can be strengthened. After completing the project summary, every two students exchange their summaries to have a peer review with the contents mentioned as parameters for evaluation.

Section 2: Project Objective

In this section, the objective of the project must be stated with clarity about what problems the project seeks to address, and whether it has sustained benefits for more than one beneficiary in a specific domain. Meanwhile, it also needs to state how this project meets the eligibility and supports the funding priority of a nominated fund, because projects cannot be carried out without the support of a corresponding fund. It is necessary to elaborate on the relevance of the project with the fund, and how the project will build the capacity of the target beneficiaries.

Samples of objective:

1. *To combine women's capacity building with the utilization of digital technology.*

2. *To offer a platform for the students in colleges or other academic institutions to realize capacity building, information exchange, and best-practice sharing.*

3. *To ensure that ICT is widely spread and thus considered an essential tool by everyone, especially the disadvantaged women.*

Section 3: Outputs and Outcomes of the Project

In this section, the outputs, outcomes, beneficiaries, dissemination, and gender are included.

Here, it is necessary to differentiate the distinction between the objective, output, and outcome. The objective is the goal of the project, which is usually described with an overall statement. The outcome is the result/effect after the completion of the project, which is in alignment with the objective. The output is the activity undertaken within the framework of the project or the product of it. There is a causal relationship between the output and the outcome. It is through the output that the outcome is achieved. The output is usually manifested in events (workshops, seminars, conferences, etc.), tools (recommendations, framework of analysis, action plan, etc.), knowledge (a research paper, survey results, an analytical report, improved abilities in a particular area, etc.), collaborations (standards, agreements, identification of next steps, networking opportunities, etc.). The outcome is a numbered list, describing the specific impacts, changes or benefits that the project is expected to deliver, which directly support the project objective. These include changes in policy, processes, or behavior in the participating institutions. Be sure that each outcome can be measured and is a direct result of the project. Outcomes must be numerically measurable and statistically analyzable.

Sample of output:

Stage One: College Women's Incubator Association of APEC

The association will mainly include two parts: 1) Mentoring Program. The program aims to offer the mentoring service for the potential students to access the academic information in STEM or ICT fields and the best practice for starting an enterprise. 2) Database. The sub-database is the product for students to record their academic achievement or internship experience to prove their qualification in relevant fields.

Stage Two: E-Commerce Assistance Plan

　　Through the online workshop, indigenous women in remote and rural areas and working in energy, fisheries, agriculture, tourism, and mining industries can access basic technology-enabled skills. The online workshop will be mainly offered by the members in the College Women's Incubator Association of APEC of Stage One.

Task 3

Directions: Match the project's objectives in Column A with the outputs in Column B. One objective may generate several outputs.

Column A

1. To innovate the productivity of small enterprises in underdeveloped countries.

2. To improve the medication of rural people in South Eastern Asia.

3. To increase rural redundant laborers' employment opportunities.

Column B

a. To hold workshops and seminars to discuss the relevant issue.

b. To provide basic working skill training.

c. To upgrade the the production line.

d. To increase the local government's annual budget for new clinic construction.

e. To pass beneficiary policies like lower tuition and lower admission grade for female students.

f. To improve the sanitary condition of the local area, such as clean water resources, and reduce air pollutant emission.

g. To increase financial support for research and innovation.

h. To send medication teams regularly to rural and remote areas.

i. To provide preferential policies to investors.

4. To empower women in their social and domestic life.

j. To pass a law stipulating the lowest ratio of female staff in enterprises.

k. To connect the research institutions with the market and facilitate the transformation of their research fruits to productivity.

Section 4: Beneficiaries

As for beneficiaries, it must be stated with clarity about who are the direct project participants and users of the outputs. Describe their qualifications, level of expertise, roles/level of responsibility, gender, organization/enterprises represented, government departments, etc.

Sample of beneficiaries

In Stage One, the female tertiary education receivers in the colleges or some other academic institutions are the direct project participants and users of the outputs. They are also the members of this "incubator", which means they may use the beneficial information and regard others' stories as the paradigms. After graduation, they can start up their own business or use the achievement in the database to seek the appropriate vocations and take the responsibility to be the one who offers help in return to share their best practice.

In Stage Two, the women working for the primary or secondary industry in the remote areas with a low education level will be the direct project users. They can utilize what they have learned through the online workshops to start their own e-commerce. Meanwhile, the trainers (i.e., the members and in the College Women's Incubator Association of APEC) are supposed to take the accountability for tracing their trainers' progress and help them do a better marketing.

Section 5: Dissemination

Dissemination is also an important part of the proposal, since you want more target beneficiaries and recipients who may be interested in reading the content of the proposal and following the ongoing process of the project. You describe plans to disseminate all output documents/reports and other results of the project, which includes the following items: (1) whether the document(s)/report(s) will be officially published and issued; (2) the number, form (Electronic publication is preferred) and content of publications; (3) channels of dissemination, such as the official websites of international organizations, government agencies, or social media; (4) the target audience of each output document/report, most of whom are the potential beneficiaries of the project.

Part III Notes from China

"Xiamen Solution" Exemplifies Harmonious Coexistence Between Man and Nature[1]

As a key birthplace and early adopter of Xi Jinping's ecological ideas, Xiamen has pursued systematic ecological governance and contributed to high-quality development through marine ecological restoration for over 30 years, fostering harmony between man and nature. Now, Xiamen has built a beautiful bay living environment, enhancing the ecological vitality of the coastal zone, and contributing the "Xiamen Solution" to domestic and international urban marine ecological protection.

A Splashing Recovery

"It was a momentous occasion for Xiamen people to undergo a consciousness awakening." Wang Yanyan, chief engineer at the Xiamen Municipal Administration of Parks and Gardens, still vividly remembers how tough the battle against environmental pollution was when it was launched in the city in 1988. In March 1988, Xi, then serving as executive vice mayor of the city, set in motion a comprehensive strategy to revitalize the lake. "The vice mayor personally spearheaded the ecological protection of a lake, and with unprecedented efforts, took out 10% of the city's annual infrastructure investment for two consecutive years—10 million yuan—for lake governance," Wang told the *Global Times*.

Xiamen, as one of the first four special economic zones in China, was also in the critical stage of the Reform and Opening-Up in the late 1980s. Despite the financial constraints, the city's leaders showed remarkable courage and commitment to the cause. "The efforts put into the lake's restoration were truly exceptional for the time," Wang emphasized. Since then, Yundang Lake has witnessed five major restoration projects, with a total investment of nearly 1.99 billion yuan ($270 million). Thanks to these measures, Yundang Lake has undergone a remarkable transformation, blossoming

---

1　The text was adapted from the Globaltimes website.

into a vibrant hub of finance, tourism, and residential living in Xiamen. The successful restoration of the lake serves as a shining example for future lake remediation projects in Xiamen, while also inspiring a collective commitment to ecological civilization across the city.

A Great Example

In January 1986, Xi emphasized at a meeting in Xiamen that "protecting natural scenic resources has far-reaching implications and great significance". In 1994, after gaining legislative power for economic special zones, Xiamen enacted its first substantive local regulation, the Xiamen Environmental Protection Regulations. Since then, Xiamen has successively enacted more than 10 maritime regulations. In addition to investing in governance and actively implementing legal safeguards, Xiamen has also implemented a series of institutional innovations, such as establishing the Municipal Government's Marine Management Office, pioneering the formation of a specialized marine cleaning team in China, strictly prohibiting the introduction of heavily polluting projects, and rationalizing the layout of industrial concentration zones.

The ecological protection of bay-type cities is a global issue. In 2002, Xi, then deputy Party chief and governor of Fujian, proposed the idea of shifting Xiamen's urban planning from island-based to bay-based. Since then, the city has undertaken a succession of comprehensive renovation and development projects in five bay areas, aiming to create a "beautiful blue bay" surrounding the city.

A Rooted Initiative

During the winter months, Xiamen becomes a haven for flocks of cormorants seeking shelter and sustenance in the tranquil waters of Xinglin Bay. Seeing these majestic birds soaring through the sky in unison is a breathtaking spectacle. "Whether the ecology is good or not, the birds know best," said Guo Qiang, a member of the Xiamen Bird Watching Association, who eagerly captures the beauty of these overwintering birds with his camera. With years of experience behind the lens, Guo said he felt lucky to see firsthand the positive impact of Xiamen's efforts to restore its marine ecosystem. There are countless dedicated bird enthusiasts like Guo in Xiamen on hand to document the birds' behaviors and movements, serving as guardians of the city's precious ecological treasures. The essence of Xi's thought on ecological civilization has truly taken root in the hearts of Xiamen residents, becoming a natural and heartfelt commitment for all, Zhang said, noting that currently in Xiamen, the focus on ecological protection has transformed from government-leading to active public action.

(659 words)

Directions: *Please discuss the following questions with your partners and provide possible answers.*

1. How did the comprehensive strategy to revitalize Yundang Lake in Xiamen serve as a symbol of remarkable courage and commitment during the critical stage of the Reform and Opening-Up in the late 1980s?

2. How has Xiamen's commitment to ecological protection and restoration efforts contributed to the city's shift towards a bay-based urban planning approach and the establishment of a "beautiful blue bay" surrounding the city?

3. Please make an investigation on the harmonious relationship between man and nature in China's urban development and tell another story about it.

Unit 6

Global Gender Equality and the IAW

Part I Reading for GC Knowledge

Text A Gender Equality: The Unfinished Business of Our Time

Warm-up

Self-Assessment of Gender Equality

Directions: *Please rate yourself on a scale of 1 to 5, where 1 = Strongly Disagree; 2 = Disagree; 3 = Neutral; 4 = Agree; 5 = Strongly Agree. Then discuss the questions that follow.*

Self-Assessment Questionnaire	Scale				
Gender Equality Awareness					
I understand the concept of gender equality and its significance in society.	1	2	3	4	5
I am aware of the disparities and inequalities that affect individuals of all genders globally.	1	2	3	4	5
I recognize the impact of global movements in advancing gender equality across different societies.	1	2	3	4	5
Engagement in Gender Equality					
I am willing to advocate for equal rights and opportunities across all genders.	1	2	3	4	5
I am prepared to challenge and address gender-based stereotypes and discrimination.	1	2	3	4	5
I respect varied gender dynamics and support policies and initiatives that promote gender equality.	1	2	3	4	5
Communication for Gender Equality					
I am mindful of how gender biases can affect communication and strive to avoid them.	1	2	3	4	5
I am sensitive to gendered language and tend to use gender-inclusive language when appropriate.	1	2	3	4	5

(Continued)

Self-Assessment Questionnaire	Scale				
I advocate for the use of social media to combat gender-based violence.	1	2	3	4	5
Global Perspective on Gender Equality					
I stay updated on international movements and discussions regarding gender equality.	1	2	3	4	5
I am conscious of the challenges and difficulties faced by marginalized genders in various cultural contexts.	1	2	3	4	5
I believe that working towards gender equality is essential for global sustainable development.	1	2	3	4	5

1. Based on your self-assessment responses, how do you define gender equality?
2. Considering your scores, would you consider yourself highly aware of gender equality? Why or why not?

Gender Equality: The Unfinished Business of Our Time[1]

❶ Women and girls represent half of the world's population and, therefore, also half of its potential. Gender equality, besides being a fundamental human right, is essential to achieve peaceful societies, with full human potential and sustainable development. Moreover, research has demonstrated that empowering women spurs productivity and economic growth. Unfortunately, there is still a long way to go to achieve full equality of rights and opportunities between men and women. Therefore, it is of **paramount** importance to end the multiple forms of gender violence and secure equal access to quality education and health, economic resources, and participation in political life for women, girls, men, and boys alike. It is also essential to achieve equal opportunities in access to employment and to positions of leadership and decision-making at all levels.

❷ The term "gender" refers to the socially constructed roles and responsibilities that societies consider appropriate for men and women. Gender equality means that men and women have equal power and equal opportunities for financial independence, education, and personal development. Women's **empowerment** is a critical aspect of

---
1 The text was adapted from the "Historical Overview and the Commission on Violence Against Women" as presented on the International Alliance of Women's official website.

achieving gender equality. It encompasses enhancing a woman's sense of self-worth, her decision-making power, her access to opportunities and resources, her power and control over her own life inside and outside the home, and her ability to effect change.

❸ The International Alliance of Women (IAW), based in Geneva, serves as a pivotal international Non-Governmental Organization (NGO) with a coalition of 41 member organizations dedicated to advancing women's human rights, gender equality, and the empowerment of women. The IAW has general **consultative** status at the UN Economic and Social Council and is accredited to many specialized UN agencies. It also has participatory status with the Council of Europe and is represented at the Arab League, the African Union, and other international organizations. Through its collaborative efforts and strategic partnerships, the IAW continues to make impactful **strides** toward creating more equitable societies.

❹ In 1902, the International Alliance of Women for Suffrage and Legal Citizenship was founded by leading American **suffragists** at a meeting in Washington attended by women from eleven countries. A second meeting in Berlin, in 1904 formally constituted the organization under the name International Woman Suffrage Alliance (IWSA), which became the preeminent international women's suffrage organization. The organization adopted yellow as its color, the color used by American suffragists since 1867 and derived from the color of the sunflower. The organization had to **temporarily** cease its operations due to the First World War. At the Congress of 1926 in Paris the name was changed to International Alliance of Women for Suffrage and Equal Citizenship, and a strong link with the League of Nations was established. In 1946 the present name, International Alliance of Women, was adopted with the sub-title "Equal Rights—Equal Responsibilities". Since 1947, the IAW has had general consultative status with the United Nations Economic and Social Council and was one of the first organizations to be granted this status.

❺ The IAW has stated that achieving gender equality and empowering women and girls is the unfinished business of our time and the greatest human rights challenge in our world. Gender equality is a human right, but our world faces a **persistent** gap in access to opportunities and decision-making power for women and men. Globally, women have fewer opportunities for economic participation than men, less access to basic and higher education, greater health and safety risks, and less political representation. Guaranteeing the rights of women and giving them opportunities to reach their full potential is critical not only for attaining gender equality, but also for meeting a wide range of international development goals. Empowered women and girls contribute to the health and productivity of their families, communities, and countries, creating a ripple effect that benefits everyone.

1. Promoting Gender Equality and Empowerment

❻ The International Alliance of Women plays a crucial role in promoting gender equality and empowering women around the globe. To further this cause, the IAW implements **targeted** strategies to close the gender gap in various sectors. Initiating comprehensive educational programs that not only focus on academic education but also on life skills and leadership training for girls and women could empower them to take on more significant roles in society. In addition, the IAW advocates for gender-sensitive policies that ensure women have equal access to healthcare, economic opportunities, and legal protections against discrimination and violence.

❼ Leveraging its international network, the IAW organizes global **campaigns** to raise awareness about the importance of women's participation in political processes and decision-making positions. By collaborating with local and international partners, the IAW supports the creation of platforms that enable women to share their experiences, learn from each other, and build strong support systems. Furthermore, the IAW champions the cause of economic empowerment by supporting women entrepreneurs through **mentorship** programs, access to finance, and market opportunities. Addressing the digital divide and promoting digital literacy among women can also be a significant step towards their empowerment, enabling them to access information, services, and opportunities in the digital world. Through these actions, the IAW contributes to building a foundation for a more equitable society where women and girls can realize their full potential and contribute to sustainable development.

2. Eliminating Gender-Based Violence

❽ Violence against women is the most devastating symbol of patriarchy; that is why the IAW would like to use the term "gender-based violence". Globally, one in three women experience physical or sexual violence, mostly within the domestic sphere. If we add psychological violence to the statistics, the number is much higher. Gender-based violence is a violation of basic human rights, and the physical, sexual, and mental consequences for women and girls are by all means **atrocious**. Death is of course the most **catastrophic** consequence of this very widespread problem: Gender-based violence is a problem of endemic proportions in every country.

❾ The IAW recognizes gender-based violence in all its forms: physical, psychological, verbal, material, economic, sexualized, digital, and honor violence. The Commission on Violence Against Women promotes programs of action and other measures to prevent and eliminate gender-based violence in all its forms. The IAW does so at national, regional, and international levels. Moreover, the IAW enacts and reinforces **legislation** and monitors its implementation.

3. Advocating for Gender-Inclusive Language

⑩ Given the key role that language plays in shaping cultural and social attitudes, the IAW champions the use of **gender-inclusive** language as a powerful tool to foster gender equality and **eradicate** ingrained gender bias. Being inclusive from a gender language perspective means speaking and writing in a way that does not **discriminate** against a particular sex, social gender or gender identity, and does not **perpetuate** gender stereotypes. Through education and policy reforms, the IAW seeks to normalize this practice, which is crucial for creating an environment where all genders can participate equally and be recognized in communication.

⑪ In conclusion, the IAW stands firm in its commitment to gender equality and women's empowerment. Through advocacy, legal frameworks, and **grassroots** activism, it strives to realize a world where gender disparities are eradicated and all individuals have equal opportunities to thrive. Upholding gender equality is not only a moral imperative but also essential for achieving a more just and prosperous society for all.

(1,185 words)

 Glossary

paramount	/ˈpærəmaʊnt/	adj.	首要的，至为重要的；至高无上的
empowerment	/ɪmˈpaʊəmənt/	n.	授权，赋权
consultative	/kənˈsʌltətɪv/	adj.	咨询的，顾问的
stride	/straɪd/	n.	大步，阔步；步伐
equitable	/ˈekwɪtəbl/	adj.	公正的，合理的
suffragist	/ˈsʌfrədʒɪst/	n.	妇女政权论者
temporarily	/ˈtemprərɪli/	adv.	暂时地
persistent	/pəˈsɪstənt/	adj.	持续的；固执的
targeted	/ˈtɑːgɪtɪd/	adj.	精准的
campaign	/kæmˈpeɪn/	n.	运动，活动
mentorship	/ˈmentɔːʃɪp/	n.	导师制；指导关系
atrocious	/əˈtrəʊʃəs/	adj.	极坏的；残暴的

catastrophic	/ˌkætə'strɒfɪk/	adj.	灾难性的
legislation	/ˌledʒɪs'leɪʃn/	n.	法律；立法
gender-inclusive	/'dʒendər ɪn'kluːsɪv/	adj.	性别包容的
eradicate	/ɪ'rædɪkeɪt/	v.	根除，消灭
discriminate	/dɪ'skrɪmɪneɪt/	v.	歧视
perpetuate	/pə'petʃueɪt/	v.	使永存，使持续存在
grassroots	/'grɑːsruːts/	n.	基层；草根

Task 1

Directions: Please read the text and fill in the blanks below with a proper word.

Gender Equality: The Unfinished Business of Our Time
What is gender equality?
• The word "gender" describes the (1) _____ roles and responsibilities that societies consider appropriate for men and women. • Gender equality means that men and women have equal power and equal (2) _____ for financial (3) _____, education, and personal (4) _____.
Why is gender equality significant?
• Women and girls represent half of the world's population and, therefore, also half of its (5) _____. • Besides being a fundamental human right, gender equality is essential to achieve (6) _____ societies, with full human potential and (7) _____ development. Moreover, it has been shown that empowering women spurs (8) _____ and economic growth.
What does women's empowerment include?
• Women's empowerment is a critical aspect of achieving gender equality. It includes increasing a woman's sense of (9) _____, her (10) _____ power, her access to (11) _____ and (12) _____, her (13) _____ and (14) _____ over her own life inside and outside the home, and her ability to effect (15) _____.

Task 2

Directions: *Please choose the best answer from the given choices.*

1. What status does the International Alliance of Women (IAW) hold with the United Nations Economic and Social Council?

    A) Specialized agency. B) General consultative status.

    C) Observer status. D) Full member status.

2. In which year did the International Alliance of Women (IAW) change its name to its current title?

    A) 1902. B) 1904.

    C) 1926. D) 1946.

3. In addition to education and healthcare, what is one of the critical areas where the IAW seeks to provide equal access to women and girls?

    A) Political life. B) Artistic expression.

    C) Sports activities. D) Entertainment industry.

4. According to the article, what is one of the significant consequences of gender-based violence?

    A) Decrease in economic growth. B) Catastrophic death.

    C) Increase in employment. D) Reduced political representation.

5. According to the text, what is the purpose of using gender-inclusive language?

    A) To promote gender stereotypes.

    B) To perpetuate discrimination.

    C) To shape cultural and social attitudes.

    D) To limit the understanding of gender roles.

Task 3

Directions: *Please read the text again and decide whether the following statements are true (T) or false (F) based on what you have learned from the text.*

_____ 1. The International Alliance of Women was originally established to promote both women's human rights and men's suffrage.

_____ 2. The IAW has had general consultative status with the UN Economic and Social Council since its inception.

_____ 3. Empowering women has no significant correlation with productivity and economic growth.

_____ 4. The IAW changed its name to the International Alliance of Women for Suffrage and Equal Citizenship after the First World War.

_____ 5. Gender equality only pertains to ensuring women have equal rights in political spheres.

_____ 6. Women currently have equal opportunities for economic participation as men.

_____ 7. The role of men and boys is not significant in achieving gender equality.

_____ 8. The IAW only works at the local and national levels.

_____ 9. The digital divide is a focal point of the IAW's efforts to empower women.

_____ 10. The IAW solely focuses on the issue of women's suffrage in modern times.

Task 4:

Directions: *Please translate the following five sentences into English using the phrases in the parentheses.*

1. 通过提供教育项目与领导力培训，国际妇女联盟赋予妇女和女童更多在社会中扮演重要角色的能力。（empower... with）

2. 国际妇女联盟认为人人有权享有一切权利和自由，不分种族、肤色和性别。（without distinction of）

3. 国际妇女联盟强调，不仅要消除性别暴力，还要确保妇女和女孩能够在政治生活中平等参与。（apart from...）

4. 鉴于语言在塑造文化和社会态度方面发挥着关键作用，使用性别包容的语言是促进性别平等和消除性别偏见的有效途径。（play a key role in...）

5. 增强妇女和女童的权能有助于提高其家庭、社区和国家的健康水平和生产力，从而产生涟漪效应，惠及每个人。（ripple effect）

Task 5

Directions: *Please discuss the following gender stereotypes and provide your solutions.*

Gender Stereotypes

Early years

Girls should play with dolls and boys should play with trucks.

Boys should be directed to like blue and green; girls toward red and pink.

During youth

Girls are better at reading and boys are better at math.

Girls should be well-behaved; boys are expected to act out.

As adults

Women are natural nurturers; men are natural leaders.

Women with children are less devoted to their jobs.

Men who spend time with family are less masculine and poor breadwinners.

---

1. Do you agree with the gender stereotypes listed above? What are the possible reasons that contribute to the formation of such stereotypes?

2. In what ways can individuals or social media platforms engage to challenge or diminish the prevalence of gender stereotypes? Are there any effective strategies or innovative approaches that could be adopted to foster a more gender-neutral environment?

Text B Technology-Facilitated Gender-Based Violence in an Era of Generative AI

 Warm-up

Directions: Look at the column below and talk about which measure you think is the most effective to create safer online space for women and girls in the digital era. Give your opinions on your choice.

Measures to Reduce Online Gender Violence	
Measure 1: Implement Stronger Legal Frameworks • Governments can enact and enforce laws specifically targeting online harassment and violence against women, providing clear definitions and consequences for perpetrators.	**Measure 6: Empower Women in Technology** • Efforts should be made to empower women and girls to participate and lead in the technology sector, ensuring their voices are heard in the design and implementation of digital tools and platforms.
Measure 2: Enhance Digital Literacy Programs • Education initiatives should be developed to teach individuals, particularly women and girls, about online safety, privacy protection, and how to respond to instances of digital violence.	**Measure 7: Raise Public Awareness** • Public awareness campaigns should be launched to raise awareness about the prevalence and impact of online gender-based violence, encouraging individuals to speak out against such behavior and support victims.
Measure 3: Establish Support Networks • Community organizations and online platforms can create support networks and resources for victims of online violence, offering counseling services, legal assistance, and emotional support.	**Measure 8: Provide Training for Law Enforcement** • Law enforcement agencies should receive specialized training on how to handle cases of online harassment and violence, ensuring that victims receive appropriate support and perpetrators are held accountable.

(Continued)

Measures to Reduce Online Gender Violence	
Measure 4: Strengthen Reporting Mechanisms • Online platforms should implement robust reporting mechanisms that allow users to easily report instances of harassment or abuse, and promptly investigate and take action against offenders.	**Measure 9: Collaborate Across Sectors** • Governments, civil society organizations, technology companies, and academia should collaborate to develop comprehensive strategies for addressing online gender-based violence, leveraging their respective expertise and resources.
Measure 5: Promote Positive Online Behavior • Educational campaigns and community outreach programs should promote positive online behavior and respectful interactions, fostering a culture of inclusivity and mutual respect.	**Measure 10: Support Research and Data Collection** • More research should be conducted to better understand the drivers and impacts of online gender-based violence, and to identify effective prevention and intervention strategies. • Efforts should be made to collect reliable data on the prevalence of online violence to inform policy and programming efforts.

Technology-Facilitated Gender-Based Violence in an Era of Generative AI[1]

❶ As digital technology mediates more and more of our daily lives, it is also facilitating new and heightened forms of gender-based violence. Online violence against women and girls, though not a new phenomenon, has escalated rapidly in recent years posing significant threats to women's safety and well-being both online and offline. This underscores the urgent need to protect and uphold women's rights in the digital era.

---

1 The text was adapted from Chowdhury, R. 2023. Technology-facilitated gender-based violence in an era of generative AI. *UNESCO Publishing*, 5–26.

What Is Tech-Facilitated Gender-Based Violence?

❷ Technology-facilitated gender-based violence is any act that is committed or **amplified** using digital tools or technologies causing physical, sexual, psychological, social, political, or economic harm to women and girls because of their gender. These forms of violence are part of a larger pattern of violence against women, occurring online and offline, including intimate image abuse, **doxing** (revealing personal information), **trolling** (online **harassment**), and the sharing of deepfake images. It also encompasses **misogynistic** hate speech and efforts to silence and **discredit** women online, including threats of offline violence.

❸ Digital violence can **exacerbate** offline forms of violence—including sexual harassment, stalking, intimate partner violence, and **trafficking**—through the use of digital tools like mobile phones, GPS, and tracking devices. For instance, traffickers often use technology to profile, recruit, and control their victims.

Why Is Tackling Online and Digital Violence Against Women and Girls a Priority?

❹ The impact of digital violence can be just as harmful as offline violence, with negative effects on the health and well-being of women and girls as well as serious economic, social, and political impacts. Digital violence can limit the participation of women online thus increasing the digital gender divide and limiting women's voices. This is a significant concern given that the majority of the estimated 2.9 billion people who remain unconnected to the Internet are women and girls.

How Prevalent Is Online and Digital Violence Against Women and Girls?

❺ According to the Institute of Development Studies, between 16% and 58% of women have experienced technology-facilitated gender-based violence. The Economist Intelligence Unit found that 38% of women have had personal experiences of online violence, and 85% of women who spend time online have witnessed digital violence against other women.

❻ The most common forms of violence reported were **misinformation** and **defamation** (67%), cyber harassment (66%), hate speech (65%), **impersonation** (63%), hacking and **stalking** (63%), **astroturfing** (58%), video and image-based abuse (57%), doxing (55%), violent threats (52%), and unwanted images or sexually explicit content (43%).

❼ Data from different regions point to a universal problem. A UN women study in the Arab States region found that 60% of women Internet users had been exposed to online violence. A study of five countries in Sub-Saharan Africa found that 28% of women had experienced online violence. A 2017 survey of women aged 18–55 in Denmark, Italy, New Zealand, Poland, Spain, Sweden, the UK and the USA found that 23% of women reported at least one experience of online abuse or harassment.

❽ The COVID-19 pandemic increased digital violence as women and girls moved online for work, school, and social activities. In Australia, there was a 210% increase in image-based abuse linked to the pandemic. Data from India, Sri Lanka, and Malaysia showed a 168% increase in the volume of misogynistic online posts during COVID-19 **lockdowns**.

❾ Prior to the pandemic, 38% of women surveyed experienced online abuse, with 27% reporting increased online abuse during the pandemic. Black and **minoritized** women reported higher rates: 50% reported online abuse before the pandemic and 38 percent reported an increase during COVID-19.

Who Is at Risk of Online and Digital Gender-Based Violence?

❿ It affects women and girls in all their diversity, but certain groups are at heightened risk. Women who face multiple forms of discrimination, including women with disabilities, black and indigenous women and other women of color, and migrant women, are all disproportionately affected.

⓫ Young women and girls, who are more likely to use technology for learning, accessing information and connecting to peers, also face increased exposure to online violence. One global study found that 58% of girls and young women have experienced some form of online harassment.

⓬ Women in public life—human rights defenders, activists, journalists and lawmakers—face increased rates of violence too. The UNESCO found that 73% of women journalists experienced online violence in the course of their work.

What More Needs to Happen to Eliminate Violence in the Digital World?

(1) Enhance cooperation between governments, the technology sector, women's rights organizations and civil society to strengthen policies.

(2) Address data gaps to increase understanding about the drivers of violence and the profiles of **perpetrators** and to inform prevention and response efforts.

(3) Develop and implement laws and regulations with the participation of survivors and women's organizations.

(4) Develop standards of accountability for Internet **intermediaries** and the technology sector to enhance transparency and accountability on digital violence and the use of data.

(5) Integrate digital citizenship and ethical use of digital tools into school curricula to foster positive social norms online and offline, **sensitize** young people—especially young men and boys—caregivers, and educators to ethical and responsible online behavior.

(6) Strengthen collective action of public and private sector entities and women's rights organizations.

(7) Empower women and girls to participate and lead in the technology sector to inform the design and use of safe digital tools and space free of violence.

(8) Ensure that public and private sector entities prioritize the prevention and **elimination** of digital violence, through human rights-based design approaches and adequate investments.

⓳ In conclusion, addressing technology-facilitated gender-based violence in the era of generative AI is imperative to ensure the safety, well-being, and equality of women and girls in the digital world. As digital technology becomes increasingly integrated into our daily lives, it also facilitates new and heightened forms of gender-based violence, posing significant threats to individuals both online and offline. The prevalence of online violence underscores the urgent need for comprehensive and collaborative efforts to protect and uphold women's rights in the digital era. Effective measures to combat online violence include enhancing legal frameworks, promoting digital literacy, strengthening reporting mechanisms, and supporting victims. Additionally, addressing data gaps, fostering cooperation between governments, technology companies, and civil society, and empowering women and girls to participate in the technology sector are crucial steps toward eliminating digital violence and creating safer online space for all. Through collective action and commitment, we can work towards a future where technology is a force for empowerment and equality, rather than a tool for perpetuating harm and discrimination.

(1,107 words)

 Glossary

amplify	/ˈæmplɪfaɪ/	v.	放大；增强
dox	/dɒks/	v.	公布（某人）的个人信息

troll	/trɒl/	v.	（在网络上）留下恶意信息
harassment	/ˈhærəsmənt/	n.	骚扰，侵扰
misogynistic	/mɪsɒdʒɪˈnɪstɪk/	adj.	厌恶女性的，憎恨女性的
discredit	/dɪsˈkredɪt/	v.	使丧失信誉，败坏名誉
exacerbate	/ɪɡˈzæsəbeɪt/	v.	恶化，加剧
traffick	/ˈtræfɪk/	v.	贩卖，交易
misinformation	/ˌmɪsɪnfərˈmeɪʃn/	n.	提供虚假信息
defamation	/ˌdefəˈmeɪʃn/	n.	诽谤，中伤
impersonation	/ɪmˌpɜːsəˈneɪʃn/	n.	冒充，伪装
stalk	/stɔːk/	v.	跟踪；悄悄接近
astroturfing	/ˈæstrəʊˌtɜːfɪŋ/	n.	营销操控
lockdown	/ˈlɒkdaʊn/	n.	封锁，禁闭
minoritize	/maɪˈnɒrɪtaɪz/	v.	成为少数派，使成为少数派
perpetrator	/ˈpɜːpətreɪtə(r)/	n.	犯罪者，行凶者
intermediary	/ˌɪntəˈmiːdiəri/	n.	中间人，调解人
sensitize	/ˈsensɪtaɪz/	v.	使敏感；使有知觉
elimination	/ɪˌlɪmɪˈneɪʃn/	n.	排除，根除

Task 1

Directions: *Please read the text and match the forms of technology-facilitated gender-based violence in Column A with their corresponding definitions in Column B.*

Column A	Column B
1. intimate image abuse	a. revealing personal information online to harass or threaten someone
2. doxing	b. coordinated efforts to share damaging content across platforms simultaneously
3. trolling	c. sending threatening messages or statements of harm
4. misogynistic hate speech	d. harassment or stalking behavior carried out through digital means
5. astroturfing	e. sharing intimate or compromising images without consent

6. hacking and stalking   f. creating fake accounts or personas to harass or deceive others

7. video and image-based abuse g. posting or circulating abusive or threatening videos or images

8. cyber harassment   h. engaging in hostile or derogatory speech towards women

9. violent threat   i. provoking or harassing others online for amusement or malicious intent

10. misinformation and defamation j. spreading false or damaging information

Task 2

Directions: Please read the text again and fill in the blanks in the summary.

The article explores the rising issue of technology-facilitated gender-based violence, highlighting its prevalence and various forms. With the increasing (1) _____ of digital technology into daily life, instances of online violence against women and girls have surged, posing significant (2) _____ to their safety and well-being. This type of violence encompasses a range of harmful acts (3) _____ by digital tools, such as intimate image abuse, doxing, trolling, and spreading misogynistic hate speech. Additionally, digital violence can (4) _____ offline forms of violence, including sexual harassment, (5) _____, and trafficking. The impact of digital violence extends beyond immediate harm, affecting the health, economic, social, and political aspects of women's lives. Studies show alarming rates of (6) _____ violence globally, with a significant proportion of women experiencing or witnessing such violence. Certain groups, including women facing multiple forms of (7) _____ and young girls, are particularly (8) _____. Addressing this issue requires collaborative efforts across governments, technology sectors, civil society, and women's rights organizations to strengthen policies, enhance (9) _____, promote digital (10) _____, and empower women and girls in technology. Ultimately, tackling technology-facilitated gender-based violence is essential to creating safer online space and upholding women's rights in the digital era.

Task 3

Directions: *Please translate the following paragraph into English.*

数字技术的普及加剧了性别暴力的形式和规模,对女性的安全和健康造成了严重威胁。各国政府有必要通过加强合作、提高意识、制定政策、推动技术行业合作以及加强法律监管等措施,最终创造一个更为安全的数字世界,使技术成为促进平等和保护妇女权益的重要力量。

Task 4

Directions: *Please debate on the following topics. You are encouraged to refer to other sources for the debate. You can use the following tables to help you organize ideas.*

Topic 1: Should social media platforms be held legally accountable for failing to prevent or adequately respond to instances of technology-facilitated gender-based violence?

Pros	Cons

Topic 2: Should educational institutions be required to offer digital citizenship courses to teach students about ethical online behavior and combat technology-facilitated gender-based violence?

Pros	Cons

Part II Drilling for GC Skills

How to Write a Project Proposal (II)

Section 6: Gender

With the progress of human civilization, gender equality has been advocated and emphasized. In your proposal, it is important to make clear these two points regarding gender: 1) how the project ensures the participation and engagement of both men and women in project activities, and 2) how the project outcomes and the project objective benefit women. In addition, regarding the specification of the project, female involvement in the project can be decided by age level, educational level, occupation, region, marital status, income level, etc. Therefore, a design of a female participation percentage table is necessary.

Sample of gender:

The project itself is mainly for the capacity and skills building of women in the digital age. However, the involvement of men should not be ignored.

In Stage One, the student's achievement in the database should be submitted to the private sector run no matter by men or women for further employment or investment offered to the students.

In Stage Two, the women's involvement in e-commerce needs the comprehension and cooperation of the male family members. Thus, the orientation and brief introduction should be included in the online workshop to make the male family members fully understand the new pattern of earning money. Meanwhile, the plan also welcomes the other males to join the team of trainers.

Section 7: Project Effectiveness

In this section, a work plan of the project is made with the stages of the project execution chronically displayed. Each stage must include a stage goal, the duration of the stage, and the output in the stage applied to achieve the stage goal. Therefore, a monitoring report per calendar year or a completion report per stage is required.

No project is perfect without jeopardy. In this section, the potential risks must be stated in advance, and possible ways of risk avoidance or alleviation should also be stated.

After the completion of the project, an effective measurement/assessment mechanism needs to be established to evaluate to what extent the project has delivered all its planned outcomes and fulfilled the objective. To guarantee the effectiveness of the evaluation, the key parameters should be carefully designed.

A sample evaluation matrix table is provided as follows:

	Evaluation Focus	Indicators	Target Goals	Evaluation Method	Reporting Method
Outputs	1. Online training	1. Contracted executed	31 Dec. 2022	Certification by PO	Contract
		2. Number of participants (speakers/experts)		Event Attendance List	Completion Report
		3. % of participating men/women (excl. speakers/experts)	x/y	Event Attendance List	Completion Report
		4. Number of speakers/experts engaged		Event Attendance List	Completion Report
		5. % of speakers/experts (men/women)	x/y	Event Attendance List	Completion Report
		6. Number of attending countries/organizations/enterprises		Event Attendance List	Completion Report

Unit 6 Global Gender Equality and the IAW

(Continued)

	Evaluation Focus	Indicators	Target Goals	Evaluation Method	Reporting Method
Outputs	2. Workshop (case studies)	1. Number of participants (excl. speakers/experts)		Event Attendance List	Completion Report
		2. % of participating men/women (excl. speakers/experts)	x/y	Event Attendance List	Completion Report
		3. Number of speakers/experts engaged		Event Attendance List	Completion Report
		4. % of speakers/experts (men/women)	x/y	Event Attendance List	Completion Report
		5. Number of attending countries/organizations/enterprises		Event Attendance List	Completion Report
	3. Project report	1. Number. of pages		Certification by PO	Email to the Secretariat
		2. Submission to the Secretariat	Date	Submission to the Secretariat	Email to the Secretariat
	4. Participants knowledge of industry-best practices and an understanding of innovative drug products	1. % of participants report substantial knowledge increase	75%	Ex-ante and ex-post evaluations	Completion Report
		2. Women report substantial knowledge increase	33%	Ex-ante and ex-post evaluations	Completion Report

(Continued)

	Evaluation Focus	Indicators	Target Goals	Evaluation Method	Reporting Method
Outputs	5. Recommendations on how to implement best practices	1. Number of recommendations made	10	Included in the Project Report	Report to the committee/ council/ organization in charge of the project
Others					

Sample of effectiveness:

- *March 2020–May 2020: Contact with the top colleges in Russia (i.e. Bauman Moscow State Technical University, Moscow State University, Saint-Petersburg State University, etc.) and invite them to join the association.*

- *June 2020–December 2020: Establish the College Women's Incubator Association in Russia for the pilot project and start the Mentoring Program.*

- *December 2020–March 2021: Submit the report of the Mentoring Program to PPWE and establish the database to record the past achievements.*

- *April 2021–July 2021: Make publicity to invite more top colleges including their alumni association and other academic institutions from other APEC economies to join.*

- *August 2021–September 2022: Build the relationship between mentors and students to ensure the information circulates smoothly and submit the annual report to reflect the achievement to PPWE.*

- *October 2022–March 2023: Connect with the target community in developing economies to confirm the Assistance Plan users and recruit and assess the eligible trainers from the Association and other males in the society.*

- *April 2023–September 2023: Investigate the local material situation and encourage the government to bolster the infrastructure and submit the application to the Women and the Economy Sub-Fund for the financial support.*

- *October 2023–September 2024: Seek the appropriate trainers for the family in need and start the online workshop.*

- *October 2024–July 2025: Summarize and assess the first year since the E-commerce Assistance Plan was launched and continuously invite more families or individuals in need to join and track trainees' following progress.*

Section 8: Budget

No project can be carried out without the support of a budget, since holding events, technical equipment, labor costs, etc. all need money. In this section, the expected budget is stated clearly, and the project is usually financed by a specific fund or sub-fund of an international organization or government agency.

Task 1

Directions: *Please decide whether the following statements are true (T) or false (F).*

_____ 1. Background introduction must be detailed with data and examples to help readers unfamiliar with the field understand.

_____ 2. The outcome must be in line with the objective of the project. Otherwise, the project is invalid.

_____ 3. The output of a project is achieved through the outcome. Therefore, output and outcome are inseparable.

_____ 4. To make the proposal persuasive, the language applied in the proposal must be vivid enough to arouse readers' emotional echoes.

_____ 5. The inclusion of a potential danger section cannot hamper the approval of a proposal since no proposal is universally perfect.

Task 2

Directions: *Based on what you have learned from "How to Write a Project Proposal (I) & (II)", answer the following questions.*

1. What are the essential sectors in a proposal?

2. What is the objective of a proposal?

3. What is the relationship between output and outcome?

4. What are the factors determining the budget?

5. What are the key evaluation methods you can come up with?

Task 3

Directions: *Discuss with your partners the following topics and complete the task.*

1. Suppose the MSMEs in the Asia Pacific region are faced with the challenge of digital

economy. Many of them are small-scale in production and lack technical advantages. You are supposed to write a proposal entitled "Development of MSMEs in Digital Age". Discuss with your team members the topic, and draw up the key points of the objective, target beneficiaries, strategies applied, parameters for evaluation, the output and expected outcomes, potential risks, etc.

2. Based on the result of your team discussion, complete a formal proposal with all the sections included.

Task 4

Directions: *Please divide the class into several teams, and each team is required to finish a proposal on a specific topic and then present the proposal to other teams. Other teams act as evaluators based on the parameters listed in the following table. The scores given to each parameter range from 0 to 10.*

Note: Before making the evaluation, the evaluators should bear the following questions in mind.

1. Is the issue typical in a few regions or common in a certain region?

2. Where did you get the resources, such as data, examples, quotations, etc.?

3. Do you think your output/strategy or some specific part of your output/strategy is approachable? Why or why not?

4. Which phase of your proposal is the most challenging or unpredictable? How can you minimize the challenge or warrant the predictability of that phase?

5. Apart from the risks mentioned in the proposal, are there other risks you can think of?

6. How do you value a proposal's success? If a proposal can be regarded as a success, to what extent the proposal's objective should be achieved?

Dimensions for Evaluation	Scores (From 0 to 10)
Clarity of Objective	
Formality of Language	
The Provision of Examples and Data	
The Alignment of Output and Outcome	
The Feasibility of the Execution Strategy	

Part III Notes from China

Empowering Dreams: Free Education for Girls in Rural China[1]

The award ceremony of the July 1st Medal, the highest honor in the Communist Party of China (CPC), was held at the Great Hall of the People in Beijing, capital of China, on June 29, 2021. President Xi Jinping presented the medals to outstanding members of the CPC, among whom Zhang Guimei gave a speech. Zhang is the principal and founder of the Huaping Senior High School for Girls, the country's first public high school that provides free education to female students, in Lijiang City, Yunnan Province. For the past 13 years, nearly 2,000 female students have graduated from this school, successfully rewriting their destinies.

The year 1995 was the darkest time in Zhang Guimei's life, losing her beloved husband to cancer after spending all their savings trying to cure him. Before that, Zhang had lost her parents. Feeling desperate, she applied to leave Dali City, Yunnan Province, where she had worked with her husband as a teacher and went to teach In remote mountainous Huaping county, Lijiang City, Yunnan Province, a totally strange place to her. "I wanted to find a place where nobody knew me or could remind me of

---

1 The text was adapted from the Chinadaily website.

any beautiful moment in my life. I was banishing myself," recalled Zhang, who was born in Heilongjiang Province in 1957, and went to Yunnan Province in 1974. That decision changed not only her life, but also numerous children living in deep mountains. Although she was in darkness, she lit up the sky for others, and was elected as a delegate to the 20th National Congress of the Communist Party of China.

In 1997, she was diagnosed with uterine fibroids. Her colleagues and students donated money to help her, which moved her deeply and she wanted to repay them. "I didn't make many contributions to the county, but brought such trouble. I felt guilty. I could only try my best to work as a teacher, and I hope to do more for the county," said Zhang. She noticed many girls dropped out of school, and after visiting their homes, she found poverty and outdated perceptions hindered parents in supporting their girls' education, and made them get married at a young age. To change the situation, she made up her mind to establish a high school, which would offer free access to local girls. She tried to collect money but failed and was regarded as a swindler by many people.

An opportunity for change came when she was elected as a delegate to the 17th CPC National Congress in 2007. After receiving an interview talking about her wish, the local government helped Zhang realize her dream and in 2008 established the Lijiang Huaping High School for Girls, with Zhang as the principal. The first year welcomed 96 students, many of whom were poorly educated before entering the school. "If girls from the mountainous area want to leave, we just offer a hand, to help them fly out to see a wider world," Zhang said. Since the school's establishment, more than 2,000 students have flown to the outside world and changed their lives, and the school has surged to be one of the best high schools in Lijiang.

Besides her work at the school, Zhang also serves as dean of the children's welfare home in Huaping, where she usually visits and cares for orphans. Over the years, Zhang has reached almost every corner of Lijiang, and changed the destiny of many families. She is alone without any children, but she has become the mother of many orphans. Zhang has devoted herself to the cause of education without caring much about her declining health. In the future, she said, she hopes to lead children from the mountains to the track of modernization. "This requires knowledge and teachers' capability, and we teachers have to improve ourselves while we teach students. But whatever it takes, we need to achieve it and not drag down our country's modernization."

(653 words)

Directions: *Please read the text above and share your thoughts about the situation of gender equality in China.*

Topic 1: Gender Equality in Education

Question: To what extent has China achieved gender equality in education? What are the major challenges that contribute to this persistent issue?

Task: Prepare a brief presentation on the current state of gender equality in education in China, highlighting key statistics and exploring the interconnected factors that contribute to the progress on this issue.

Topic 2: Economic Disparities and Discrimination

Question: In China, what role does economic disparity play in perpetuating gender inequality in education? How can the Chinese government address and rectify these economic imbalances?

Task: Prepare a presentation outlining the economic challenges faced by women and girls in China, focusing on access to education and employment opportunities. Propose solutions to address these issues.

Unit 7

Global Culture and the UNESCO

Part I Reading for GC Knowledge

Text A 1982–2022: Cultural Policies at the Heart of International Debate

 Warm-up

Self-Assessment of Global Competence

Directions: *Please rate yourself on a scale of 1 to 5, where 1 = Strongly Disagree; 2 = Disagree; 3 = Neutral; 4 = Agree; 5 = Strongly Agree. Then discuss the questions that follow.*

Self-Assessment Questionnaire	Scale				
I am familiar with the cultural policies of my country.	1	2	3	4	5
Cultural preservation is very important for our society.	1	2	3	4	5
I actively participate in cultural events such as art exhibitions, theater performances, or music concerts.	1	2	3	4	5
I understand the impact of cultural policies on the development of artistic and creative industries.	1	2	3	4	5
I know a few government initiatives to support and promote cultural diversity.	1	2	3	4	5
I am interested in learning about different cultures and their traditions.	1	2	3	4	5
I believe that cultural policies should prioritize the preservation of traditional art forms and encourage the creation of contemporary art.	1	2	3	4	5
I actively engage in cultural activities in our community.	1	2	3	4	5
I know many cultural organizations and institutions in our country.	1	2	3	4	5
I am fully aware of the role of culture in fostering social cohesion and inclusivity.	1	2	3	4	5

1. Based on your self-assessment, are you aware of the significance of culture for social development? In which aspect do you think culture affects our social development?
2. Considering your score, would you say that you have a good understanding of culture and its relevant policies? Can you list governmental initiatives to support and promote cultural diversity?

1982–2022: Cultural Policies at the Heart of International Debate[1]

❶ The first UNESCO World Conference on Cultural Policies, held in Mexico City in 1982, was a genuine turning point. It laid the **groundwork**, for decades to come, for the fundamental concept of the functional links between culture and the development of societies. And alongside the growing material manifestations of culture grew their interdependence with immaterial expressions. This in turn opened the way for the protection of all the manifestations of culture that **punctuate** our ways of life, and through which knowledge and values are transmitted from one generation to the next.

❷ This broader concept led to the UNESCO Recommendation on the Safeguarding of Traditional Culture and Folklore (1989) and opened up the field of human heritage to "living culture" and to synergies with other fields of development, such as well-being and education. Languages, music, dance, rituals, and crafts are now included in the field of culture, while their socioeconomic importance is increasingly gaining recognition. As the **embodiment** of the collective memory of communities, this living and evolving heritage strengthens the sense of identity and belonging, as well as resilience and the ability to project oneself into the future.

Link Between Culture and Development

❸ Considered a mirror of the evolution of societies, culture has **progressively** been integrated into the international agenda, while its role in sustainable development and the defense of human rights is increasingly recognized, notably through its contribution to social cohesion, employment, and innovation. The promotion of cultural diversity in the 1990s stimulated a **revitalization** of creative resources, centered around the idea that development efforts have often failed due to the **omission** or neglect of the human element—the complex web of relationships and beliefs, the variety of values and aspirations, creative expression, and imagination. This new impetus draws on the capacity of culture to expand "people's choices...individual opportunities for being

---

[1] The text was adapted from Ziemiszewska, A. July–September 2022. Cultural policies at the heart of international debate. *The UNESCO Courier*.

healthy, educated, productive, creative and enjoying self-respect and human rights" (*Our Creative Diversity*, 1996).

❹ The UNESCO Universal Declaration on Cultural Diversity, adopted in 2001, was a milestone in reaffirming the **indivisible** link between culture and development. The principles of the Declaration have inspired a series of **normative** texts, adopted by the UNESCO member states, which have extended the scope of culture to the protection of underwater cultural heritage (2001), the safeguarding of intangible cultural heritage (2003), the protection and promotion of the diversity of cultural expressions (2005) and the conservation of historic urban landscapes (2011). Another step forward was the adoption of the Declaration concerning the Intentional Destruction of Cultural Heritage in October 2003.

Recreating Social Links

❺ This evolution in the appreciation of the role of culture is not purely conceptual. In 2004, during the reconstruction of the Mostar Bridge, destroyed in 1993 during the war in Bosnia and Herzegovina, the challenge was not only to restore a monument, but also to overcome the collective **trauma** by involving the various cultural, ethnic, and religious communities in the reconstruction. The Dayton Peace Accords (1995), which put an end to the fighting in Bosnia and Herzegovina, included a section on the protection of cultural heritage in their **provisions** on respect for human rights. For the first time, cultural heritage was recognized as a fundamental element in peacebuilding.

❻ More recently, in 2014, the UNESCO's vast project in Timbuktu (Mali) on the reconstruction of destroyed mausoleums and the conservation of ancient manuscripts illustrated once again the need to integrate culture into peace efforts. The support for the reconstruction of the city of Mosul in Iraq, in the framework of the UNESCO project "Reviving the Spirit of Mosul", or the measures to safeguard the cultural heritage and educational system of Beirut in Lebanon, coordinated by the UNESCO, are examples of initiatives aimed at enabling communities to recreate social links through the reconstruction of historical monuments and entire neighborhoods.

The Rise of Globalization

❼ Over the years, from one international conference on cultural policies to another, other themes have emerged. At the 1998 conference in Stockholm (Sweden), in a context characterized by the rapid growth of globalization, topics such as access to culture, freedom of expression, participatory governance, and the trade in cultural products came to the fore. The development of digital technologies was starting to profoundly change cultural consumption and distribution. But, while these new technologies allow **unprecedented** access to content—leading to a boom in cultural and creative industries—they also come with challenges, such as the **deregulation** of markets, the need for more equitable **remuneration** for artists and cultural professionals, economic concentration, the digital divide, and cultural normalization. These are issues that remain highly topical.

❽ The future of our societies is now being played out on a global scale. Mass tourism, uncontrolled urban growth, and the effects of climate change threaten a number of **emblematic** sites **inscribed** on the World Heritage List, whether it is Venice and its lagoon, the rice terraces of the Philippine Cordilleras, the Galapagos Islands (Ecuador), the Great Barrier Reef in Australia or the Forest of the Cedars of God (Horsh Arz el Rab) in Lebanon.

Rethinking Our Relationship with the World

❾ During the COVID-19 pandemic, culture demonstrated its capacity for adaptation and resilience, highlighting solidarity within the sector and across other fields, such as the economy, health, and education, during times of lock down. However, it also highlighted the persistent **fragilities** of the cultural sector, urging us to rethink its core foundations.

❿ The concepts forged over the past forty years also provide a conceptual foundation for the UNESCO's normative and programming work. In the wake of the 2030 Agenda for Sustainable Development and beyond, the UNESCO must take on a key role, leading the international dialog on emerging challenges. Issues such as cultural diplomacy, the fight against **illicit trafficking** in cultural property and return and **restitution** of these properties to their countries of origin, the status of the artist, freedom of expression, creative economy, the impact of digital transformation, sustainable cultural tourism, and the role of culture in climate action will be center-stage in discussions at the Mexico Conference. Its objective is not only to clarify our future action, but also to **reposition** culture as a global public **good**.

The Increasingly Recognized Role of Culture in Sustainable Development

⓫ Access to culture—including online—must be ensured to all, cultural diversity as part of the global **commons** must be safeguarded, and full cultural rights must be guaranteed in the face of new challenges. To address these **imperatives**, local and national commitments need to be accompanied by a global and concerted effort by the international community as a whole. To build inclusive and supportive societies, it is essential to acknowledge the transformative role of culture as a global good. It is vital to take culture fully into account when designing this new social contract. Culture is our reservoir of meaning, our creative energy; it **forges** our sense of belonging, frees our imagination, our power of innovation, and our commitment towards a more sustainable future for the benefit of all humanity.

(1,164 words)

 Glossary

groundwork	/ˈɡraʊndwɜːk/	n.	基础
punctuate	/ˈpʌŋktʃueɪt/	v.	强调
embodiment	/ɪmˈbɒdimənt/	n.	体现
progressively	/prəˈɡresɪvli/	adv.	逐步地
revitalization	/riːˌvaɪtəˈlaɪzeɪʃn/	n.	复兴，振兴
omission	/əˈmɪʃn/	n.	疏忽
indivisible	/ˌɪndɪˈvɪzəbl/	adj.	不可分的
normative	/ˈnɔːmətɪv/	adj.	规范的，标准的
trauma	/ˈtrɔːmə/	n.	精神创伤，心理创伤
provision	/prəˈvɪʒn/	n.	规定
unprecedented	/ʌnˈpresɪdentɪd/	adj.	前所未有的
deregulation	/ˌdiːˌreɡjuˈleɪʃn/	n.	撤销管制，解除控制
remuneration	/rɪˌmjuːnəˈreɪʃn/	n.	报酬
emblematic	/ˌembləˈmætɪk/	adj.	象征的；可当标志的
inscribed	/ɪnˈskraɪbd/	adj.	记名的
fragility	/frəˈdʒɪləti/	n.	脆弱
illicit	/ɪˈlɪsɪt/	adj.	非法的
trafficking	/ˈtræfɪkɪŋ/	n.	非法交易
restitution	/ˌrestɪˈtjuːʃn/	n.	归还
reposition	/ˌriːpəˈzɪʃn/	n.	使复位
good	/ɡʊd/	n.	用处；好处，益处
commons	/ˈkɒmənz/	n.	共享资源
imperative	/ɪmˈperətɪv/	n.	重要紧急的事
forge	/fɔːdʒ/	v.	锻造

Unit 7　Global Culture and the UNESCO

Task 1

Directions: Please read the text and fill in the blanks below with a proper word.

1982-2022: Cultural Policies at the Heart of International Debate
Link between culture and development
• Culture has (1) _____ been integrated into the international agenda. • The promotion of cultural diversity in the 1990s stimulated a(n) (2) _____ of creative resources. • The principles of the Declaration have inspired a series of (3) _____ texts.
Recreating social links
• This evolution in the appreciation of the role of culture is not purely (4) _____. • The challenge was not only to restore a monument, but also to overcome the collective (5) _____. • The conservation of ancient manuscripts illustrated once again the need to (6) _____ culture into peacebuilding.
The rise of globalization
• These new technologies allow (7) _____ access to content. • Mass tourism, uncontrolled urban growth, and the effects of climate change threaten a number of (8) _____ sites (9) _____ on the World Heritage List.
Rethinking our relationship with the world
• Culture highlighted (10) _____ within the sector and across other fields. • Culture also highlighted the persistent (11) _____ of the cultural sector. • Its objective is also to (12) _____ culture as a global public good.
The role of culture in sustainable development is increasingly recognized.
• Cultural diversity as part of global (13) _____ must be safeguarded. • To address these (14) _____, local and national commitments need to be accompanied by a global and (15) _____ effort by the international community as a whole.

Task 2

Directions: *Please read the text again and decide whether the following statements are true (T) or false (F) based on what you have learned from the text.*

_____ 1. The promotion of cultural diversity in the 1990s led to the neglect of the human element in development efforts.

_____ 2. Normative texts adopted by the UNESCO member states have extended the scope of culture to the protection of underwater cultural heritage.

_____ 3. The Dayton Peace Accords recognized cultural heritage as a fundamental element in peacebuilding.

_____ 4. The UNESCO project "Reviving the Spirit of Mosul" aimed at safeguarding the cultural heritage of Beirut in Lebanon.

_____ 5. The challenges posed by new technologies include the deregulation of markets and economic concentration.

_____ 6. The future of societies is being influenced by global factors such as mass tourism and climate change.

_____ 7. The COVID-19 pandemic highlighted the weaknesses of the cultural sector.

_____ 8. The Mexico Conference will not discuss the role of culture in climate action.

_____ 9. Global and concerted efforts are not necessary to address the imperatives of cultural rights.

_____ 10. Culture does not contribute to a more sustainable future for humanity.

Task 3

Directions: *Please translate the following five sentences into English using the words or phrase in the parentheses.*

1. 土家族服饰艺术是土家族文化最具特色的显性表征，是土家族特有的审美追求和审美心理的自然体现。（embodiment）

2. 历史悠久的闹市区的复兴为曾经衰落的地区注入了新的活力，翻新的建筑、熙熙攘攘的商店和充满活力的艺术场景，吸引了当地人和游客来体验丰富的文化遗产。（revitalization）

3. 文化创伤是指暴力、压迫或流离失所的集体经历对一个社会的文化认同、习俗和价值观产生的深刻而持久的影响。（trauma）

4. 这些复杂的雕刻和象形文字镌刻在一个被遗忘的文明的古老遗址中，不仅是一扇通往过去的窗户，而且还记载了他们文化的兴衰。(inscribe)

5. 在一场毁灭性的自然灾害之后，各社区在重建家园、振兴地方经济、治愈灾难性事件造成的情感创伤时，比以往任何时候都更加强大和团结。(in the wake of)

Task 4

Directions: *Please discuss the following questions in groups and role-play the following situation with your solution.*

> ***Situation***
>
> Under the impact of artificial intelligence (AI), Lucas, a talented artist, found himself unemployed. With galleries closed and art events cancelled, his passion for painting became an uncertain source of income. Desperate to support himself and his family, Lucas reached out to Minister of Culture in his country, Dr. Thompson, seeking assistance.
> …

1. What difficulty was Lucas confronted with in this story?

2. Suppose you were Dr. Thompson in this story, what measures would you take to help people like Lucas in the age of AI?

Text B Cultural Selection: The Diffusion of Tea and Tea Culture Along the Silk Roads

 Warm-up

Directions: *Look at the options below and share your ideas about the significance of tea culture along the Silk Roads.*

1. **Ritual and Ceremonial Importance:** Tea became deeply ingrained in the cultural practices and rituals of various civilizations along the Silk Roads. Tea ceremonies, with their specific procedures and etiquette, were developed and passed down through generations, reflecting the values of hospitality, respect, and harmony in different cultures.

2. **Social Bonding:** Tea served as a catalyst for social interactions and community

bonding. Tea houses and tea gardens became popular gathering places where people from different backgrounds could come together, share stories, exchange ideas, and build social connections. Tea drinking became a symbol of friendship, unity, and mutual understanding.

3. **Art and Aesthetics:** Tea had a profound influence on various art forms along the Silk Roads. The appreciation of tea and tea-related objects, such as tea utensils, tea bowls, and tea sets, gave rise to the development of tea-related art, including ceramics, calligraphy, painting, and poetry. Tea aesthetics, such as the simplicity and tranquility of the tea ceremony, inspired artistic expression.

4. **Philosophy and Zen Buddhism:** Tea played a significant role in shaping philosophical and spiritual beliefs along the Silk Roads. The practice of tea became intertwined with Zen Buddhism, emphasizing mindfulness, meditation, and the appreciation of the present moment. Tea ceremonies were seen as a means to attain inner peace, enlightenment, and spiritual awakening.

5. **Symbol of Status and Prestige:** Tea became a symbol of wealth, prestige, and social status along the Silk Roads. The availability and consumption of tea were often associated with the ruling elite and the upper classes. Tea became a luxury item and a demonstration of refined taste, contributing to social hierarchies and cultural aspirations.

Cultural Selection: The Diffusion of Tea and Tea Culture Along the Silk Roads[1]

❶   The history of tea **stretches** back over thousands of years and spans not only the vast regions encompassed by the Silk Roads but much of the globe. It is well known that tea has been at the center of intercultural exchanges taking place between European ports and the far Eastern regions of the Silk Roads from the 16th century CE onwards. However, tea, as well as its **associated** drinking culture, has been at the foreground of Silk Roads interactions stretching back much further to the earliest days of these routes. Tea is derived from the plant Camellia sinesis, and, although today there are numerous types of tea and many different ways of preparing and drinking it, whether black, oolong, green, or white, they all originate from this one plant. Camellia sinesis has a number of possible places of origin but it is generally accepted that it originates from Central Southeast Asia in the region at the intersection of what is today North East India, Northern Myanmar, and South West China.

1　The text was adapted from the UNESCO website.

❷ Tea has been **consumed** in China for thousands of years with some of the earliest references to tea drinking on record dating from the Shang Dynasty (1500 BCE–1046 BCE), where it was consumed in Yunnan Province primarily as a **medicinal** drink. By the Tang Dynasty (618 CE–907 CE), tea had become popular and was widely enjoyed as a **refreshing** beverage, prepared from leaves that had been **moistened** and shaped into a dense brick. **Anecdotal** evidence from the 8th century CE reports that the city of Chang'An had a large number of flourishing tea shops, many of which advertised the health benefits of tea drinking. Later, during the Song Dynasty (960 CE–1279 CE) the brick form of tea was replaced in popularity with loose leaves which were often ground into fine powder and, increasingly, flavored with different substances. Over time tea houses began to appear across large cities, making tea more accessible outside of the elite society. As it grew in popularity and accessibility, thanks to the development of **sophisticated** trade routes, tea became associated with homeliness, and was drunk daily as well as served to guests to welcome them. From China tea spread across the Eastern Silk Roads to Japan and the Korean Peninsula. In Japan, the beverage developed close **connotations** with religious and social rituals owing to the fact that it was commonly consumed by Buddhist priests. In the 6th century CE envoys were sent from Japan to China to learn about tea and its associated culture and seeds were imported via the Silk Roads in order for the plant to be cultivated in Japan.

❸ Indeed, the dynamic exchanges and social rituals associated with tea were, and remain, important parts of everyday life and community. Tea soon became prominent in creative spheres, including within poetry and literature, as poets and artists wrote about the joy of tea and explored tea customs and associated traditions in their work. As a result, tea's popularity quickly rose throughout the Eastern regions of the Silk Roads, in particular an aesthetic culture developed around tea drinking that achieved a considerable amount of **notoriety** in medieval Japan in the 14th and 15th centuries CE. The art of tea making as well as drinking, was not only passed down through generations but was also diffused to the West and across various continents around the world. Ultimately, the tea trade spread from China and Mongolia to the Indian Subcontinent, Anatolia, the Iranian Plateau and beyond eventually reaching Europe and North Africa. Tea was also intricately linked to another flourishing Silk Roads trade that became the basis for a number of complex interactions within the arts, that of **ceramics**, and, specifically, **porcelain**. During the Ming dynasty (1368 CE–1644 CE) tea wares became a major art form and teapots and other ceramics were produced in various styles. Many of these ceramics were exported as desirable luxury trade items across the Silk Roads.

❹ Although there are many regional **variations**, many cultures along the Silk Roads share tea-drinking customs and traditions. Today, cultures and regions around the world have continued to adapt the ubiquitous product according to their own societal norms, with brewing processes, flavoring, and social rituals varying from place to place. Some examples of the different variations of tea found across the Silk Roads include "kahwa", a tea popular in the northern Indian Subcontinent that is often served at special occasions such as weddings and festivals. It is prepared in a samovar with added cardamom, cinnamon, almonds, and saffron. In what is today Afghanistan, an elaborate tea called "qymaq chai" is prepared for special occasions such as weddings and engagements, it is pinkish in color with added milk and cardamom. The British and Dutch also **incorporated** the beverage into their lifestyles, where it developed connotations linked to **hospitality**, mutual understanding, local tradition, and community.

❺ The complex intercultural exchanges associated with tea and tea culture were the direct result of the movement of traders, missionaries, and physicians along the Silk Roads. As they traveled across the vast regions of Eurasia, different elements of culture were transmitted both to the East and the West. Tea culture is just one excellent example of the new **imports** and social practices that were often later transformed and reconceptualized according to the specificities of the societies into which they were introduced. The effects of this free flow of ideas, goods, and artistic elements along the Silk Roads constitute an important shared heritage in the contemporary world.

❻ On November 29, 2022, China's traditional tea-making was added to the intangible cultural heritage list of the UNESCO. The item "Traditional Tea-Processing Techniques and Associated Social Practices in China" passed the examination at the 17th session of the UNESCO Intergovernmental Committee for the Safeguarding of the Intangible Cultural Heritage ongoing here in the Moroccan capital. China now has 43 items on the intangible cultural heritage list, continuing to be the most enlisted country in the world. Wang Yongjian, head of the Chinese delegation to the UNESCO session, told Xinhua that the **inscription** will make this cultural heritage more visible to the public and help promote respect for cultural diversity and human creativity. "We will apply for and promote more of the intangible cultural heritage projects with Chinese characteristics and showcasing Chinese spirit and wisdom, so as to better promote Chinese culture to go global," he added.

(1,078 words)

 Glossary

stretch	/stretʃ/	v.	延续
associated	/əˈsəʊʃieɪtɪd/	adj.	有关联的，相关的

consume	/kən'sjuːm/	v.	吃，喝
medicinal	/mə'dɪsɪnl/	adj.	药用的
refreshing	/rɪ'freʃɪŋ/	adj.	使人精神振作的
moistened	/'mɔɪstənd/	adj.	弄湿的
anecdotal	/ˌænɪk'dəʊtl/	adj.	轶事的，传闻的
sophisticated	/sə'fɪstɪkeɪtɪd/	adj.	复杂巧妙的；先进的，精密的
connotation	/ˌkɒnə'teɪʃn/	n.	内涵意义，隐含意义，联想意义
notoriety	/ˌnəʊtə'raɪəti/	n.	知名度
ceramic	/sə'ræmɪk/	n.	陶瓷制品，陶瓷器；制陶艺术
porcelain	/'pɔːsəlɪn/	n.	瓷；瓷器
variation	/ˌveəri'eɪʃn/	n.	变化，变动
incorporate	/ɪn'kɔːpəreɪt/	v.	包含，合并
hospitality	/ˌhɒspɪ'tæləti/	n.	殷勤款待，好客
import	/'ɪmpɔːt/	n.	输入，引进
inscription	/ɪn'skrɪpʃn/	n.	（石头或金属上）刻写的文字，碑文

Task 1

Directions: *Please read the text and fill in the blanks in the summary.*

> The history of tea (1) _____ back over thousands of years and spans not only the vast regions encompassed by the Silk Roads but much of the globe. And it is generally accepted that tea (2) _____ from Central Southeast Asia. Tea has been (3) _____ in China for thousands of years. In the Shang Dynasty, it primarily was a(n) (4) _____ drink, and a(n) (5) _____ beverage in the Tang Dynasty. Thanks to the development of (6) _____ trade routes, tea was drunk daily and served to guests to welcome them. From China, tea spread across the Eastern Silk Roads to Japan and the Korean Peninsula and it developed close (7) _____ in Japan for it was consumed by Buddhist priests. As an aesthetic culture developed around tea drink, tea achieved a considerable amount of (8) _____ in medieval Japan. Ultimately, the art of tea making as well as drinking, was (9) _____ to the West and the whole world. Although there are many regional (10) _____, many cultures along the Silk Roads share tea-drinking customs and traditions.

Task 2

Directions: *Please read the text again and match different teas and tea cultures in Column B with various historical periods and locations in Column A. You may use one letter more than once.*

Column A	Column B
1. In the Shang Dynasty in China	a. tea-wares became a major art form and teapots and other ceramics were produced in various styles
2. By the Tang Dynasty in China	b. tea was consumed in Yunnan Province primarily as a medicinal drink
3. In the Song Dynasty in China	c. a popular tea "kahwa" is often served at special occasions such as weddings and festivals
4. In the 6th century CE in Japan	d. tea had become popular and was widely enjoyed as a refreshing beverage, prepared from leaves that had been moistened and shaped into a dense brick
5. In medieval Japan	e. an elaborate tea called "qymaq chai" is prepared for special occasions such as weddings and engagements; it is pinkish in color with added milk and cardamom
6. During the Ming Dynasty in China	f. tea's popularity quickly rose throughout the Eastern regions of the Silk Roads, in particular an aesthetic culture developed around tea drinking
7. In the northern Indian Subcontinent	g. the brick form of tea was replaced in popularity with loose leaves which were often ground into a fine powder and, increasingly, flavored with different substances
8. In Afghanistan	h. envoys were sent from Japan to China to learn about tea and its associated culture and seeds were imported via the Silk Roads in order for the plant to be cultivated in Japan

Task 3

Directions: *Please translate the following paragraph into English.*

文化是一幅丰富的挂毯（tapestry），将一个社会的信仰、习俗、传统和艺术表达编织在一起。它包含（encompass）了共同的价值观、仪式和行为，塑造了我们的身份，培养（foster）了归属感。文化是承载我们祖先故事的容器，将我们与我们的遗产联系起来，并为后代提供基础。正是通过文化，我们庆祝（celebrate）多样性，促进（promote）理解，拥抱（embrace）我们的差异之美。

Task 4

Directions: *Please discuss with your partners the topic below and finish a group report. You are encouraged to refer to other resources for the report.*

How can a society improve the atmosphere of cultural diversity?

Part II Drilling for GC Skills

How to Write a Position Paper (I)

1. Overview

A position paper is a diplomatic statement of your country's position on the issues under consideration by a committee. Each nation-state is required to submit a position paper—an essay detailing the country's policies on the topic being discussed.

A solid position paper has three parts:

- The country's position on the topic;
- The country's relation to the topic;
- Proposals of policies to pass in a resolution.

Position papers are usually one page in length. It should include a brief introduction followed by a comprehensive breakdown of the country's position on the topic(s) that are being discussed by each of the committees. A good position paper will not only provide facts but also make proposals for resolutions.

In detail, a good position paper will include:

- A brief introduction to the country and its history concerning the topic and committees;
- How the topic affects the country;
- The country's policies with respect to the issue and the country's justification for these policies;
- Quotes from the country's leaders about the issue;
- Statistics to back up the country's position on the issue;
- Actions taken by the government with regard to the issue;
- Conventions and resolutions that the country has signed or ratified;
- UN actions that the country supported or opposed;
- What the country believes should be done to address the issue; and
- What the country would like to accomplish in each committee.

Goals of a position paper include:

- Showing your country's unique understanding of the issue being discussed;
- Showing your country's previous relationship with the topic (preferably with relevant examples).
- Showing policies and ideas that your country would like to see in the resolution.

Task 1

Directions: *Please read the text and decide whether the following statements are true (T) or false (F).*

_____ 1. A solid position paper consists of three parts: the country's position on the topic, the country's relation to the topic, and proposals of policies to pass in a resolution.

_____ 2. Position papers are typically one-page long and should include a brief introduction followed by a comprehensive breakdown of the country's position on the topic(s) being discussed.

_____ 3. A good position paper should only provide facts and not make any proposals for resolutions.

_____ 4. A good position paper may include a brief introduction to the country's history concerning the topic and committees, as well as quotes from the country's leaders about the issue.

_____ 5. The actions taken by the government with regard to the issue and the conventions and resolutions that the country has signed or ratified are not relevant in a position paper.

2. Structuring Your Position Paper

(1) Establishing Your Position on the Topic Being Discussed

To answer the question or how to start a position paper, keep in mind that you are not only sharing your position, but also introducing the reader to see the topic being discussed from your eyes. To establish your position, start with a brief history of the situation/problem the committee will be discussing (How you see the situation/your position on the topic).

Define what you see as the challenge to the global community (or at least what some of them face). Keep in mind that your goal is to meet this challenge by the end of the paper. Frame the issue to be discussed as something that pertains not only to your country but, ideally, also the other countries to support your policy. It helps keep in mind that you will not get support for your clauses, or pass a resolution, alone. It is only when other countries see the topic the same way as you do that they will want to join you to implement your solution.

Task 2

Directions: *Please read the example of establishing your position and answer the questions below.*

Country: Angola

Committee: The Food and Agriculture Organization (FAO)

Topic: Improving Access to Clean Water

The Republic of Angola believes consistent access to clean water is a basic human right. Some countries have an abundance of water, such as Canada, Scotland, and Switzerland. Others have next to no water, such as Yemen, Libya and Djibouti, or low rainfall like Namibia and Sudan which creates water scarcity and desertification. The solution to all of these problems is the weather control that comes from cloud-

(Continued)

> seeding, with richer countries already reaping the benefits. The National Center of Meteorology and Seismology (NCMS) witnessed an increase in rainfall of 10%–15% in polluted air and 30%–35% in clean air. China uses cloud-seeding over several increasingly arid regions. In 2017, the United Arab Emirates launched 235 cloud-seeding operations by five cloud-seeding planes based in Al Ain. The use and success prove the technology works, but it is only accessible to those who can afford setting up the mechanisms to cloud seeding, or pay for the chemicals from companies like Bayer and DowDuPont Inc., who control the patents and sales rights.

1. What is the position of Angola on the topic of improving access to clean water?
2. What solution does Angola propose for addressing water scarcity and desertification?
3. What are some challenges or limitations associated with the proposed solution?

(2) Stating Your Country's Relation to the Topic

It is a presentation of the policies that your country has used to deal with the issue in the past. You should also describe the successes or failures of those policies (Your country's previous relation to the topic and the precedents it set). In the cases where your country has a strong link to the issue, the examples in the second paragraph should be about your country's connection to the specific issue. If your country has no direct relation, see if similar countries to yours, or countries with similar positions, have a relation to the topic. You can also conduct research to find out if your country has a relation to a similar topic, from where you can draw inspiration and a direction to justify your policies.

Note: This is also the place to write previous actions your committee has with the topic only if it is relevant to how your country introduces itself. Otherwise, you are repeating factual information that is not related to you introducing your position. Writing facts that do not forward your case is a trap many fall into.

Task 3

Directions: *Please read the example of stating the country's relation to the topic and discuss the questions below in pairs or groups.*

> Country: Angola
>
> Committee: The Food and Agriculture Organization (FAO)

(Continued)

> Topic: Improving Access to Clean Water
>
> Angola's history is scarred with conflicts arising from the abuse and mismanagement of natural resources, such as iron ore, petroleum, uranium, and diamonds. Angola is oil-rich while our people are dirt-poor. We stand at 149 out of 186 on the 2016 Human Development Index poverty scale. In rural areas, which contain 11.4 million people (38.5% of our total population), only 6% of households have access to electricity and 38% do not have access to safe water sources. Approximately 15 out of every 100 children do not survive beyond the age of five, leaving us with a child mortality rate around 17%. These challenges are especially difficult for our President Joao Lourenco, who entered the office in September 2017. President Lourenco's biggest challenge is reforming 38 years of cronyism and corruption under former President José Eduardo dos Santos. During his 38 years in power, infrastructure has not been developed while tens of billions of petrodollars disappeared. The 2014 oil slump made our situation worse reaffirming that we are unable to pull ourselves up on our own. Additionally, we do not get enough rain. We only get 32 days of rain with more than 0.1mm of rainfall meaning only 2.7 days of quality rain, sleet, and snow per month. Not enough to maintain adequate crop yields.

1. How does Angola's history of resource abuse and mismanagement contribute to the challenges it faces in improving access to clean water?

2. What are the key challenges faced by President Joao Lourenco in reforming Angola's infrastructure and addressing the issues related to poverty, child mortality, and inadequate rainfall?

3. According to the statement, in what ways is Angola related to the severe issue of clean water?

(3) Providing Extra Supporting Material

Sometimes, a position paper will need a fourth paragraph of extra supporting material covering additional angles that don't fit into the main three. This can be a case study, some topic-specific information about your (or another) country. It can be hard data needed to support Paragraph 2 or justify Paragraph 3; this fourth paragraph still comes before the final paragraph where you describe your desired policies.

The key is that the fourth paragraph needs to display a clear contribution to the position paper, show clear thinking and, in the end, support the call to action/policy that is being advocated for. Collectively, all of the paragraphs of the position paper should show how the delegates' unique, country-specific research and analysis furthers the understanding of what was originally read in the committee study guide.

Task 4

Directions: *Please read the example of providing extra supporting material and match the following companies in Column A with the agricultural sectors they strongly influence in Column B.*

Country: Angola

Committee: The Food and Agriculture Organization (FAO)

Topic: Improving Access to Clean Water

The global system that depends on technologies provided by companies like Corteva is strongly entrenched in the Sub-Saharan agriculture sector, as well as all over the world. The four biggest companies, Bayer-Monsanto, ChemChina, Corteva, and Syngenta have 59% of the world's patented seeds and 64% of all pesticides, and hold near-monopolies over other agrichemicals. The use of these crops and chemicals has become fundamental to growing corn in Tanzania, potatoes in Kenya and other crops in Sub-Saharan Africa throughout their diverse range of crops and terrains. This position of power persists because the Sub-Saharan farmers are similar in their lack of access to best practices, techniques, technologies, finances, and markets. This lack of skills combined with limited resources, results in the agriculture sector that is as under-development in agriculture as it is dependent on companies like ChemChina.

Column A	Column B
1. Bayer-Monsanto	a. corn production in Tanzania
2. ChemChina	b. potato cultivation in Kenya
3. Corteva	c. Sub-Saharan agriculture sector
4. Syngenta	d. global monopolies over agrichemicals and patented seeds

(4) Proposal—What You Want to Pass in a Resolution

In the proposal paragraph, you can either commit to one strong call to action, a few different policies or two extreme red lines, which you say you intend to work between. Remember, while you do not need to fully commit yourself to what you write in a position paper, it is important that you show the margins within which you will be operating at the conference. Doing this shows there is thought behind your actions and gives you more credit with the chairs for diplomatic progress. It is thus strongly advisable that you not write something that you will directly contradict through your actions in committee sessions.

Task 5

Directions: *Please read the example of writing a proposal and fill in the blanks with a proper word.*

Country: Angola

Committee: The Food and Agriculture Organization (FAO)

Topic: Improving Access to Clean Water

Angola advocates for a UN-sanctioned policy that gives permission to dry developing countries to make generic replicas of their patented chemicals at a fraction of the cost to achieve water independence. An example of these technologies belongs to German rainfall enhancement leader WeatherTec Services GmbH. WeatherTec's cutting-edge technologies to improve water access are cheaper than many of their competitors but the operating costs start at 11–15 million Euros a year. Angola does not believe the UN should subsidize the cost of the chemicals, as the subsidy is a temporary solution and it would take funds from other important programs while leaving the corporations with the same level of control. Today, aside from South Africa, none of us can afford cloud-seeding. We can cloud seed on our own if freed from the shackles of patent laws that benefit the rich. Dupot made net sales of $62.5 billion in 2017, by charging prices which the poorer dry countries could never afford. The UN should allow the relevant member states to locally produce WeatherTec's technologies so we can join the ranks of self-sufficient nations who can provide for themselves the basic water needs to survive.

---

1. The main argument presented in the passage is that Angola advocates for an UN-sanctioned policy that allows developing countries to produce generic replicas of

patented chemicals in order to achieve _____.

2. The passage supports the main argument by providing the following evidence: WeatherTec's technologies for improving _____ are cheaper than those of many competitors.

3. The proposed content of the policy is for the UN to allow relevant member states to produce WeatherTec's technologies locally, enabling them to provide for their own basic _____.

4. According to the passage, the current patent laws prevent poorer dry countries from accessing _____ solutions for improving water access.

5. Angola proposes that relevant member states should be allowed to locally produce WeatherTec's technologies to achieve _____ in providing for their basic water needs.

Task 6

Directions: *Please read the four examples again and figure out how the author presents and supports his or her arguments. Answer the following questions.*

1. How is the position introduced? Is the topic clearly stated?

   _____
   _____

2. How are the arguments organized? Are they presented in a logical sequence?

   _____
   _____

3. Are there any transitional phrases or linking words that help connect the ideas?

   _____
   _____

4. How does the author use evidence and examples to support his or her claims?

   _____
   _____

5. Does the position paper conclude with a persuasive statement summarizing the main points?

   _____
   _____

(5) The PReP Formula for Successful Position Papers

PReP stands for Position, Relation, extra & Proposal, which are the essential parts of every position paper. PReP will help you remember the formula.

- **Position**—Your view/interpretation of the issue being discussed. (Paragraph 1)

- **Relation**—Your connection to the topic being discussed. (Paragraph 2)

- **Extra**—The optional third paragraph which can contain extra information you feel is critical to your case, but doesn't naturally fit into one of the other three paragraphs. This paragraph still comes before the one containing your policies.

- **Proposal**—The practical policies you would want to see in the resolution. (Paragraph 3)

Tooltip: With the Proposal (Paragraph 3), you solve the issue shown in your Position (Paragraph 1) with the tools and relevance you set up in your Relation (Paragraph 2). The policy outlined in the final paragraph of the position paper should show ideas that address the issues outlined in your position associated with the committee topic, as should have been specified in the first paragraph. This position should be justified by the country's relation to the topic (Paragraph 2). These should be used to justify the policy proposals you outline in Paragraph 3. Each of these paragraphs should try to have as much unique information as possible that can't be found in the committee study guide because everyone in the committee should theoretically know that information. Obviously, your paper should have some connections to the main issues of the topic.

Task 7

Directions: *Please compose a position paper on China's diplomatic strategies, focusing on the theme of "Cultural Diplomacy: Bridging Nations Through Shared Heritage and Cooperation".*

In your position paper, you should follow the PReP formula with the following key points. Remember, these are just brief prompts for each key point. You can expand on each point by providing examples, evidence, and analysis to support your position. You are encouraged to work in groups and refer to other resources for this writing task.

1) **Position** (Paragraph 1):

- Highlight the significance of cultural diplomacy as a powerful tool for building bridges between nations.

- Emphasize China's commitment to promoting cultural exchange and understanding through the preservation and promotion of shared heritage.

2) **Relation** (Paragraph 2):

- Discuss the historical and cultural ties between China and other nations, emphasizing the commonalities that exist in terms of traditions, values, and historical legacies.

- Explain how cultural diplomacy can strengthen diplomatic relations, foster mutual respect, and deepen cooperation between nations.

3) **Extra** (Optional paragraph):

- Explore China's efforts in preserving and promoting its own cultural heritage, showcasing its rich history, traditions, and artistic achievements.

- Highlight the success stories of cultural exchange programs, festivals, and exhibitions organized by China, demonstrating the positive impact of cultural diplomacy on enhancing people-to-people connections.

4) **Proposal** (Paragraph 3):

- Propose concrete measures and initiatives for further enhancing cultural diplomacy, such as expanding cultural exchange programs and fostering collaborations in the fields of arts, education, and tourism.

- Advocate for the establishment of cultural centers, joint research projects, and exchange programs to facilitate the sharing of knowledge, ideas, and experiences between nations.

Country: China

Committee: General Assembly of the United Nations

Topic: Cultural Diplomacy: Bridging Nations Through Shared Heritage and Cooperation

(Position)

_____

_____

_____

(Relation)

_____

_____

_____

                                                    Unit 7   Global Culture and the UNESCO

                                                                    (Continued)

(Extra)
_____
_____
_____

(Proposal)
_____
_____
_____

Pro Tip: There is no set amount of space each paragraph needs to have. But no paper can miss any of the sections (except the extra part) and each one should be developed to at least 25% of the paper.

Part III   Notes from China

Chinese Culture Pursues "Not King, But Jade"[1]

On December 4, 2023, embracing more than 300 guests from around the world, the first Liangzhu Forum had its grand finale in Hangzhou, Zhejiang Province. Besides the main forum on Sunday, my journalistic experience of the event has been sweetened by two sub-events. The first one was crowded with 43 young Sinologists from around the globe, while the second one embraced art creators from 83 countries to depict China in their eyes. Sitting side by side with participants from countries such as Poland and Uganda, I was impressed to see overseas Sinologists discuss Chinese subjects that were even too profound for locals to understand as well as view global artists' deft paintings on traditional Chinese rice paper, known as *xuanzhi*. On Friday, the "Dialog of Young Sinologists in the New Era" agenda was launched. Several topics covering a wide range of areas such as history, philosophy, sociology, and media studies about China were discussed.

---

1 The text was adapted from the Globaltimes website.

It was interesting to see that most of the experts' opinions about China's development were bundled with topics such as history and modernity and archaeology and nature. Those cross-fielded opinions alerted those in attendance that Chinese civilization has never been purely about culture. Its evolution has been comprehensive to include all-round progress, which is why German expert Hannes Wolfgang Reinhard said that no text can thoroughly explain the complexity of China. Filippo Costantini, an expert representing the Belt and Road Initiative (BRI) partner country Costa Rica, told the *Global Times* that thanks to the BRI, Costa Rican locals who could once only vaguely differentiate between China, Japan, and South Korea have now fallen in love with Chinese culture through co-published books and the China-Costa Rica research center. "Our cooperation is inspiring and needed," Costantini said, adding that he believes ancient Chinese philosophy can still guide our lives today.

What makes overseas countries want to collaborate with China? This was the question I pondered after hearing the speeches from the many Sinologists in attendance. I was fortunate to be able to find the answer at the forum. It came from Adil Kaukenov, the chief researcher of the Kazakhstan Institute for Strategic Studies, who summed it up as mutual trust. As an expert contributing to Kazakhstan's strategic development, Kaukenov said that China and Kazakhstan's similar cultures, such as their shared love for naan flatbread, bring the two countries emotionally closer. With China's fast development, "China-Kazakhstan exchanges can even influence the entirety of Central Asia," he emphasized.

Cultural exchange may indeed sound abstract, but Albert Kozik, a young Polish Sinologist studying Comparative Asian-Western history in Warsaw, said there are many young people who are falling in love with Chinese culture through digital channels. At the venue, there were many visitors taking pictures with their phones. One young visitor from Thailand said that he had visited the nearby Liangzhu Museum and that the "likes" he got on X after posting his photos were beyond his expectations. "I could not believe how incredible those jade wares were. I think the world needs to see the magic of China," the Thai visitor said.

Other than the Sinologist forum, the event Silk Road Artists' Rendezvous was the most impressive part of the entire Liangzhu agenda. The program offers international artists tours of Chinese cities like Hangzhou, Shaoxing, and Huzhou, where local art teachers introduce traditional Chinese art forms like landscape paintings and calligraphy. *Ubuntungumuntu*, a painting whose title means "I am, because we are" in Ugandan, attracted people's attention during the tour. Ruganzu Bruno, T., the work's artist, added an extra layer of "bark cloth", a type of tree bark indigenous to Uganda, to the painting to symbolize the tombs from the ancient Liangzhu culture. He said that art allowed him to see the connection between China and Africa. "I'm overwhelmed by the whole Liangzhu legacy and cried when looking at Zao Wou-Ki's art. I guess that's the power of sharing humanity," Kate, a painter from New Zealand, said when showing me a photo of her new silk work made by using Chinese brooms as a paint brush.

The "Liangzhu" in the Liangzhu Forum refers to China's more than 5,000-year-old archaeological ruins that have become known for its jade culture. Jade, with its genteel sheen, symbolizes the humble and harmonious nature of Chinese people. There is an interesting saying I grasped at the event to describe the Chinese cultural spirit: "Not a 'king', just 'jade.'" This is an analogy describing the Chinese people's spirit of seeking harmony instead of hegemony.

(749 words)

Directions: *Please discuss the questions below with your partners.*

1. According to the author, what motivates overseas countries to seek to collaborate with China?

2. What role does cultural exchange play in fostering collaboration between overseas countries and China?

3. What does jade symbolize in Chinese culture? How can we better promote jade culture overseas? Can you design a project on the promotion of jade culture?

Unit 8

A Community of Shared Future for Mankind (I)

Part I Reading for GC Knowledge

Text A The Belt and Road Initiative as a Strategy to Promote and Sustain Growth

 Warm-up

Directions: *Suppose you have a takeover week to engage in work concerning the Belt and Road Initiative, please discuss with your partners the questions below.*

Jobs on the Takeover Week	
Job 1: Docent in French Silk Museum • Learn about silk production in China and France. • Guide tourists to visit the museum about the origin, history, and technological process of silk.	**Job 4: Coordinator in a wind power station in Greece** • Learn about the cooperation between China and Greece on energy projects. • Communicate with the project manager in Greece.
Job 2: Staff on China Railway Express to Madrid • Conduct customs declaration for the goods. • Check the goods, including their packing, weight, quantity, safety, etc.	**Job 5: Promotor of overseas Chinese medicine program** • Promote the value of traditional Chinese medicine overseas. • Organize some skill demonstrations, like acupuncture and moxibustion therapy.
Job 3: Train conductor of China-Laos Railway • Learn about the construction process and multi-dimensional significance of China-Laos Railway.	**Job 6: International Chinese teacher** • Teach Chinese and Chinese culture to foreigners to help them better communicate in Chinese contexts.

(Continued)

Jobs on the Takeover Week	
• Communicate with the counterpart authorities and individuals in Laos. • Promote a closer tie between the countries and people.	• Organize targeted cultural festivals to enhance diverse cultural communication.

1. How much do you know about China's Belt and Road Initiative and relevant projects?

2. How can your major contribute to the development of the Belt and Road Initiative?

3. Please choose a job in the table below that you are interested in and give your opinions.

The Belt and Road Initiative as a Strategy to Promote and Sustain Growth[1]

❶   In March 2015, China issued an action plan which described the main objectives of the Belt and Road Initiative (BRI). The BRI-participating economies represent more than one-third of global GDP and over half of the world's population. While infrastructure investment is a key aspect of the BRI, China states that it is much broader in its objectives, encompassing all aspects of sustainable growth for itself and including more balanced regional growth, the upgrading of its industry, and greener economic growth at home.

Specific Objectives for the BRI: Growth Through Connectivity

❷   As stated by China, the focus on connectivity within the BRI is both about facilitating trade and investment, and thereby the development of neighboring countries, as well as strategically shoring up its own security of energy, resources, and food by taking a regional leadership role with its most important neighbors. It has a very broad scope encompassing economic, strategic, and cultural connectivity.

- To increase trade and investment in the BRI: We will improve the bilateral and multilateral cooperation mechanisms of the Belt and Road Initiative focusing on policy communication, infrastructure connectivity, trade facilitation, capital flow, and **people-to-people exchanges**.

---

1 The text was adapted from OECD Business and Finance Outlook 2018—"China's Belt and Road Initiative in Global Trade, Investment and Finance Landscape".

- Free trade zones along the Silk Road: We will speed up efforts to implement the free trade area strategy, gradually establishing a network of high-standard free trade areas. We will actively engage in negotiations with countries and regions along the routes of the BRI on the building of free trade areas.

- To enhance financial cooperation in the region to fund infrastructure: We will strengthen cooperation with international organizations including international financial organizations and institutions, work actively to promote the development of the **Asian Infrastructure Investment Bank** and the **New Development Bank**, put the Silk Road Fund to effective use, and attract international capital for the creation of a financial cooperation platform that is open, **pluralistic**, and mutually beneficial.

- To gain access to natural resources: We will strengthen international cooperation on energy and resources and production chains, and increase local processing and **conversion**.

- To strengthen transport infrastructure in the BRI corridors: We will advance the development of multi-modal transportation that integrates expressways, railways, waterways, and airways, build international **logistics thoroughfares**, and strengthen infrastructure development along major routes and at major ports of entry. We will work to develop Xinjiang as the core region for the Silk Road Economic Belt and Fujian as the core region for the 21st Century Maritime Silk Road.

- To deepen cultural exchanges in the region: We will conduct extensive international cooperation in the areas of education, science, technology, culture, sports, tourism, environmental protection, healthcare, and traditional Chinese medicine.

The Six Economic Corridors of the BRI

❸   Thinking about development in terms of economic corridors has been an important aspect of China's development model. Infrastructure investment along the Belt and Road is concerned with six economic corridors covering a large energy- and resource-rich part of the world.

- New Eurasia Land Bridge: involving rail to Europe via Kazakhstan, Russia, Belarus, and Poland.

- China, Mongolia, Russia Economic Corridor: including rail links and the **steppe road**—this will link with the land bridge.

- China, Central Asia, West Asia Economic Corridor: linking to Kazakhstan, Kyrgyzstan, Tajikistan, Uzbekistan, Turkmenistan, Iran, and Turkey.

- China-Indochina Peninsula Economic Corridor: Vietnam, Thailand, Lao People's Democratic Republic, Cambodia, Myanmar, and Malaysia.

- China, Pakistan Economic Corridor: Xinjiang Uygur **Autonomous** Region will be most affected. This important project links Kashgar City (free economic zone) in landlocked Xinjiang with the Pakistan port of Gwadar, a deep water port used for commercial and military purposes.

- China, Bangladesh, India, Myanmar Economic Corridor: This is likely to move more slowly due to mistrust over security issues between India and China.

Sustainable Development Motivations

❹ China is proposing a holistic implementation of the BRI, covering a number of broad aspects that will be important for achieving the 2030 Sustainable Development Goals. Aspects of this much broader approach include:

- Peace: All countries should respect each other's **sovereignty**, dignity and **territorial integrity**, each other's development paths and social systems, and each other's core interests and major concerns.

- Ecology and environment: China will improve green and low-carbon operation, management and maintenance of infrastructure by clarifying environmental protection requirements in infrastructure construction standards and enforcing environmental standards and practices in such sectors as green transportation, green building, and green energy. China will jointly create eco-industrial parks with a focus on enterprise **agglomeration**s, eco-industrial chains, and service platforms. Environmental protection facilities will be constructed, centralized **sewage** treatment and recycling and corresponding demonstrations will be promoted, and public service platforms on eco-environmental information, technology, and business will be put in place in industrial parks.

- Water conservation: The Chinese government **proactively** promotes policy coordination, technology sharing, and engineering cooperation with neighboring countries in the protection and development of cross-border rivers. It has launched joint studies with the countries concerned on the protection and use of water resources of cross-border rivers, in order to better protect these resources. China encourages the sharing of **hydrological** data during the flood season and has established a Sino-Russian mechanism for cooperation in flood prevention and control.

- Civil society: We should establish a multi-tiered mechanism for cultural and people-to-people exchanges, build more cooperation platforms and open more cooperation channels. Educational cooperation should be boosted, and more exchange students should be encouraged and the performance of cooperatively run schools should be enhanced. Efforts should be made to establish **think tank** networks and partnerships in cultural, sports, and health sectors. Historical and cultural heritage should be fully tapped to jointly develop tourist products and protect heritage.

❺ All in all, China's BRI is affecting the global investment, trade, and finance landscape in significant ways:

- Investment: Many BRI-participating economies see benefits in a strong role for the state and commercial relationships in line with the **Bandung Principles**. An important part of the hardware-first strategy is connectivity in energy supplies and **electricity grids** along the Belt and Road. There are multiple sources of energy across the BRI, and how best to link these up and price them is also an important issue. China has leadership in **ultra-high voltage** lines. China is also well advanced in 5G **broadband** that is expected to play an important role in the use of big data and in the development of smart grids and cities, remote transport, and other projects.

- Trade: Trade creation is greater in regions where connectivity is likely to be less **problematic**, and **extra-bloc** effects on imports and exports for BRI-participating economies are strong when they originate from trade blocs where either China or the United States are members. This underlines the need for investment that promotes greater connectivity and China's role in the BRI is especially important given the gravity effects of its economy.

- Finance: China alone cannot fund all of the infrastructure needs of developing Asia; these needs are very large and China faces its own financial constraints at home. This means that there is a need for more effort by OECD countries to engage with those of the BRI and vice versa. The future of all economies is improved when well-being rises around the world. This requires a sound investment environment to attract the capital required and to ensure that host countries get the best value for money.

(1,220 words)

Glossary

pluralistic	/plʊərə'lɪstɪk/	adj.	多元的
conversion	/kən'vɜːʃn/	n.	转换，转化
logistics	/lə'dʒɪstɪks/	n.	物流
thoroughfare	/'θʌrəfeə(r)/	n.	要道
autonomous	/ɔː'tɒnəməs/	adj.	自治的，自主的

sovereignty	/ˈsɒvrənti/	n.	主权
agglomeration	/əˌglɒməˈreɪʃn/	n.	集聚
sewage	/ˈsuːɪdʒ/	n.	（下水道的）污水
proactively	/ˌprəʊˈæktɪvli/	adv.	主动地
hydrological	/ˌhaɪdrəˈlɒdʒɪkəl/	adj.	水文学的
broadband	/ˈbrɔːdbænd/	n.	宽带
problematic	/ˌprɒbləˈmætɪk/	adj.	成问题的

Useful Expressions

people-to-people exchanges	人文交流
Asian Infrastructure Investment Bank	亚洲基础设施投资银行
New Development Bank	金砖国家新开发银行
steppe road	草原之路
territorial integrity	领土完整
think tank	智库
Bandung Principles	万隆会议十项原则
electricity grids	电网
ultra-high voltage	超高压
extra-bloc	集团外的

Task 1

Directions: *Please read the text and fill in the blanks below with a proper word.*

Achieving Sustainable Growth Through the BRI
Development through connectivity
• To increase trade and (1) _____, and build free trade zones along the Silk Road;   • To enhance international (2) _____ to fund and build (3) _____;   • To gain access to natural (4) _____ and increase local processing and (5) _____;   • To deepen cultural (6) _____ through intercultural communication and cooperation.

(Continued)

Achieving Sustainable Growth Through the BRI
Development through six economic corridors
• New (7) _____ Land Bridge;
• China, Mongolia, Russia Economic Corridor;
• China, Central Asia, West Asia Economic Corridor;
• China-Indochina (8) _____ Economic Corridor;
• China, (9) _____ Economic Corridor;
• China, Bangladesh, India, Myanmar Economic Corridor.
Sustainable development motivations
• All countries should work together to build a(n) (10) _____ world;
• China will implement a series of (11) _____ operations to achieve ecological (12) _____;
• The Chinese government encourages water (13) _____;
• A multi-tiered (14) _____ for cultural exchanges will be established to construct (15) _____ society.

Task 2

Directions: *Please read the text again and decide whether the following statements are true (T) or false (F) based on what you have learned from the text.*

_____ 1. Less than one-third of the world's population is included in the BRI-participating economies.

_____ 2. The objectives of connectivity involve a wide range, covering economic, strategic, and cultural aspects.

_____ 3. International cooperation is indispensable for infrastructure construction along the Silk Road.

_____ 4. The Asian Infrastructure Investment Bank and the New Development Bank are two important organizations for the effective use of the Silk Road Fund.

_____ 5. The six economic corridors of the BRI span Asian, European, and African continents.

_____ 6. More challenges have to be overcome to construct the China, Bangladesh, India, Myanmar Economic Corridor.

_____ 7. Research on 5G broadband has witnessed continual progress in China and it will play a key role in the projects of the BRI.

_____ 8. Improvement in water conservation requires technological upgrading and sharing.

_____ 9. It is not encouraged to share hydrological data during the flood season in case of any possible safety risks.

_____ 10. China alone can satisfy the infrastructure needs of the developing countries in Asia without help from the developed countries.

Task 3

Directions: *Please translate the following sentences into English using the words in the parentheses.*

1. "一带一路"倡议提出十年以来，中国已与五大洲的150多个国家、30多个国际组织签署了200多份合作文件，该倡议成为深受欢迎的国际公共产品和国际合作平台。（global public good）

2. "一带一路"国际合作涵盖政治互信、基础设施互联互通、经贸合作、人文交流等重点领域。（encompass）

3. 全球化智库（Center for China & Globalization, CCG）报告建议，参照APEC峰会的方式，在参与"一带一路"的国家轮流举办"一带一路"国际合作高峰论坛，进一步推进多边合作机制。（multilateral）

4. 目前，"一带一路"发展已进入绿色转型的新阶段，在项目设计与推进中充分考虑碳排放、生物多样性等环境问题。（conversion）

5. 过去几年中，"一带一路"经济合作既成果丰硕，同时也存在诸多困难，例如新冠疫情的冲击、贸易保护主义等。（problematic）

Task 4

Directions: *Please work with your partners and finish the project assignment below.*

The Annual Belt and Road Forum for International Cooperation is going to be held in Beijing next month. Suppose you are chosen as a volunteer to assist the representatives of relevant international organizations during their stay in Beijing.

One item on their schedule is to have a culture tour in Beijing, such as a visit to some cultural heritage sites, high-tech companies, or some relevant institutions that have some connections with the international organization you are offering voluntary work.

Please design a recommended route and serve as a tour guide for them. Based on your designed route, prepare some China's stories about the highlights of the tour.

Text B The Chinese Express Train Running in East Africa

 Warm-up

***Directions:** Please discuss the following questions with your partners.*

1. What's your impression of Kenya concerning its history, culture, ecology, people's livelihood, etc.?
2. What do you know about China-Kenya cooperation in infrastructure construction?
3. What challenges do you think are likely to emerge during railway construction and operation in East Asia?

The Chinese Express Train Running in East Africa[1]

❶ It has now been more than half a century since Kenya gained its independence. Under the Vision 2030, President Uhuru Kenyatta aims to develop Kenya into a diversified, robust, and competitive industrialized country. A new railway was a century-old dream for the country and people of Kenya.

❷ Mombasa and Nairobi were previously connected by **The Lunatic Express**, the old Kenya-Uganda meter-**gauge** railway, which was built by the British in 1896. Due to **disrepair** and aging of equipment, the railway could run at a mere 22 km/h on average and the entire journey would take 21 hours. Besides, its operation was unstable. Any breakdown would keep it out of service for days and there were frequent accidents such as **derailments** and **collisions** with animals.

❸ Financed mainly by China and constructed by China Road and Bridge Corporation (CRBC), the 480-km Mombasa-Nairobi Standard Gauge Railway (SGR) connecting

---
1 The text was adapted from the Chinadaily website.

Mombasa, the largest port in East Africa, and Kenya's capital city of Nairobi is a **flagship** project under the China-proposed Belt and Road Initiative (BRI), and is Kenya's largest infrastructure project since its independence in 1963.

A Railway of Development Running Through East Africa

❹ It took three years for the Chinese company to complete the Mombasa-Nairobi line, which was put into operation in 2017 and began to take both passengers and **cargo** almost at the same time. Since its operation, the SGR has promoted the growth of the local logistics industry. Goods loaded in Mombasa in the morning will arrive in Nairobi in the afternoon, with logistics costs **slashed** by up to 40%. Transportation of goods from the port to the **hinterland**s of East Africa has become much more efficient. As the railway network and supporting infrastructure in East Africa improve, the logistics industry throughout the region will be **galvanized**, and economic cooperation and cultural exchanges between countries will reach a new height. The Mombasa-Nairobi SGR is projected to contribute 2%–3% to Kenya's GDP, and the railway has become a dominant player in Kenya's pursuit of inclusive growth, as it has revolutionized the transportation of passengers and **bulk cargo**, stimulated commerce and investments, and fostered job creation for local youth.

❺ The integrated development of the Mombasa-Nairobi Railway, the Port of Mombasa and the Mombasa Special Economic Zone is unveiling an exciting scene of industrialization. As President Uhuru Kenyatta said, the SGR will "reshape the story of Kenya for the next 100 years". As a strategic infrastructure project, the SGR is adding the realization of Kenya's two flagship socioeconomic transformation blueprints—Vision 2030 and the Big Four Agenda, said Philip Mainga, managing director of Kenya Railways Corp.

A Railway of Ecological Protection

❻ The SGR **traverses** the Tsavo National Park, Kenya's largest wildlife reserve. The destination, Nairobi, is one of the few capital cities in the world that has a nature reserve. The vast areas along the railway are home to almost all African animal species, representing an extraordinarily valuable natural environment. How to ensure that the railway runs in harmony with the wildlife and build the SGR into a railway of nature that cares for animals—this question stayed on the mind of the builders since the very beginning.

❼ During the construction, China Road and Bridge Corporation adopted extremely **stringent** standards and hired specialist companies for environmental impact assessments.

Digging and other works along the line were carried out during the day only, and construction was prohibited at night so as not to disturb animals. In order to avoid collision with wild animals at the Tsavo National Park, the SGR tracks are not laid on the ground like the narrow-gauge railway. It employed an enclosed design and built **viaducts** so that wild animals could pass safely.

❽ To protect the **migrating** herds, the builders painstakingly designed 14 large **underpasses** that are seven meters tall, enough to allow giraffes to pass without lowering their necks. They also built over 100 **culverts**, which gave animals like zebras access to water and served as underpasses for small animals. Protective fences and **embankments** were built at the parks and **swamp** sections, to prevent animals from climbing onto the tracks and running into the trains.

❾ Besides wildlife, **mangrove** forests are also well protected. Ali Mohamed, a 44-year-old resident of a **serene** village overlooking a mangrove swamp on the northwestern edges of Mombasa, said that besides regulating coastal weather, the **installation** of overpasses and culverts has ensured that there was minimal disturbance to the mangrove forest, which is an important fish breeding site. The SGR has earned **accolades** from local officials and conservationists for prioritizing ecological protection along its corridor since its launch.

A Railway of Friendship for China-Africa Cooperation

❿ Since the launch of the SGR, the Chinese company has been providing Kenyan employees with training tailored to their specific backgrounds, professions, and roles. It is committed to transferring China's railway technologies, selecting talent in Kenya, and building up a talent pool for Kenya's railway sector. Close to 80% of the employees are hired locally. On the 1,000th day of the SGR's operation, the head of the Africa Star Railway Operations Co., Ltd. announced that technology transfer has been done across 123 types of skilled work, marking an effective transfer throughout the industrial chain. Kenya has thus been provided with technologies and capabilities to develop railway transportation independently. The Kenyan employees have started to work in major skilled posts independently. The **well-groomed** and graceful **stewardesses** trained with Chinese standards have become a beautiful sight on the SGR. The training of skilled personnel for the SGR is an overseas training program by the Chinese railway industry that features the longest duration, the largest number of trainees, and the most distinctive **vocational** characteristics.

⓫ Philip Mainga, managing director of Kenya Railways Corp., said the SGR is also benefiting the local people as skills transfer has reached 80%–90%. "Now our people are able to run the operations, to drive their **locomotives**, to carry on with signal work, to repair and maintain our wagons."

⑫ Recruited in 2017 by SGR operator Africa Star Railway Operation Company, Harrison Kinyanjui, a 26-year-old economics major, has received **rigorous** training on railway operations and management from Chinese **mentors**, and progressed quickly to become the first Kenyan to work at the SGR **dispatch center** in Nairobi.

⑬ Kinyanjui, the assistant **superintendent** of the center, said the work is to organize train operations using a centralized traffic control system in the center, which is the brain and heart of all SGR train operations. "The Chinese experts have taught us very well. They now have the confidence to leave us to work independently. We are very, very proud that we came here not knowing anything about train dispatching, but we are now very competent," he said.

(1,111 words)

Glossary

gauge	/ɡeɪdʒ/	n.	（铁道的）轨距
disrepair	/ˌdɪsrɪˈpeə(r)/	n.	破败；破损
derailment	/dɪˈreɪlmənt/	n.	脱轨
collision	/kəˈlɪʒn/	n.	碰撞，相撞
flagship	/ˈflæɡʃɪp/	n.	旗舰
cargo	/ˈkɑːɡəʊ/	n.	货物
slash	/slæʃ/	v.	大幅降低
hinterland	/ˈhɪntəlænd/	n.	内陆
galvanize	/ˈɡælvənaɪz/	v.	使振奋，激励
traverse	/trəˈvɜːs/	v.	穿过
stringent	/ˈstrɪndʒənt/	adj.	严格的
viaduct	/ˈvaɪədʌkt/	n.	高架桥
migrate	/maɪˈɡreɪt/	v.	迁徙
underpass	/ˈʌndəpɑːs/	n.	地下通道
culvert	/ˈkʌlvət/	n.	涵洞
embankment	/ɪmˈbæŋkmənt/	n.	路堤
swamp	/swɒmp/	n.	沼泽
mangrove	/ˈmæŋɡrəʊv/	n.	红树林
serene	/səˈriːn/	adj.	平静的；宁静的

installation	/ˌɪnstəˈleɪʃn/	n.	安装；设置
accolade	/ˈækəleɪd/	n.	荣誉
well-groomed	/ˌwel ˈgruːmd/	adj.	梳妆整洁的
stewardess	/ˌstjuːəˈdes/	n.	女乘务员
vocational	/vəʊˈkeɪʃənl/	adj.	职业的
locomotive	/ˌləʊkəˈməʊtɪv/	n.	机车；火车头
rigorous	/ˈrɪgərəs/	adj.	严格的
mentor	/ˈmentɔː(r)/	n.	导师
superintendent	/ˌsuːpərɪnˈtendənt/	n.	主管，负责人

Useful Expressions

The Lunatic Express	疯狂铁路
bulk cargo	散装货物
dispatch center	调度中心

Task 1

Directions: *Please read the text and fill in the blanks in the summary.*

The article addresses the Chinese-built Mombasa-Nairobi Standard (1) _____ Railway (SGR) with three distinctive features, including (2) _____ of East Asia, (3) _____ protection, and friendship for China-Africa (4) _____. The SGR took three years to complete and since its operation, the SGR has promoted the growth of the local (5) _____ industry. Transportation of passengers and bulk cargo has been (6) _____. During the railway construction, as the SGR traverses Kenya's wildlife (7) _____, stringent standards are set to evaluate its influence on the environment. A series of measures were also implemented to protect animals. For example, to ensure the safety of migrating herds and zebras' access to water, builders designed (8) _____ and (9) _____ respectively. Besides, since the launch of the SGR, the Chinese company has provided Kenyan employees with professional training (10) _____ to their specific backgrounds and roles. They now feel proud and confident to work on the train.

Unit 8　A Community of Shared Future for Mankind (I)

Task 2

Directions: *Please read the text again and choose the best answer from the four choices marked A), B), C) and D) based on what you have learned from the text.*

1. Built by the British in 1896, The Lunatic Express in Kenya _____.

   A) could take 25 hours from Mombasa to Nairobi on average

   B) has the problem of disrepair and aging of equipment

   C) still has few accidents during operation currently

   D) could run fast enough to keep pace with people's demand

2. Which of the following is NOT correct about the SGR?

   A) The infrastructure project is largely financed by China.

   B) The SGR is a flagship project under the China-led BRI.

   C) The SGR was put into operation after five years' construction.

   D) The completion of the SGR met the dream of the Kenya people.

3. Because of the SGR, transportation of goods from the port to the hinterlands of East Africa has become much more _____.

   A) expensive   B) laborious

   C) time-consuming   D) efficient

4. The connectivity between Mombasa and Nairobi through the SGR helps boost the development of the following fields EXCEPT _____.

   A) aesthetic judgment   B) cultural exchanges

   C) logistics industry   D) economic cooperation

5. As the SGR traversed Kenya's largest wildlife reserve, the builders wanted to construct it into a railway _____.

   A) without animals seen along the way

   B) with the fastest running

   C) without any disturbance

   D) caring for animals

6. According to Ali Mohamed, besides regulating coastal weather, the installation of overpasses and culverts has ensured _____.

   A) minimal disturbance to the mangrove forest

   B) the safety of villagers

   C) less noise from animals

   D) the breath of fish

7. On the 1,000th day of the SGR's operation, the head of the Africa Star Railway Operations Co., Ltd. announced that _____.

   A) the Chinese company would provide Kenyan employees with training

   B) technology transfer has been done across 123 types of skilled work

   C) the SGR would contribute to 2%–3% of Kenya's GDP

   D) the SGR would reshape the story of Kenya for the next years

8. Chinese mentors have offered _____ training for the Kenya employees to have them work independently on the SGR.

   A) caring and warm-hearted   B) knowledgeable and polite

   C) rigorous and tailored   D) practical and simple

9. Staff on SGR trains are now _____ enough to carry out their work after receiving training from Chinese experts.

   A) smart   B) graceful

   C) talented   D) competent

10. The writer's attitude toward China-Kenya cooperation on the SGR project is _____.

    A) supportive   B) negative

    C) indifferent   D) neutral

Task 3

Directions: *Please translate the following five sentences into English using the words and phrases in the parentheses.*

1. 由于这条铁路贯穿世界上最脆弱的生态系统，在建设期间和建成后都采取了生态保护措施。(traverse)

2. 本届APEC峰会的主题是如何通过加强合作来促进包容性增长和推动全球经济的复苏。

（inclusive）

3. 全面融合了中国标准和中国智慧的雅万高铁（The Jakarta-Bandung HSR）是中国高铁首次全系统、全要素、全产业链的海外建设项目。（integrate）

4. "一带一路"倡议提出十年以来，基础设施互联互通一直是该倡议的首要目标之一。（prioritize）

5. 铁路领域有严格的安全标准监管，以最大限度保障乘客的人身和财产安全。（rigorous）

Task 4

Directions: *Please discuss with your partner and write a report on China's contribution in boosting the world's connectivity under the BRI. You are supposed to investigate one typical example based on your major at your university or the field you are interested in.*

Part II Drilling for GC Skills

How to Write a Position Paper (II)

1. Writing Your Position Paper

In most cases, a position paper should be written in diplomatic language. That is, it should express your position on the issues in the most favorable and respectful light possible. A position paper consists of a short introductory paragraph, followed by a body paragraph on the topic and a conclusion paragraph.

- **Introductory paragraph:** This paragraph lists the topics your committee will discuss and summarizes the country's basic approach to the topics by referring to the relevant international organizations to which the country belongs and the relevant treaties it has signed.

- **Body paragraph:** For each topic your committee will discuss, you will need to write three paragraphs. Below is a description of each paragraph.

- **Conclusion paragraph:** The final paragraph of a position paper emphasizes your claims and summarizes your paper. You might also include information about the impact of this issue.

(1) The First Paragraph—History

a. This paragraph should provide a short introduction to the topic, the previous work of the UN on the topic, and current issues that need to be addressed, from your country's point of view.

b. It should refer to important treaties or past resolutions that your country has supported.

(2) The Second Paragraph—Position

a. This paragraph should state your country's position on the topic.

b. It should refer to your country's work on the issue within its borders, with allies, with regional partners, and/or within the world community.

c. It should explain why your country is a shining example, or needs assistance, or has made progress, or can help other countries on this topic.

(3) The Third Paragraph—Proposal

a. This paragraph should summarize your country's proposal for addressing the issues related to this topic.

b. It should assess the progress that has been made on this issue, describe areas for improvement, and suggest specific measures.

c. Conclude with a strong, forward-thinking sentence.

2. The Expressions to Help Develop Your Structure and Flow

(1) Introduction of the Issue

Introducing the topic:

- The matter at hand...
- The subject under consideration...
- The focal point of discussion...
- The core issue being addressed...
- The central theme revolves around...

Significance of the issue:

- Given its paramount importance...

- In light of its critical nature...
- Considering its profound implications...
- Acknowledging its far-reaching consequences...
- Recognizing its pivotal role in...

Thesis statement:

- It is the contention of this paper that...
- The central argument posited here is...
- This paper asserts that...
- The overarching thesis of this position paper is...
- The stance adopted in this discourse is encapsulated by the thesis that...

(2) Body Paragraph

Presenting arguments:

- Firstly, it is imperative to address...
- An integral aspect to consider is...
- From a broader perspective...
- A cogent argument in favor of...
- Supporting this viewpoint is the notion that...

Providing evidence:

- Empirical evidence underscores...
- Statistical data substantiates...
- Noteworthy examples elucidate...
- A comprehensive study reveals...
- Authoritative sources authenticate...
- Addressing counterarguments...
- While it may be contended that...
- It is essential to acknowledge the viewpoint that...
- An opposing argument suggests that...
- Despite these considerations, it is essential to recognize...

- In response to potential counterarguments...

Transition phrases:

- Transitioning to the next facet of the discussion...
- Shifting the focus to another critical element...
- Turning our attention to...
- Having examined the aforementioned, let us now delve into...
- This brings us to the next pivotal point...

(3) Conclusion

Summarizing key points:

- In summation...
- To recapitulate...
- In conclusion...
- To summarize...
- To encapsulate...

Reinforcing the stance:

- Reiterating the central argument...
- Emphasizing the thesis...
- Underscoring the importance of...
- Affirming the position taken...
- Strengthening the conviction that...

Proposing action or solutions:

- Advocating for proactive measures...
- Proposing tangible solutions...
- Suggesting a course of action...
- Encouraging a concerted effort toward...
- Putting forth actionable recommendations...

Unit 8　A Community of Shared Future for Mankind (I)

Task 1

Directions: *Please fill in the blanks with the expressions provided above.*

1. _____ lies in the need for immediate action to address climate change.

2. _____ is the contention of this paper that sustainable development offers viable solutions.

3. From a broader perspective, _____ is crucial to understanding the interconnectedness of environmental issues.

4. Empirical evidence _____ the urgency of implementing renewable energy solutions.

5. Despite _____ that economic growth may suffer, transitioning to renewable energy is imperative.

6. Transitioning to _____, let's explore the role of individual responsibility in combating climate change.

7. In _____, it is crucial to emphasize the importance of international cooperation.

8. An opposing argument suggests that _____ may lead to job losses in certain sectors.

9. To _____, advocating for policy changes to promote renewable energy is essential.

10. Given its _____, it is essential to acknowledge the need for long-term planning.

11. The _____ of the discussion is now focused on adaptation strategies for vulnerable communities.

12. _____ to another critical element, let's discuss the importance of education in climate change mitigation.

13. This brings us to the next pivotal point, _____ the importance of community engagement.

14. In _____, it is crucial to propose actionable recommendations for policy-makers.

15. _____, it is imperative to reinforce the stance that climate change requires urgent and decisive action.

Task 2

Directions: *Please fill in the blanks with the proper linking phrase from the box below.*

> in addition to this   on the contrary   at the same time   has also   by the same token

1. China has steadfastly upheld world peace and security; _____, it has dedicated itself to resolving differences through dialogs.

2. China firmly opposes the willful threat or use of force; _____, it advocates for resolving international disputes through peaceful dialogs.

3. Over the past 50 years, China's cooperation with the UN has not only expanded but _____, it has engaged in fruitful cooperation across a wide range of areas.

4. Over the past 50 years, China has not only contributed to economic development but _____ played a key role in initiatives aimed at improving global health and environmental protection.

5. While China emphasizes the importance of multilateralism and the upholding of international laws; _____, it stands firmly against unilateral actions and sanctions that undermine the collective decision-making processes of the international community.

Task 3

Directions: *Please craft a position paper focusing on China's governance strategies for the Belt and Road Initiative, centering on the theme "Sustainable Development and Mutual Benefits". You are suggested to analyze and articulate the efforts and impact of governance in the context of rural development with approximately 500 words.*

Task 4

Directions: *Please read a position paper on China versus the United States and answer some questions by scanning the QR code.*

Part III Notes from China

President Xi's Reply Letters to Student Representatives from BRI Countries[1]

I

Chinese President Xi Jinping has replied to a letter from representatives of Kenyan students and alumni at Beijing Jiaotong University, encouraging them to continue contributing to the friendship between China and Kenya and between China and Africa.

In his reply on January 17, 2024, Xi noted that China and Kenya enjoy a time-honored friendship. The Belt and Road Initiative has turned the ideals of development and revitalization of China and Kenya into reality, and closely linked the well-being of the two peoples. The Mombasa-Nairobi Standard Gauge Railway (SGR) is a flagship project and a successful example of China-Kenya Belt and Road cooperation.

"I am glad to see that you have bonded with China through this road to happiness. You have witnessed and benefited from the China-Kenya and China-Africa friendship and cooperation, and you have helped build and spread the friendly cooperation between China and Kenya and between China and Africa," Xi said.

Looking ahead, the magnificent picture of the Belt and Road Initiative and the grand blueprint of the China-Kenya comprehensive strategic cooperative partnership need more promising young people to realize, Xi stressed.

"It is hoped that you can learn professional knowledge well, continue the traditional friendship, devote yourself to bilateral cooperation, tell well stories of China-Africa friendship, and make greater contributions to the building of a high-level China-Africa community with a shared future," Xi said.

Recently, representatives of Kenyan students and alumni at Beijing Jiaotong University wrote a letter to President Xi, expressing their great pleasure in coming to China to learn railway operation and management knowledge. They also expressed their hope to serve as a bridge of friendship between Kenya and China and contribute to enhancing friendship and cooperation between the two countries and building a community with a shared future for mankind.

---

1 The text was adapted from the Chinadaily website.

II

Recently, students from Central Asian countries at China University of Petroleum (Beijing) wrote to Chinese President Xi Jinping, telling about their studies and lives in China and expressing their determination to study hard, strengthen cooperation, and contribute to building a China-Central Asia community with a shared future. President Xi replied to the letter on May 15th, 2023, encouraging them to make greater contributions to the promotion of ties between China and Central Asian countries.

In his reply, Xi said that China and Central Asian countries are linked by mountains and rivers, and that they have profound friendships and a shared future. "In 2013, I put forward the initiative of jointly building the Silk Road Economic Belt in Central Asia," Xi said. He noted that over the past decade, China-Central Asia relations have been brought to a new level, and cooperation in various fields has moved onto the fast track, delivering benefits to the peoples. Friendly relations between China and Central Asian countries need to be carried forward from generation to generation by ambitious and promising young people, Xi said.

Xi said the students have witnessed and benefited from China-Central Asia relations and, more importantly, that they have helped boost China-Central Asia relations. He urged them to take an active part in promoting friendships between China and Central Asian countries, carry forward the Silk Road spirit, tell Chinese stories and Central Asian stories well, act as envoys of friendship and bridges of cooperation, and contribute to building an even closer China-Central Asia community with a shared future.

(552 words)

Directions: *Please read the passage above and finish either of the two assignments below.*

1. Please make an investigation on China-Kenya (or any other country in Africa) cooperation in certain fields by referring to various resources, and tell one China-Africa friendship story via making a 5-minute short video. The short video is supposed to include solid content, personal perspective as well as English and Chinese subtitles.

2. Please make an investigation on China-Central Asia exchanges and cooperation since the ancient time by referring to various resources, and tell one China-Central Asia friendship story via making a 5-minute short video. The short video is supposed to include solid content, personal perspective as well as English and Chinese subtitles.

A Community of Shared Future for Mankind (II)

Part I Reading for GC Knowledge

Text A Poverty Alleviation: China's Experience and Contribution

Warm-up

Self-Assessment of Poverty Alleviation

Directions: *Please rate yourself on a scale of 1 to 5, where: 1 = Strongly Disagree; 2 = Disagree; 3 = Neutral; 4 = Agree; 5 = Strongly Agree. Then discuss the questions that follow.*

Self-Assessment Questionnaire	Scale				
Poverty is one of the major challenges in "The UN 2030 Agenda for Sustainable Development".	1	2	3	4	5
128,000 impoverished villages, 832 designated poor counties, and 98.99 million people in rural areas shook off poverty in China's battle against poverty.	1	2	3	4	5
I know the importance of China's poverty alleviation.	1	2	3	4	5
I know the general goal of China's poverty alleviation.	1	2	3	4	5
I know some targeted measures of China's poverty alleviation.	1	2	3	4	5
I know some experience of other countries in poverty alleviation.	1	2	3	4	5

1. Based on your self-assessment, how much do you know about China's poverty alleviation campaign?

2. Have you made any contribution to China's poverty alleviation, such as donating your belongings, volunteer teaching in rural areas, purchasing some specialty products from poverty-stricken areas, etc.?

3. What do you think are some important elements in lifting individuals or areas out of poverty?

Poverty Alleviation: China's Experience and Contribution[1]

❶ Identifying those truly in need is a universal problem in countries with a large population in poverty. **Accurate** identification of the poor and targeted measures is central to any effort to eradicate poverty. In its poverty elimination effort, China has actively learned from international experience, fully considered its actual conditions, and launched a series of guidelines and measures to increase efficiency, summarized as accomplishing "Targeted Efforts in Six Areas" (identify the poor accurately, arrange targeted programs, utilize capital efficiently, take household-based measures, dispatch first Party secretaries based on village conditions, and achieve the set goals), taking "Five Measures for Poverty Eradication" (boosting the economy to provide more job opportunities, relocating poor people from **inhospitable** areas, compensating for economic losses associated with reducing ecological damage, improving education in **impoverished** areas, and providing **subsistence allowances** for those unable to shake off poverty through their own efforts alone), and addressing "Five Questions in Poverty Alleviation" (who should help, who should be helped, how to help, how to evaluate whether someone has emerged from poverty, and how to ensure those people stay free from poverty).

❷ There are many different types of poverty and the causes vary from case to case. We cannot address the root cause without the right **remedies**. In practice, China has adopted categorized and targeted measures to reduce poverty, based on the situation of individual households, local conditions, and the causes for and types of poverty. These targeted measures include:

❸ First, boosting the economy to provide more job opportunities. Poverty alleviation through economic development is the most direct and effective method, the fundamental way to give poor areas the capacity for independent development and help the poor find employment locally. With this in mind, China has supported and guided poor areas in developing economic activities geared to their available resources, and encouraged poverty alleviation through new forms of business and new industries such as e-commerce, photovoltaic (PV) power generation, and tourism, and through the consumption of products and services from poor areas. Relying on collaboration on poverty alleviation between the eastern and western regions, China has facilitated the transfer of food processing, clothes manufacturing, and other labor-intensive industries from the east to the west. With the growth of such **specialty** industries, poor areas have gained economic **momentum**. More than 300,000 industrial bases have been built,

---

1 The text was adapted from a white paper entitled "Poverty Alleviation: China's Experience and Contribution", released on April 6, 2021 by the State Council.

leading to the creation of new industries with distinctive features and greater capacity to facilitate poverty alleviation efforts. China has created 12,000 local **agro-product** brands, 14,400 leading enterprises above the city level, and 719,000 rural cooperatives operated by farmers. A total of 72.6% of poor households have formed close ties with new types of agribusiness entities, and almost every poor household has been covered by policy support for boosting the economy.

❹ Second, relocating poor people from inhospitable areas. Some people lived in **uninhabitable** areas suffering from harsh natural conditions and subject to frequent natural disasters. It would be very difficult for them to shake off poverty if they remained where they were, so the government **relocated** them to other areas. The government respected these people's wishes, and only relocated those who were **eligible** and agreed to move. The reasons for relocation were explained to them but no **coercion** was used. The conditions and needs of target relocation groups were given full consideration, the scale of relocation was determined through research, and **feasible** plans were worked out and implemented in steps. As a result, more than 9.6 million people from inhospitable areas have shaken off poverty through relocation. Their former homes have been turned into farmland or planted with trees, to improve the eco-environment in these areas. In the **resettlement** sites, support facilities, industrial parks, and workshops have been built to create jobs for the relocated population, to ensure that they have stable incomes and equitable access to basic public services. Measures have been taken to ensure smooth relocation and resettlement, and make sure that those involved have the means to better themselves.

❺ Third, shaking off poverty through compensations for economic losses associated with reducing ecological damage and getting eco-jobs. Clear waters and green mountains are invaluable assets. Laying equal emphasis on poverty alleviation and eco-conservation, China has strengthened ecological **restoration** and environmental protection in poor areas, increased government transfer payments to key eco-areas, and expanded the scope of those eligible for **preferential** policies. Poor people with the ability to work have thus been employed in eco-work, for example as forest **rangers**. Since 2013, a total of 4.97 million ha (hectare) of farmland in poor areas has been returned to forest and grassland. A total of 1.1 million poor people have become forest rangers, and 23,000 poverty alleviation **afforestation** teams have been formed. By participating in projects for afforestation, turning reclaimed farmlands into forests or grasslands, restoring and protecting forests, grasslands and wetlands, and growing woody oil plants and working in forest tourism, the poor population have increased their incomes and made a major contribution to improving the eco-environment in poor areas, with mutually beneficial results.

❻ Fourth, improving education in impoverished areas. Through education, poverty can be prevented from passing down from generation to generation. The government has continued to increase support for schools in poor areas to improve their conditions, standard of teaching, faculties, and financial resources. The state ensures compulsory education for all school-age children. All the 200,000 **dropouts** from compulsory education coming from poor families have returned to school. Favorable policies have been leveraged to enroll more poor students from **designated** areas, expand employment for graduates, and help students shake off poverty through vocational education. More than 8 million middle and high school graduates from poor families have received vocational training, 5.14 million poor students have received higher education, and key institutions of higher learning have admitted some 700,000 students from designated rural and poor areas. All this has opened up more channels for poor students to emerge from poverty and move upwards in society. The government has offered training on standard spoken and written Chinese language to 3.5 million rural teachers and young farmers and **herdsmen** in ethnic minority areas, in an effort to make poor people from these areas more competitive in the job market. A pilot campaign has been launched to teach standard Chinese to preschool children in Liangshan Yi Autonomous **Prefecture**, and Mabian Yi Autonomous County, Ebian Yi Autonomous County, and Jinkouhe District in Leshan City, Sichuan Province, involving 430,000 children.

❼ Fifth, providing subsistence allowances for those unable to shake off poverty through their own efforts alone. China focuses on the needs of the most vulnerable groups and provides them with subsistence allowances. Services and facilities to support people living in extreme poverty have been upgraded, with a greater capacity to provide care in service centers. The rural subsistence allowances framework has been effectively **dovetailed** with poverty alleviation policies, and the per capita yearly subsistence allowances in rural areas grew from CNY 2,068 in 2012 to CNY 5,962 in 2020, an increase of 188.3%. The departments in charge of poverty alleviation and civil affairs compare data and **verify** information on a regular basis, to ensure full **coverage** of support for eligible groups.

❽ China has also implemented many other forms of support for poverty alleviation that are consistent with local conditions. The government has redoubled its efforts to boost employment for the poor, through means such as offering free training on vocational skills, strengthening collaboration in the labor market between the eastern and western regions, supporting leading enterprises and workshops in poverty alleviation to create more jobs, encouraging **entrepreneurial** individuals to start businesses in their hometowns or villages, creating public welfare jobs for the rest of the unemployed, etc.

(1,269 words)

Glossary

accurate	/ˈækjərət/	adj.	精确的，准确的
inhospitable	/ˌɪnhɒˈspɪtəbl/	adj.	不适宜居住的
impoverish	/ɪmˈpɒvərɪʃ/	v.	使贫困
subsistence	/səbˈsɪstəns/	n.	生存，存活
allowance	/əˈlaʊəns/	n.	（定期发给的）津贴，补助
remedy	/ˈremədi/	n.	解决方法；治疗方法
specialty	/ˈspeʃəlti/	n.	特色食品，特产
momentum	/məˈmentəm/	n.	势头；冲劲；动力
agro-product	/ˈægrəʊ ˈprɒdʌkt/	n.	农产品
uninhabitable	/ˌʌnɪnˈhæbɪtəbl/	adj.	不适合居住的
relocate	/ˌriːləʊˈkeɪt/	v.	搬迁，重新安置
eligible	/ˈelɪdʒəbl/	adj.	符合条件的；合适的
coercion	/kəʊˈɜːʃn/	n.	强迫，逼迫
feasible	/ˈfiːzəbl/	adj.	可行的
resettlement	/ˌriːˈsetlmənt/	n.	重新定居，移居，重新安置
restoration	/ˌrestəˈreɪʃn/	n.	恢复，修复
preferential	/ˌprefəˈrenʃl/	adj.	优惠的，优待的
ranger	/ˈreɪndʒə(r)/	n.	护林员
afforestation	/əˌfɒrɪˈsteɪʃn/	n.	植树造林
dropout	/ˈdrɒpaʊt/	n.	辍学者，退学者
designate	/ˈdezɪgneɪt/	v.	指定，指派
herdsman	/ˈhɜːdzmən/	n.	牧人
prefecture	/ˈpriːfektʃə(r)/	n.	辖区，省，县
dovetail	/ˈdʌvteɪl/	v.	吻合，切合
verify	/ˈverɪfaɪ/	v.	核实，查清
coverage	/ˈkʌvərɪdʒ/	n.	覆盖
entrepreneurial	/ˌɒntrəprəˈnɜːriəl/	adj.	具有企业家素质的

Unit 9 A Community of Shared Future for Mankind (II)

Task 1

Directions: *Please read the text and fill in the blanks below with a proper word.*

Five Measures for Poverty Eradication
• **Boost the economy to provide more job opportunities**
Poverty alleviation through (1) _____ development is the most direct and effective method, the (2) _____ way to give poor areas the capacity for independent development and help the poor find employment locally.
• **Relocate poor people from (3) _____ areas**
The government respected people's wishes, only relocating those who were (4) _____ and agreed to move. The reasons for relocation were explained to them but no (5) _____ was used.
• **Compensate for economic losses associated with reducing (6) _____ damage**
Laying equal emphasis on poverty alleviation and eco-conservation, China has strengthened ecological (7) _____ and environmental protection in poor areas, increased government transfer payments to key eco-areas, and expanded the scope of those eligible for (8) _____ policies.
• **Improve (9) _____ in (10) _____ areas**
The government has continued to increase support for schools in poor areas to improve their conditions, standard of teaching, faculties and (11) _____ resources. The state ensures (12) _____ education for all school-age children.
• **Provide (13) _____ allowances for those unable to shake off poverty through their own efforts alone**
China focuses on the needs of the most (14) _____ groups. Services and facilities to support people living in extreme poverty have been (15) _____, with a greater capacity to provide care in service centers.

Task 2

Directions: *Please read the text again and decide whether the following statements are true (T) or false (F) based on what you have learned from the text.*

_____ 1. Accurate identification of the poor and targeted measures is central to any effort to eradicate poverty.

_____ 2. China has launched a series of guidelines and measures to eliminate poverty without learning from international experience.

_____ 3. Only with the right remedies can we address the root cause of poverty.

_____ 4. Improving education is the fundamental way to give poor areas the capacity for independent development and help the poor find employment locally.

_____ 5. The former homes of people who are relocated have been turned into factories to improve the economy.

_____ 6. Eco-conservation is as important as poverty alleviation.

_____ 7. The government has offered training on standard spoken and written Chinese to make poor people from ethnic minority areas more competitive in the job market.

_____ 8. China provides all the poor people with subsistence allowances.

_____ 9. The rural subsistence allowances framework has been effectively dovetailed with poverty alleviation policies.

_____ 10. China has implemented many forms of support for poverty alleviation that are consistent with local conditions.

Task 3

Directions: *Please translate the following five sentences into English using the words or phrases in the parentheses.*

1. 贫困是人类社会的顽疾，是全世界面临的共同挑战，消除贫困是人类梦寐以求的理想。（eradicate）

2. 占世界人口近五分之一的中国全面消除绝对贫困，不仅是中华民族发展史上具有里程碑意义的大事件，也是人类减贫史乃至人类发展史上的大事件。（milestone events）

3. 不便的交通、恶劣的气候条件、较低的受教育水平等多重因素一直是很多边远地区贫困的主要原因。（impoverish）

4. 当地政府积极推进职业技能培训、无息贷款等系列优惠政策来吸引在外务工的年轻人回乡创业，打造生态旅游、电商等项目。（preferential）

5. 践行绿水青山就是金山银山的理念，不仅恢复了当地脆弱的生态系统，而且大幅度提高了当地居民的收入。（vulnerable）

Unit 9 A Community of Shared Future for Mankind (II)

Task 4

Directions: *Please work with your partners on the assignment below to finish a speech draft. You are encouraged to refer to other resources for the draft.*

"FLTRP Cup" English Speech Contest is going to be held next month in your university, and the topic for the prepared speech is "The Chinese Path to Modernization". Suppose you are going to participate in the speech contest, please compose a speech draft from the perspective of poverty alleviation in achieving the Chinese path to modernization.

Text B Poverty Reduction in Sub-Saharan Africa

 Warm-up

Directions: *Please discuss the following questions with your partners and provide possible answers.*

1. What do you know about Sub-Saharan Africa?
2. What are the possible challenges of poverty reduction in Sub-Saharan Africa?
3. Do you know any China-Africa cooperation in poverty reduction? What effects have been achieved via the cooperation?

Poverty Reduction in Sub-Saharan Africa[1]

❶ Sub-Saharan Africa (SSA) is the part of the African continent south of the Sahara Desert. It consists of the **overwhelming** majority of Africa's **landmass**, including four geographic regions: West Africa, Middle Africa, East Africa, and Southern Africa. The total population of the countries in SSA is over 1.1 billion. East Africa is the most **populous** sub-region of SSA, with a population of 455 million. Southern Africa has the smallest population in SSA, with just 68 million people. The most populous country in SSA is West Africa's Nigeria, which has a population of more than 206 million. Ethiopia in the East African is the second most populous country, as it is home to more than 114 million people.

❷ Sub-Saharan Africa, a region comprising most of the world's least developed countries (LDCs), whose income **threshold** falls **approximately** under USD 1,000

---
[1] The text was adapted from Mahmood, M. 2022. *Growth, Job and Poverty in Sub-Saharan Africa*. Palgrave Macmillan.

per capita. SSA accounts for 32 of the global 47 LDCs, reflecting the development and structural challenges outlined for LDCs by several global initiatives, preeminent being the United Nations Istanbul Program of Action and the goals set out in 2011. SSA also includes a number of higher-income countries, ten low and middle-income countries (LMICs), falling approximately between USD 1,000 and USD 4,000, and six emerging economies (EEs), falling between USD 4,000 and USD 12,000. Although the region should not be defined by the structural **parameters** and opportunities of LDCs, it is tightly constrained in the quality of its growth, employment, and poverty outcomes.

❸ Poverty reduction has to comprise the **trinity** of **macro-objectives** along with growth and jobs. The weak outcomes observed for SSA in the growth of gross domestic product (GDP), and job quality and incomes, can be expected to generate a weak outcome for the primary and secondary distributions of income, including transfers. In turn, the primary and secondary distributions of income can be expected to give a weak outcome for poverty reduction over time in SSA.

❹ Poverty in Africa has come down from 48% of the population in 2005 to 41% by 2012 (International Labor Organization, 2016). The comparative numbers for Asia and the Pacific are 25% and 12%, and for Latin America 10% and 6%. Africa did not meet the Millennium Development Goal (MDG) set in 2000 of **halving** poverty by 2015. The subsequent Sustainable Development Goal (SDG) was to end poverty by 2030. Given that most of the world's poor are now in Africa, especially in SSA, it is important for the policy agenda to focus on eradicating this mass poverty in the region.

❺ Rather than regional poverty numbers, which are too **aggregate**, what is needed are country poverty **headcounts**. The World Bank's PovcalNet data set provides these estimates for each country that has had a living standards measurement study (LSMS) for that year, which means that poverty is not being aggregated and generalized across countries. Each country has its own estimates at different points in time. The table on Pages 222–223 gives these headcounts for each country in SSA from 2000 to 2019 for each LSMS year. We see that all countries except one, Burundi, have had more than one LSMS over this period, permitting an exact estimate of the change in poverty over time in each case.

❻ The table shows that, for the 26 least-developed countries (LDCs) in SSA for which these poverty estimates are available, 20 have reduced their poverty headcounts over time, while for the six LDCs, the poverty headcounts have increased. Of the ten lower-and-middle-income countries (LMICs) in SSA, eight have reduced their poverty headcounts over time. of the five emerging economies (EEs) in SSA, all five have reduced their poverty headcounts over time. This means that 33 countries out of the 41 in SSA for which these poverty estimates are available, reduced their poverty headcounts between 2000 and 2019. In eight cases, however, the poverty headcounts rose.

❼ For LDCs, their rate of poverty reduction left the most recent headcounts available in a band range of 60%–78.8% of each of their populations, which gives an average of 47.8%, indicating a disturbingly high set of poverty headcounts. For LMICs, the rate of poverty reduction left the most recent headcounts available in a band range of 3.4%–77.2% of each of their populations. This gives an average of 33.4%, which is also quite high. For EEs, their rate of poverty reduction from 2000 to 2019 left the most recent headcounts available in a band range of 0.2%–18.7% of each of their populations. The average of these headcounts comes to 10.1% of each of their populations.

❽ The **humanitarian** and policy challenge of poverty reduction in SSA has to be viewed from the perspective of the starting points and the rates of poverty reduction. For the 20 LDCs that reduced their headcounts between 2000 and 2019, the average rate of poverty reduction was −18.9% of each of their populations. This gives their best rate of poverty reduction of approximately 20% in 20 years, implying that their current rate of poverty reduction (to eliminate the average remaining headcount of 47.8% of their population) will take another 40–50 years, on average. This rate does not take into account the poverty increases in six LDCs.

❾ For the eight LMICs that reduced their headcounts over these two decades, the average rate of poverty reduction was −12.5% of each of their populations. This gives their best rate of poverty reduction of approximately 13% in 20 years, implying that their current rate of poverty reduction (to eliminate the average remaining headcount of 33.4% of their populations) will take another 25 years, not accounting for the increases in poverty in two countries.

❿ Finally, for the five EEs that reduced their headcounts, the average rate of poverty reduction was −10.7% of each of their populations. This gives their rate of poverty reduction of approximately 11% in 20 years, implying that their current rate of poverty reduction (to eliminate the remaining headcount of 10.1% of their populations) will take another 20 years.

⓫ These large remaining poverty headcounts in SSA pose **immense** humanitarian and policy challenges. The current rates of poverty reduction imply that eliminating poverty in SSA will take anywhere from 20 to 50 years—a far cry from meeting the SDG of eliminating global poverty by 2030. The current strategy of poverty reduction in SSA is thus simply not acceptable. Reversing the LSPF (Lewis-Singer Prebisch-Fallacy) model and its effect on the primary and secondary distributions of income is a structural goal for the long run. Poverty is an immediate goal. Therefore, what needs to be examined

Table Poverty Headcount 2000–2019 for SSA Countries

	2000	2001	2002	2003	2004	2005	2006	2007	2008	2009	2010	2011	2012	2013	2014	2015	2016	2017	2018	2019
EEs																				
Botswana			28.17																	
Gabon						7.97				17.24								3.39		
Mauritius							0.43						0.55					0.21		
Namibia				32.59						23.47						13.79				
Seychelles							0.37							1.15					0.45	
South Africa	34.77					25.68			16.74		16.17				18.7					
LMICs																				
Cabo Verde		16.58						8.36								3.35				
Cameroon		26.01						31.78							25.97					
Congo						55.09						39.57								
Republic of Congo					94.28								77.15							
Republic of Cote d'Ivoire			24.38						30.44							29.83				
Eswatini	48.94									43							29.17			
Ghana						23.36							11.16				12.66			
Kenya						43.9										37.08				
Nigeria				55.94						56.4										
Zimbabwe												21.36						33.86	39.09	
LDCs																				
Angola	36.37								34.45										49.91	
Benin				51.43								53.19				49.61				
Burkina Faso				57.4						55.41					43.84					
Burundi							78.6							72.8						

Unit 9 A Community of Shared Future for Mankind (II)

(Continued)

	2000	2001	2002	2003	2004	2005	2006	2007	2008	2009	2010	2011	2012	2013	2014	2015	2016	2017	2018	2019
Central African Republic									65.87											
Chad				59.99								38.08								
Comoros					14.98										19.07					
Ethiopia					38.55						35.57					30.8				
Gambia				46.14							25.35					10.3				
Guinea-Bissau			56.62								68.39									
Guinea			64.5					58.36					36.09							
Lesotho			61.94															27.22		
Liberia								71.39							41.72		44.43			
Madagascar		68.42				71.72					78.18		78.84							
Malawi					72.53						71.1						69.21			
Mali	58.81						52.11			50.29										
Mauritania	20.41				16.9				10.9						5.97					
Mozambique			79.81						69.65						63.68					
Niger						75.27		72.36			50.64				45.4					
Rwanda	78					69.13					63.21			57.9			56.48			
Sao Tome and Principe	31.38										34.59							35.64		
Senegal		49.49				38.29						38.53								
Sierra Leone				73.02								54.67							42.99	
Tanzania	86.23						60.25					49.64						49.37		
Togo							56.55					55.02				51.14				
Uganda			65.57		57.03					45.32			35.74				41.35			
Zambia			52.05		58.37		62.14				65.82					58.75				

is a policy that can influence the primary and secondary distributions of income in the shorter run to meet the humanitarian challenge of poverty reduction more immediately.

(1,120 words)

 Glossary

overwhelming	/ˌəʊvəˈwelmɪŋ/	adj.	数量巨大的；压倒性的
landmass	/ˈlændmæs/	n.	大陆，陆块，地块
populous	/ˈpɒpjələs/	adj.	人口众多的，人口稠密的
threshold	/ˈθreʃhəʊld/	n.	界限，阈；门槛；开端
approximately	/əˈprɒksɪmətli/	adv.	大约，近似
parameter	/pəˈræmɪtə(r)/	n.	界限；范围；参数
trinity	/ˈtrɪnəti/	n.	三位一体
macro-objective	/ˈmækrəʊˌəbˈdʒektɪv/	n.	宏观目标
halve	/hɑːv/	v.	把……减半
aggregate	/ˈæɡrɪɡət/	adj.	总计的，合计的
headcount	/ˈhedkaʊnt/	n.	人数统计
humanitarian	/hjuːˌmænɪˈteəriən/	adj.	人道主义的；博爱的
immense	/ɪˈmens/	adj.	广大的，巨大的

Task 1

Directions: *Please write down the full name of the terms based on the text and translate them into Chinese.*

	Full Name	Chinese Translation
SSA		
LDC		
LMIC		
EE		
GDP		
MDG		
SDG		
LSMS		

Task 2

Directions: *Please read the text again and decide whether the following statements are true (T) or false (F) based on what you have learned from the text.*

_____ 1. East Africa is the most populous country in SSA.

_____ 2. SSA is a region comprising most of the world's least-developed countries.

_____ 3. SSA doesn't include any higher-income countries.

_____ 4. Poverty reduction has to comprise the trinity of macro-objectives along with growth and jobs.

_____ 5. Africa did not meet the SDG set in 2000 of halving poverty by 2015.

_____ 6. Country poverty headcounts are more needed than regional poverty numbers.

_____ 7. Each country has its own estimates at different points in time, and poverty is not being aggregated and generalized across countries.

_____ 8. All the five emerging economies (EEs) in SSA have reduced their poverty headcounts over time.

_____ 9. The current rate of poverty reduction of LMICs to eliminate the remaining headcount of 10.1% of their populations will take another 20 years.

_____ 10. The large remaining poverty headcounts in SSA pose slight humanitarian and policy challenges.

Task 3

Directions: *Please translate the following five sentences into English using the words or phrase in the parentheses.*

1. 减贫对人口众多且气候多样的撒哈拉以南非洲来说是一项艰巨的任务。(populous)

2. 这项援助非洲农业技术的提案引起了诸多高校和企业的关注。(generate)

3. 相关国际组织每年向非洲的一些最不发达国家提供巨大的人道主义援助。(immense)

4. 中非从来都是命运共同体，在减贫发展的道路上，中非将始终携手前行。(community with a shared future)

5. 中非合作释放的红利，成为非洲摆脱贫困的福利，赢得非洲赞誉和国际社会高度肯定。(collaboration)

Task 4

Directions: *Please work with your partners on the assignment below, and you are encouraged to refer to other resources for the proposal.*

An international forum on China-Africa Cooperation—Poverty Reduction and Development Conference will be held in Beijing next month. Suppose you are the invited representatives from related international organizations to the conference, and you are going to give a brief talk, present your proposal, and seek more collaboration on behalf of your organization.

Part II Drilling for GC Skills

How to Give a Formal Presentation (I)

1. Setting an Objectives/Purpose for the Presentation

Understanding the purpose of a presentation allows the presenter to tailor the content as well as delivery manners to ensure the presentation can meet the goals. Specific circumstances may vary, but as a general indication, the common purpose for a formal presentation is usually to inform, persuade, inspire or instruct the audience. Before preparing for the presentation, the presenter should be clear about the objective of the presentation.

- **Informative presentation:** Such kind of presentation focuses on helping the audience to understand a topic, issue, or technique clearly. It is to share ideas with the audience, increase their understanding, influence their perceptions, or help them gain new skills. Typical scenarios for informative presentations include academic assignments, conference presentations, etc.

- **Persuasive presentations:** Persuasion is an act or process of presenting arguments to move, motivate, or change your audience. A persuasive presentation aims to stimulate thought, convince the audience, call to action, increase consideration, or develop tolerance of alternate perspectives from the audience. Typical scenarios for persuasive presentations include job interviews, commercial sales, etc.

- **Inspirational presentations:** This type of presentation attempts to inspire audiences and encourage them to overcome obstacles or challenges. It generates interest in a topic while providing the audience with a specific viewpoint and message. This type of presentation may have elements of persuasion, and it often deals more with the audience's emotions, seeking a higher emotional level. In such presentations, the presenter can share stories of challenges and hardships, and how these were overcome, appealing to the common bond of humanity and heart and creating a closer tie. Such kind of presentation can often be used in working places, from encouraging employees, business cooperation to political exchanges, etc.

- **Instructional presentations:** This type of presentation aims to provide the audience with specific directions or orders and deliver key information to help them in their work so that the audience can understand a certain topic better and further take certain actions. Webinars and training workshops are examples of instructional presentations that present audiences with new information and teach them new skills.

Task 1

Directions: *Please define an objective/purpose for each presentation situation listed below. You will probably be able to think of several, as some types of presentations have multiple objectives / purposes.*

Situation 1: A presentation in high-tech product launch event.

Situation 2: A presentation about your current research at an international conference.

Situation 3: A keynote speech on behalf of a certain international organization at an international summit.

2. Analyzing the Audience

An audience analysis can help the presenter in many aspects, such as choosing proper topics, selecting appropriate points of emphasis, developing useful levels of details, preparing appropriate visual aids as well as creating a tone that is sensitive to your audience's circumstance, etc.

In analyzing the audience, the presenter can ask himself/herself the following questions:

- Who are the targeted audiences? How about the demographic features of the audience, such as age, gender, educational background, occupations, as well as some sensitive factors like race or religious belief?
- What does the audience know about the topic? What would be an appropriate level to design the content of the presentation? Is it too difficult?

- What occasion is the presentation made for? Is it a formal occasion or not? Is it for professionals or not? For example, if a presenter is invited to give a talk about his/her research field, but what he/she presents is supposed to be different in an academic conference or scientific knowledge propagation meeting.
- What are the possible situational elements? Such as the size of the audience, the audience's potential attitudes towards the topic as well as some unexpected factors.

Suppose you are a young scholar in the field of traffic and transportation, and you are invited to give a presentation on traffic safety in the situations below:

Situation 1: Promoting traffic safety among primary school students and their parents.

You may focus on the following points for this group of audience:

- the alarming statistics of traffic accidents in recent years;
- the traffic rules both parents and students have to obey;
- how to deal with traffic accidents or emergencies;
- …

Situation 2: Discussing how to enhance traffic safety with professionals of this field in a seminar.

You may discuss the following points with this group of audience:

- professional elements like road or rail design standards, traffic signal control, etc.;
- uncertain parameters like weather conditions, mechanical errors probability, etc.;
- some cutting-edge directions or breakthroughs in traffic safety research worldwide;
- …

Task 2

Directions: *Assume you are going to give a presentation on the theme of "Poverty Reduction Worldwide in the 21st Century", and your presentation will be different based on different audience groups or situations. Please make a list of major points for each presentation.*

Situation 1: Suppose you are a representative from the International Poverty Reduction Center in China, and you are going to give a presentation at the China-AU International Forum on poverty reduction.

Unit 9 A Community of Shared Future for Mankind (II)

Situation 2: Suppose you are chosen as spokesperson to tell your hometown's changes under China's poverty alleviation actions, and you would like to make a video and post it on social media to share your hometown's changes.

3. Choosing and Refining the Topic

As you begin to think about choosing a presentation topic, there are a few key factors to consider, including the purpose of the speech, its projected time length, the appropriateness of the topic for your audience, and your knowledge or the amount of information you can access on the topic. Below are the processes to choose a topic.

Step 1 Brainstorming

- To generate a variety of ideas without evaluation;
- To select relevant, objective, and feasible ideas;

Step 2 Refining a topic

Mostly, the topic from brainstorming tends to be general and broad, and the presenter can refine it in the following ways:

- Focus on a particular aspect of this topic that interests you or you know well;
- Focus on a particular aspect of this topic that is important to the target audience;
- Focus on a specific time period about the topic you want to cover.

For example, your team is required to give a presentation on "Approaching the Second World War" in a course seminar. The topic is quite broad, because all students can find their space in presenting this topic. However, each presentation from student teams is supposed to be specific and well-focused. Students can refine the topic in the following ways:

If you and your teammates are history and military fans, you can design the presentation based on your team interest, and refine the topic as "Landmark Campaigns in the Second World War", or you can further specify the topic as "Landmark Campaigns During the Second World War in Asia/Europe Battle Field". You can also focus on the international organizations in the war if you are good at international relations and refine the topic as "the Second World War Two and the Inception of the UN".

If the students are science and engineering majors in universities, the topic can also be possibly refined as "The Evolution of Military Technology in the Second World War". If the audience are mainly female, you can possibly refine the topic as "Women's Role in the Second World War" or "Women rights Trigged by the Second World War", for women contributed to the Second World War immensely not only at battlefield front but at home front.

Task 3

Directions: *Please discuss the following presentation topics with your partners, refine them if necessary, and explain the reasons.*

1. Scientific and Technological Innovation in the Digital Age

2. "Going Global" of China's HSR (High-Speed Railway)

3. Green Development: A Promising Future

4. Poverty Reduction in the Developing World

5. People-to-People Exchanges Between China and Central Asia Under BRI

4. Gathering, Evaluating Materials, and Developing Supporting Evidence

Gathering materials is an essential step in preparing a presentation, which can make the presentation more solid credible, for a presentation in a formal occasion is definitely more than individual common sense and simple generalizations. Gathering and evaluating specialized materials will make the presentation more relevant and convincing to particular audience.

Evaluating the materials is crucial before using them in your presentation, for well-assessed materials can guarantee the validity and credibility of the presentation. In evaluating the materials collected, a presenter can ask himself/herself the following questions:

- Is the material collected authoritative or up-to-date?
- Is the material relevant and competent in supporting the argument?
- Is the source of the material credible? Is it biased or perceived as biased?
- Is the information quoted accurately and objectively?
- Is there any sensitive or even forbidden element in the materials collected?
- …

To support the argument/claim of the presentation, the frequently used methods include examples, statistics, testimony, etc.

(1) Examples

Examples can be used to clarify, reinforce or personalize ideas, and the examples used should be vivid and richly textured. For instance, the presenter would like to illustrate how photovoltaic projects (PVP) contributed to China's targeted poverty alleviation. The example can be described as below:

As clearly promulgated by the OLGPAD of the State Council in 2015, photovoltaic projects (PVP) were listed as one of ten major programs of targeted poverty alleviation, initiating a new era of development for the solar photovoltaic industry in helping eradicate poverty. PVPs should be implemented by fully utilizing the abundant solar energy in impoverished regions. China has abundant but unevenly distributed solar energy due to significant geographical differences. The average sunshine hours of the North, Northeast and Northwest districts are higher than the national average, and of all provinces in these regions, only the sunshine hours of Shaanxi Province are lower than the national average. Moreover, the average solar insolation values of the Northwest and North districts are the only ones higher than the national average, with only the solar insolation of Shaanxi Province being slightly lower than the national average. In the Northeast, although the sunshine hours are quite high, the solar insolation is slightly lower than the national average.

In China, the initiation of photovoltaics for poverty alleviation can be traced back to China's Brightness Program commenced in May 1997, which aimed to provide electricity to 23 million impoverished people in rural and remote areas by utilizing renewable resources such as solar photovoltaic and wind power by 2010. Additionally, impoverished people greatly benefited from subsidies to solar roofing and the Golden Sun Program. In March 2014, PVPPA (photovoltaic projects for poverty alleviation) were first deployed in Jinzhai County, Anhui Province, to build household-type distributed solar photovoltaic systems for 1008 families at 3 kw a piece. By the end of 2014, there were 2008 household-type distributed solar photovoltaic systems installed in Jinzhai County, Anhui Province.

(2) Statistics

Statistics is an effective method in various types of formal presentations. Audiences tend to trust data more than personal predictions, and data or diagrams on visual aids can enhance audience's comprehension on the presentation topic. Although using statistics creates much benefits both for presenters and audiences, keep in mind that using too much of them will make the presentation monotonous and boring, and it may discourage or distract the audience's attention. While using statistics, remember to identify the source and make sure the source is authoritative and competent in the field of your topic; meanwhile, explain the statistics when necessary and present the statistics in charts or diagrams to achieve a better visual effect.

Example 1

Today, estimates for global poverty are approximately 8.6% of the world as reported by the World Population Review (WPR). This means that 736 million people live in extreme poverty, surviving on less than US$1.90 per day. 413 million of these people live in Sub-Saharan Africa while 19 countries worldwide have poverty rates over 50 percent.

While many poorer countries are still languishing in poverty amid the COVID-19 pandemic, China has defeated extreme poverty within its borders with a precise and targeted poverty alleviation program and strategy. In 2012, there were around 832 poor counties, 128,000 poor villages, and nearly 100 million people living in absolute poverty in China. In just eight years, this number has been reduced to zero. Nearly 1.6-trillion-yuan (US$246 billion) worth of fiscal funds have been invested into poverty alleviation over the past eight years, with more than 90% of impoverished Chinese receiving some form of employment assistance from the government. To date, all 832 registered counties have formulated industrial plans to fight poverty, with over 300,000 industrial bases in farming, planting, and processing constructed on-site. Also, more than 96 million registered people have moved into over 2.66 million newly constructed houses, all equipped with water, electricity, gas, and Internet. Transportation has also improved with the building of better roads.

Example 2

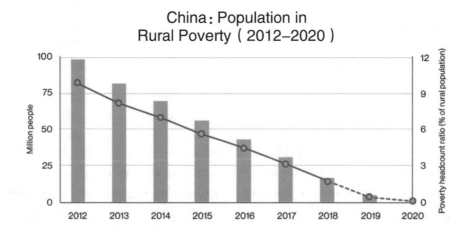

Source: China's National Bureau of Statistics, China's State Council Leading Group Office of Poverty Alleviation and Development

(3) Testimony

A testimony is a statement or endorsement given by someone who has a logical connection to the topic and who is a credible source. Testimony can be used to either clarify or prove a point, and is often used by referring to the research of experts.

There are three major types of testimonies, ranging from expert to peer testimony.

- **Expert authorities:** If an expert supports your position, it usually adds credibility. If you are giving a presentation on a medical issue and can find support for your position in prestigious medical reviews such as *The New England Journal of Medicine* or *The Lancet*, it would probably be a good idea to cite those authorities.

- **Celebrities and other influential figures:** Presenters can also refer to celebrities and other influential figures, especially in less formal or less academic presentations. For example, when recommending books for the public reader, the presenter can refer to Oprah Winfrey's recommendation, for her recommendations are neither too professional nor too entertaining, and the books are often in the best-seller list, influencing the book-buying habits for thousands of people.

- **Antiauthority/peers:** Presenters can also refer to people or events around them as peer testimony, because it comes from a source that is neither an expert nor a celebrity, but similar status to the audience. For example, in a roundtable on poverty alleviation strategies and cases, presenters can cite the example of some rural women who have lifted their family out of poverty via their ethnic style embroidery, agro-product livestreaming as well as the building of sisterhood in developing the local specialty. Such testimonies are even more powerful than expert testimonies in such occasions.

Task 4

***Directions**: Suppose you are preparing for a formal presentation on "How FAO Contributes to Global Poverty Reduction" and you have collected the following materials. Please evaluate whether it is appropriate to use them in your presentation.*

1. An unidentified file download from the Baidu Wenku website or general information from the Wikipedia website.

2. A passage taken from the official website of FAO.

According to FAO's latest figures, hunger in the Arab states reached its highest value since the start of the millennium in 2022, with 59.8 million undernourished people. This represents a 75.9% increase from 2000, which corresponds to 12.9% of the population, well above the global average of 9.2%. The situation has since reached a critical point in Gaza, where the population is experiencing catastrophic levels of conflict-induced food insecurity and a high risk of famine.

During his address to the FAO Regional Ministerial Conference for the Near East and North Africa, QU Dongyu, the Director-General of the Food and Agriculture Organization of the United Nations, emphasized the crucial role played by FAO in Gaza, particularly in terms of providing emergency relief and participating in rebuilding efforts. FAO is part of the joint UN flash appeal and is closely coordinating with the wider UN family and partners in responding most appropriately and effectively, in line with its mandate. FAO has also issued a call for $20 million in the November 2023 UN Interagency Flash Appeal and plans to reactivate the production of perishable, highly nutritious food that cannot be imported as food aid, including fresh milk, meat, and vegetables, Qu said.

3. A passage on gender equality taken from the UN's The Sustainable Development Goals Report 2023: Special Edition.

Agricultural land ownership and legal protection of women's land rights remain low. Available data from 46 countries for 2009–2020 show that many women and men involved in agricultural production lack ownership and/or secure tenure rights over agricultural land. In one-third of these countries, less than 50% of women and men have land ownership or secure rights. Meanwhile, in almost half of these countries, the share of men with ownership is at least twice that of women. When it comes to legal frameworks, close to 60% of the 71 reporting countries have no or low levels of protection for women's land rights. However, positive examples of laws and policies promoting women's land rights exist in all regions, particularly in marital property and inheritance. Moreover, 51% of the 41 countries with laws recognizing customary law or customary land tenure explicitly protect women's land rights. Many also provide mandatory quotas to ensure women's representation in land management and administration institutions. Nonetheless, there is a need for stronger protection, policies and enforcement of laws to safeguard women's land rights.

4. One chapter taken from a book authored by the Food and Agriculture Organization of the United Nations—*The Unjust Climate—Measuring the Impacts of Climate Change on Rural Poor, Women and Youth*. Rome, 2024.

Chapter 6   Priorities and recommendations for inclusive climate

6.3   Tailoring extension services to the needs of vulnerable people

To promote the widespread implementation of climate-adaptive actions by rural people, access to adequate advisory services is critical. How such services are delivered, and the types of support that are associated with them, determines the degree to which they include vulnerable groups. Indeed, information is not socially neutral, and specific attention must be paid to how and by whom information is delivered to specific populations to achieve sustainable and inclusive climate change adaptation. For example, in Ethiopia and India, extension services specifically acknowledge and address the constraints that female farmers face in participating in agricultural extension events. They foresee the timing of training sessions in the function of women's schedules, take account of seasonal variations in women's work burdens, organize training sessions in accessible locations and include the provision of child care during training sessions. As a result of this approach, women's participation in extension activities has increased, as has their uptake of improved practices.

...

The inclusiveness of climate actions is also determined by who delivers the extension services. Increasing the number of female extension agents, for example, was found to boost the adoption rate of sustainable land management practices by women farmers in Mozambique. Meanwhile, peer-to-peer mentorship programs have been shown to help young farmers develop social networks to share information on best practices and strategies to improve farm incomes. Leveraging these types of approaches in the context of climate actions is likely to be more beneficial than using traditional extension approaches.

5. A quotation or testimony from academic research

Some scholars' analysis revealed that while economic growth generally was an important contributor to poverty reduction, the sector mix of growth mattered substantially, with growth in agricultural incomes being especially important.

4. Organizing the Outline of the Presentation

The most effective speakers are those who strategically gain command of each fundamental speech element: the introduction, body, and conclusion. Before composing the introduction and conclusion, determine what your main points will be. The main points should be logical and convincing to help the audience remember the message, anticipate doubts, and remove controversial materials. The presentation should have smooth transitions and keep repeating the message to help the audience track where you are going. The following elements should be considered while organizing the body of presentation:

- The layouts of major points shouldn't be more than five;
- Each major point should separate from one another;
- Certain logical order should be built while organizing the major points, such as order of importance, order of causal effect chain, etc.;
- Each major point should be supported by relevant and credible evidence;
- Connectives should be used to help audience follow up the speaker's major points.

When preparing for a presentation, there are a number of ways you can ensure that you share relevant ideas. One tool to help presenters give talks is a presentation outline. Presentation outlines give him/her the ability to organize his/her thoughts and create a logical flow in his/her discussion. A presentation outline is a synopsis of a talk or pitch. The outline summarizes what the presenter plans to share with his/her audience members. Finally, the presenter can use the outline to keep the audience on track when giving the presentation.

Some common organizational patterns, such as the enumeration pattern, the causal-effect pattern, comparison and contrast pattern, etc., are often used in developing presentation outlines.

For example, if the focus of your presentation is the major applications of 5G technology currently in China, you can use the enumeration pattern in developing the outline in parallels:

- The application of 5G in daily entertainment;
- The application of 5G in educational scenarios;
- The application of 5G in intelligent manufacturing;
- …

With the major points listed, relevant examples or programs can be sorted out to support this major point, making the point rich and solid in content.

Meanwhile, if the focus of your presentation intends to demonstrate some differences between the chosen targets, the pattern of comparison and contrast can be used to develop your presentation outline. For example, you work as an industry expert and currently you are invited to give a talk on "Why EVs (electric vehicles) prosper in

China". You would like to compare EV development both in China and globally. While comparing different items, the presenter should follow either of the two comparison methods—point-by-point comparison or side-by-side comparison. Here is an example of a point-by-point comparison:

	EVs in China	EVs in Developed Countries
The breakthroughs of key technologies in EVs		
The governmental policies		
The matched infrastructure construction		
The public acceptance		
…		

Task 5

Directions: *Suppose you work as a representative from IPRCC (International Poverty Reduction Center in China) and you are going to attend an international roundtable themed "Poverty Reduction Contributes to the Well-being for All". Please collect relevant materials and design an outline for your talk at the roundtable.*

Part III Notes from China

Anji Solution in China's Rural Revitalization[1]

Anji is a county in northwest Zhejiang Province. It is located in the center of the Yangtze River Delta region, where the Huangpu River originates. Covering an area of 1,886 square kilometers, Anji has a population of 470,000. It is home to abundant bamboo forests and produces white tea. It has 67,300 hectares of bamboo forest, and about 75% farmers here depend on bamboo for their livelihoods. "Flat plain stretching

---

[1] The text was adapted from the Weixin and Chinakeywords websites.

over 25 kilometers, half covered by elegant bamboo forests," Gan Yuanding, a Ming Dynasty scholar, wrote about Anji.

Anji had fallen behind in development. Still a poor county in the late 20th century, it tried to escape poverty through industrial development. Paper mills, chemical plants, building material factories, and printing and dyeing businesses mushroomed. The local GDP skyrocketed, but the local environment suffered serious damage.

Anji began to improve its environment in 2001. It decided to abandon the traditional model of "destruction first, restoration second", and adopt a new model. Notable results were achieved and the environment of its villages improved. But its economic performance still lagged behind other counties.

Xi Jinping visited Anji twice during his tenure as secretary of the CPC Zhejiang Provincial Committee. On his first trip in April 2003, Xi pointed out that environmental conservation would be the right path for Anji. When he visited Yucun Village in Anji in August 2005, he put forward the idea that "lucid waters and lush mountains are invaluable assets". Over the years that followed, Anji has acted upon this vision, and pursued sustainable development to provide a pleasant environment, prosperous businesses, and a better life to local residents. A beautiful countryside has become a reality in Yucun.

Now Anji is also pioneering a new practice with bamboo forests to address climate change. With abundant bamboo resources, Anji explores a diverse range of methods to cope with climate change. The county has joined hands with an expert team from Zhejiang A & F University to develop a bamboo forest carbon flux observation system, bamboo carbon sink credits, etc. The collaboration has yielded extensive results.

In December 2021, Anji established a trading platform for bamboo carbon credits to pool the local resources together. Thus, carbon sinks turn into money-makers, placing Anji on a green, low-carbon, and sustainable pathway to common prosperity. Anji develops a bamboo forest management system, promotes carbon sequestration technology, launches a digital bamboo carbon sink platform, tracks life-cycle product footprint, and transforms bamboo forest management models. Through scientific cultivation methods, bamboo forests can capture an additional six tonnes of carbon dioxide per hectare every year, which significantly improves the environment.

With constant efforts to develop and optimize bamboo-based products, companies now offer around 3,000 products of eight categories in the market. Bamboo proves to be an ideal alternative to wood, plastic or steel used in daily goods, which can help to reduce logging and avoid carbon-intensive products. Compared with the conventional process, the carbon transfer ratio of bamboo panels is about 52.4%–74.4%, instead of 37.0%.

Unit 9 A Community of Shared Future for Mankind (II)

Anji sets up a benefit-sharing mechanism for business, village cooperatives, and farmers, making sure that resources taken off the hands of farmers are reciprocated by benefits. Farmers are also encouraged to get involved in the process and benefit from rent, shares, and salary in the value chain.

Anji follows the concept of "lucid waters and lush mountains are invaluable assets", develops bamboo forest carbon sinks, enhances ecological value, and improves local farmers' income by making good use of bamboo. With ecology and economy going forward hand-in-hand, the county creates a virtuous development cycle and contributes the unique "Anji solution" not only to Chinese rural revitalization but to the global reduction of greenhouse gas emissions.

(613 words)

Directions: *Please finish the assignments below based on the passage you have read.*

1. What is Anji solution in China's rural revitalization?
2. What is Anji's pioneering practice in addressing climate change?
3. Please make an investigation on how the concept of "lucid waters and lush mountains are invaluable assets" has been implemented in your hometown or the city you are studying in currently.

Unit 10

A Community of Shared Future for Mankind (III)

Part I Reading for GC Knowledge

Text A China's Three Global Initiatives

Warm-up

Self-Assessment of China's Global Initiatives

Directions: *Please rate yourself on a scale of 1 to 5, where 1 = Strongly Disagree; 2 = Disagree; 3 = Neutral; 4 = Agree; 5 = Strongly Agree. The discuss the questions that follow.*

Self-Assessment Questionnaire	Scale				
I understand the current international situations remain intricate and complex.	1	2	3	4	5
I understand the concept of building a global community of shared future as proposed by China.	1	2	3	4	5
I know at least one initiative proposed by China in recent years to build a community of shared future.	1	2	3	4	5
I understand the objectives of China's Global Development Initiative (GDI).	1	2	3	4	5
I know GDI stays committed to a people-centered and innovation-driven approach in development.	1	2	3	4	5
I understand the objectives of China's Global Security Initiative (GSI).	1	2	3	4	5
I understand GSI includes some non-traditional domains, such as climate change, cybersecurity, and biosecurity.	1	2	3	4	5
I understand China's Global Civilization Initiative and its objectives (GCI).	1	2	3	4	5
I respect the diversity of civilizations, and countries should uphold equality, mutual learning, dialog, and inclusiveness among civilizations.	1	2	3	4	5

Unit 10   A Community of Shared Future for Mankind (III)

1. To what extent do you understand China's role in the current international situations as well as China's role in advancing a shared future for humanity?
2. As for the three global initiatives mentioned in the questionnaire, which one are you interested in most and willing to have a further investigation? Why?

China's Three Global Initiatives[1]

❶   This is an era of promise, and an era of challenges. At yet another crossroads in history, we have to choose between unity and division, between opening up and closing off, between cooperation and **confrontation**. With the overall interests of humanity **at stake**, this choice tests the wisdom of all countries.

❷   To build a **global community of shared future** is to pursue openness, **inclusiveness**, mutual benefit, equity, and justice. The goal is not to replace one system or civilization with another. Instead, it is about countries with different social systems, **ideologies**, histories, cultures, and levels of development coming together to promote shared interests, shared rights, and shared responsibilities in global affairs. The vision of a global community of shared future stands on the right side of history and on the side of human progress. It introduces a new approach to international relations, provides new ideas for global governance, opens up new prospects for international exchanges, and draws a new blueprint for a better world.

❸   The vision of a global community of shared future is the outcome of China's wisdom in handling contemporary international relations from the perspective of world peace and development—a Chinese plan for improving global governance, and a Chinese proposal to address various challenges in the 21st century. Vision guides action and direction determines the future. The international community should work together to turn the grand blueprint into a roadmap, and a beautiful vision into reality step by step.

I

❹   The **Global Development Initiative (GDI)** was proposed by Chinese President Xi Jinping at the 76th Session of the **UN General Assembly** in September 2021. It was put forward with the hope that countries would work together to overcome the impact of COVID-19 on global development, accelerate the implementation of the 2030 Agenda

---
1   The text was adapted from "A Global Community of Shared Future: China's Proposals and Actions", from the State Council Information Office website.

for Sustainable Development, and build a **global community of development with a shared future**. Six proposals are included in the initiative:

- Staying committed to development as its first priority. Putting development front and center in the global macro policy framework, boosting policy coordination among major economies, ensuring policy continuity, consistency, and sustainability, fostering global development partnerships featuring greater equality and balance, coordinating multilateral development cooperation to generate synergy, and accelerating the implementation of the UN's 2030 Agenda for Sustainable Development.

- Staying committed to a **people-centered approach**. Ensuring and improving people's well-being and protecting and promoting human rights through development, ensuring that development is for the people and by the people and that its fruits are shared by the people, ensuring a stronger sense of fulfillment, happiness, and security for the people, and pursuing the **people's well-rounded development**.

- Staying committed to inclusiveness and benefits for all. Addressing the special needs of developing countries, supporting developing countries—especially vulnerable countries facing exceptional difficulties—by means such as **debt suspension** and development aid, and addressing imbalanced and inadequate development among and within countries.

- Staying committed to innovation-driven development. Seizing the historic opportunities created by the latest round of revolution in science and technology and industrial transformation, speeding up efforts to harness scientific and technological achievements to boost productivity, creating an open, fair, equitable, and non-discriminatory environment for scientific and technological advances, unleashing new impetus for post-pandemic economic growth, and joining hands to achieve leapfrog development.

- Staying committed to harmony between humanity and nature. Improving global environmental governance, actively responding to climate change, building a community of life for humanity and nature, accelerating the transition to green and low-carbon development, and achieving green recovery and development.

- Staying committed to results-oriented actions. Increasing the input of development resources, prioritizing cooperation in areas such as poverty reduction, food security, pandemic response and **vaccines**, financing for development, climate change and green development, industrialization, the digital economy, and connectivity, and building a global community of development.

Unit 10 A Community of Shared Future for Mankind (III)

II

❺ The **Global Security Initiative (GSI)** is another global public good offered by China. The initiative was proposed by President Xi Jinping when he delivered a keynote speech via video at the opening ceremony of the Boao Forum for Asia (BFA) Annual Conference in April, 2022. It contributes Chinese solutions and wisdom to solving security challenges facing humanity.

❻ China officially released The Global Security Initiative Concept Paper in 2023. The document further **elaborates** the core concepts and principles of the initiative, **elucidates** its key **avenues** for cooperation, and presents recommendations and ideas concerning its cooperation platforms and mechanisms. This has demonstrated China's awareness of its duty to maintain world peace and its firm determination to safeguard global security. Six proposals are included in the initiative:

- Staying committed to the vision of common, comprehensive, cooperative, and sustainable security, and working together to maintain world peace and security;

- Staying committed to respecting the sovereignty and territorial integrity of all countries, upholding non-**interference** in others' internal affairs, and respecting the independent choices of development paths and social systems made by people in different countries.

- Staying committed to abiding by the purposes and principles of the **UN Charter**, rejecting the Cold War mentality, opposing **unilateralism,** and saying no to **bloc politics** and camp-based confrontation.

- Staying committed to taking the **legitimate** security concerns of all countries seriously, upholding the principle of indivisible security, building a balanced, effective, and sustainable security architecture, and opposing the pursuit of one's own security to the **detriment** of others' security.

- Staying committed to peacefully resolving differences and disputes between countries through dialog and consultation, supporting all efforts **conducive** to the peaceful settlement of crises, rejecting double standards, and opposing the **arbitrary** use of unilateral sanctions and long-arm **jurisdiction**.

- Staying committed to maintaining security in both traditional and non-traditional domains, and working together to address regional disputes and global challenges such as terrorism, climate change, **cybersecurity**, and biosecurity.

III

❼ President Xi made the remarks while delivering a keynote speech at the opening ceremony of the CPC in Dialog with World Political Parties High-Level Meeting via video link in March 2023 and proposed the **Global Civilization Initiative (GCI)**. Through the initiative, China calls for jointly advocating respect for the diversity of civilizations, jointly advocating the **common values of humanity**, jointly advocating the importance of continuity and evolution of civilizations, and jointly advocating closer international people-to-people exchanges and cooperation. The Global Civilization Initiative makes a sincere call for the world to enhance inter-civilization exchanges and dialog, and promote human progress with inclusiveness and mutual learning, inspiring the building of a global community of shared future. Four proposals are included in the initiative:

- Jointly advocating respect for the diversity of civilizations. Countries should uphold equality, mutual learning, dialog, and inclusiveness among civilizations, and let cultural exchanges transcend **estrangement**, mutual learning transcend conflict, and inclusiveness transcend **supremacy**.

- Jointly advocating the common values of humanity. Peace, development, equity, justice, democracy, and freedom are shared aspirations of people across the world. Countries should be open to appreciating different perceptions of values by different civilizations, and refrain from imposing their own values or models on others and from **stoking** ideological confrontation.

- Jointly advocating the importance of continuity and evolution of civilizations. Countries should fully harness the relevance of their histories and cultures to the present times, and push for creative transformation and innovative development of their fine traditional cultures in the course of modernization.

- Jointly advocating closer international people-to-people exchanges and cooperation. Countries should explore the building of a global network for inter-civilization dialog and cooperation, enrich the contents of exchanges and expand avenues of cooperation to promote mutual understanding and friendship among people of all countries, and jointly advance the progress of human civilization.

(1,239 words)

 Glossary

| confrontation | /ˌkɒnfrʌnˈteɪʃn/ | n. | 对抗；对峙；冲突 |

Unit 10　A Community of Shared Future for Mankind (III)

inclusiveness	/ɪnˈkluːsɪvnəs/	n.	包容性，兼容并蓄
ideology	/ˌaɪdiˈɒlədʒi/	n.	思想（体系）；思想意识
vaccine	/ˈvæksiːn/	n.	疫苗
elaborate	/iˈlæbərət/	v.	详尽阐述；详细描述
elucidate	/iˈluːsɪdeɪt/	v.	阐明；解释；说明
avenue	/ˈævənjuː/	n.	选择；途径；手段
interference	/ˌɪntəˈfɪərəns/	n.	干涉；干预；介入
unilateralism	/ˌjuːnɪˈlætrəlɪzəm/	n.	单边主义
legitimate	/lɪˈdʒɪtɪmət/	adj.	合法的；法律认可的；法定的
detriment	/ˈdetrɪmənt/	n.	伤害；损害；造成伤害的事物
conducive	/kənˈdjuːsɪv/	adj.	有助于；便于
arbitrary	/ˈɑːbɪtrəri/	adj.	任意的；武断的；随心所欲的
jurisdiction	/ˌdʒʊərɪsˈdɪkʃn/	n.	司法权；审判权；管辖权
cybersecurity	/ˌsaɪbəsɪˈkjʊərəti/	n.	网络（空间）安全
inter-civilization	/ˌɪntərˌsɪvəˌlaɪˈzeɪʃn/	n.	文明之间，跨文明
estrangement	/ɪˈstreɪndʒmənt/	n.	疏远；分离
supremacy	/suːˈpreməsi/	n.	至高无上；最大权力；最高地位
stoke	/stəʊk/	v.	煽动；激起
at stake			有风险；处于危急关头

 ## Useful Expressions

global community of shared future	人类命运共同体
Global Development Initiative (GDI)	全球发展倡议
UN General Assembly	联合国大会
global community of development with a shared future	全球发展共同体
people-centered approach	以人民为中心
people's well-rounded development	人的全面发展
debt suspension	暂停偿债
Global Security Initiative (GSI)	全球安全倡议
Global Civilization Initiative (GCI)	全球文明倡议
UN Charter	《联合国宪章》
bloc politics	集团政治
common values of humanity	全人类共同价值

Task 1

Directions: *Please read the text and fill in the blanks below with a proper word.*

China's Three Global Initiatives
I. The Global Development Initiative (GDI)
• The GDI aims to accelerate the (1) _____ of the 2030 Agenda for Sustainable Development. It emphasizes fostering global development partnerships featuring greater (2) _____ and (3) _____. The GDI advocates for an open, fair, equitable, and non-discriminatory environment for scientific and (4) _____ advances. One of its goals is to achieve (5) _____ recovery and development.
II. The Global Security Initiative (GSI)
• The GSI emphasizes the vision of common, comprehensive, cooperative, and sustainable (6) _____. It opposes bloc politics and camp-based (7) _____. The GSI advocates for peacefully resolving differences through (8) _____ and consultation. It addresses both traditional and non-traditional security concerns such as terrorism, climate change, (9) _____, and (10) _____.
III. The Global Civilization Initiative (GCI)
• The Global Civilization Initiative calls for jointly advocating respect for the diversity of civilizations, ensuring (11) _____, mutual learning, dialog, and (12) _____ among civilizations. It promotes the common values of humanity, including peace, development, equity, (13) _____, democracy, and freedom. The initiative emphasizes the importance of (14) _____ and the evolution of civilizations in the modern era. It aims to promote mutual understanding and friendship among people of all countries through closer international (15) _____ exchanges and cooperation.

Task 2

Directions: *Please read the text again and decide whether the following statements are true (T) or false (F) based on what you have learned from the text.*

_____ 1. The passage suggests that the current era presents both opportunities and challenges.

_____ 2. According to the passage, the choice between unity and division tests the wisdom of all countries.

_____ 3. The vision of a global community of shared future aims to replace existing systems and civilizations with a new one.

_____ 4. The Global Development Initiative (GDI) was proposed at the 76th Session of the UN General Assembly in September, 2021.

_____ 5. One of the proposals in the GDI focuses on boosting policy coordination among major economies.

_____ 6. China released The Global Security Initiative Concept Paper in 2022.

_____ 7. The GSI aims to promote bloc politics and camp-based confrontation.

_____ 8. According to the passage, the Global Civilization Initiative emphasizes the imposition of one civilization's values over others.

_____ 9. President Xi Jinping proposed the Global Civilization Initiative at the CPC in Dialog with World Political Parties High-Level Meeting.

_____ 10. The Global Civilization Initiative encourages countries to explore the building of a global network for inter-civilization dialog and cooperation.

Task 3

Directions: *Please translate the following five sentences into English using the words or phrase in the parentheses.*

1. 人类只有一个地球，各国共处一个世界，没有哪一个国家能够独自应对人类面临的各种挑战，人类是休戚与共的命运共同体。（community of shared future）

2. 无论是"一带一路"倡议还是全球发展倡议，中国都致力于推进不同经济体之间的协同效应，以加快实现全球可持续发展的目标。（accelerate）

3. 这份调研报告详细描述了当地如何将绿色发展的理念融入有机农业、旅游业和中小微企业的发展。（elaborate）

4. 全球文明倡议倡导尊重文明的多样性，为不同文明冲突时有发生的当今世界营造了有利于文化和人文交流的氛围。（conducive）

5. 这个非政府组织致力于全面赋能年轻人的成长，鼓励青年人超越社会、经济和政治边界为全球性问题寻找可能的解决路径。（transcend）

Task 4

Directions: *Please compare the proposals in China's Global Development Initiative with some of the goals of the UN's 2030 Agenda for Sustainable Development in the following table and discuss the following questions with your partners.*

1. To what extent are China's proposals in GDI consistent with the goals of the UN's 2030 Agenda for Sustainable Development?

2. Please choose one of the goals shared by both the UN and China, such as food security, climate change, green development, etc., and discuss with your partners how to achieve this goal by listing the possible proposals and actions.

	UN's 2030 Agenda for Sustainable Development	China's GDI
Goal-1	End poverty in all its forms everywhere.	
Goal-2	End hunger, achieve food security and improved nutrition and promote sustainable agriculture.	
Goal-3	Ensure healthy lives and promote well-being for all at all ages.	
Goal-4	Ensure inclusive and equitable quality education and promote lifelong learning opportunities for all.	
Goal-5	Achieve gender equality and empower all women and girls.	
Goal-6	Ensure availability and sustainable management of water and sanitation for all.	
Goal-7	Ensure access to affordable, reliable, sustainable and modern energy for all.	
Goal-8	Promote sustained, inclusive and sustainable economic growth, full and productive employment and decent work for all.	

(Continued)

UN's 2030 Agenda for Sustainable Development		China's GDI
Goal-9	Build resilient infrastructure, promote inclusive and sustainable industrialization and foster innovation.	
Goal-10	Reduce inequality within and among countries.	
Goal-11	Make cities and human settlements inclusive, safe, resilient and sustainable.	
Goal-12	Ensure sustainable consumption and production patterns.	
Goal-13	Take urgent action to combat climate change and its impacts.	
Goal-14	Conserve and sustainably use the oceans, seas and marine resources for sustainable development.	
Goal-15	Protect, restore and promote sustainable use of terrestrial ecosystems, sustainably manage forests, combat desertification, and halt and reverse land degradation and halt biodiversity loss.	
Goal-16	Promote peaceful and inclusive societies for sustainable development, provide access to justice for all and build effective, accountable and inclusive institutions at all levels.	
Goal-17	Strengthen the means of implementation and revitalize the global partnership for sustainable development.	

Text B The Influence of Ancient Chinese Cultural Classics in France

 Warm-up

Directions: Please read the following table and discuss the questions with your partners.

Table: Representative Elements of Chinese Culture
(Unit %)

	China	Overseas overall	Developed country	Developing country	Overseas 18–35 years old	Overseas 36–50 years old	Overseas 51–65 years old
food (Chinese food)	60 / 57	53 / 55	53 / 56	53 / 54	48 / 50	55 / 56	60 / 62
traditional Chinese medicine	60 / 67	47 / 50	41 / 44	54 / 57	39 / 42	49 / 52	57 / 61
Chinese kongfu	41 / 58	43 / 46	36 / 39	51 / 55	39 / 42	45 / 47	46 / 51
products	9 / 8	29 / 29	20 / 21	39 / 37	30 / 28	30 / 29	28 / 29
natural scenery	35 / 29	27 / 28	25 / 25	28 / 30	24 / 25	27 / 27	32 / 33
scientific and technological inventions	21 / 18	27 / 24	19 / 17	36 / 32	28 / 25	27 / 23	26 / 24
traditional calendar, festivals, zodiac signs	44 / 54	26 / 28	22 / 24	30 / 31	27 / 28	25 / 27	26 / 29
calligraphy and painting	43 / 46	26 / 28	25 / 27	27 / 29	25 / 26	26 / 27	28 / 31
Confucius, Confucianism	59 / 69	25 / 27	25 / 27	26 / 28	21 / 21	25 / 28	33 / 36
clothes	24 / 21	25 / 26	19 / 20	32 / 32	26 / 25	24 / 26	26 / 27
architecture	25 / 22	24 / 24	20 / 20	28 / 29	24 / 24	23 / 23	25 / 26
music and dance	13 / 15	20 / 21	17 / 18	24 / 25	20 / 20	21 / 20	22 / 25
cultural classics	48 / 53	19 / 21	16 / 17	23 / 25	20 / 22	19 / 20	19 / 21
Taoism	25 / 34	17 / 19	16 / 17	19 / 21	16 / 16	18 / 19	19 / 24
folk arts and acrobatics	30 / 35	15 / 15	14 / 14	16 / 15	12 / 12	16 / 14	19 / 19
literary works	23 / 21	12 / 11	10 / 9	14 / 13	13 / 12	11 / 10	10 / 10
film and television works	11 / 9	11 / 10	7 / 7	16 / 15	13 / 11	12 / 11	8 / 8

Sample size: 10,500 overseas samples,
500 Chinese samples

■2019   ■2018

Question: Which of the following aspects do you think best represents Chinese culture?

Note: The table was taken from the "2019 China National Image Global Survey" compiled by the Center for International Communication Studies, Academy of Contemporary China and World Studies.

1. What are the top three cultural elements that are considered most representative of Chinese culture among overseas young people according to the table? Why do you think these elements stand out?

2. How about the overseas reception of Chinese cultural classics as well as Confucianism?

3. What are the possible strategies to boost the dissemination and reception of Chinese culture overseas? Can you think of any particular examples about Chinese cultural exports that have gained increasing popularity?

The Influence of Ancient Chinese Cultural Classics in France[1]

❶ If we can locate any **vestiges** of the **Sinophile** in Michel de Montaigne (1533–1592), then the real contact between France and "the Central Empire" may be traced back to the late 19th century when Louis XIV sent Jesuit **missionaries** to the imperial court ruled by Emperor Kangxi (1662–1722). Thanks to these exchanges, the so-called "**chinoiseries**"—porcelain, jade ware, **lacquer** ware, screens, and fans—made their way into the French royal family's residence. Other writings from China—dictionaries, encyclopedias, Chinese historical geographies, inscriptions, and **bibliographic** collections—have formed the material basis for the birth of French **Sinology**.

❷ In 1697, the French Jesuit priest Joachim Bouvet (1656–1730) returned to Europe from Beijing, bringing with him more than 50 books that Emperor Kangxi gifted to Louis XIV. These books were incorporated into the Royal Library and formed the foundation of the museum's Sinology collection. This series quickly **amassed** thousands of volumes.

❸ In the 18th century, when Chinese **sensibilities** were mainly displayed in the decorative arts, Chinese literature came to France via a 13th-century Yuan Dynasty play called *The Great Revenge of the Orphan of Zhao*. Voltaire was inspired to write a tragedy based on this masterwork, and the original drama was passed on to future generations. More broadly speaking, the Age of **Enlightenment** philosophers drew upon China as an ideal example in their discussions on religion, the state, and morality.

❹ In the 19th century, the France interested in China was replaced by a powerful empire that exerted its rule by force. The **looting** of the Old Summer Palace (Yuanmingyuan) in 1860 is one of the most well-known **ransackings** in Chinese history. However, it was also in the 19th century that French institutions focused on Sinology research were founded. In 1814, the French Academy established the "Chair of Chinese,

---

1 The text was adapted from Rabut, I. 2022. The influence of ancient Chinese cultural classics in france. In Zhange Xiping (Ed.), *A Study of Ancient Cultural Classics Abroad in the 21th Century*, Economic Science Press & Springer: 83–88.

Manchu and **Tartars** Languages and Literatures". Thirty years later, in 1843, the Chair of Modern Chinese was established in the School of **Oriental** Languages. At that time, instructors' knowledge of Chinese language and literature **emanated** from books, and they particularly valued ancient Chinese or **dialect** literature. At the beginning of the 20th century, various translations of the stories from Pu Songling's (1640–1715) *Strange Tales from a Chinese Studio* surfaced.

❺ The late 19th and early 20th centuries **ushered** in an era of exploration. At the turn of the century, **archaeology** became an important field thanks to the contributions of Sinologists Paul Pelliot (1878–1945), Edouard Chavannes (1865–1918) and Victor Segalen (1878–1919). As in other parts of the world, military personnel involved in colonial expansion sometimes took up exploration. General Henry d'Ollone (1868–1945), who completed several studies on non-Han ethnic minority groups in China, serves as a case in point. Although the First World War somewhat **hampered** the progress of Sinology, the discovery of the **Dunhuang Grottos** has continued to inspire Sinology research, in the realms of religious studies, medicine, literature, and even economics.

❻ The Sinologists in the first half of the 20th century included a sizeable **cohort** of missionaries, who completed **ethnographic** writings on non-Han ethnic minorities (especially in Yunnan Province). Père Alfred Liétard (1872–1912), for instance, conducted an in-depth study on the Axi Yi people. Similar studies were carried out in French Indochina, such as a study of the Yi minority of Haut-Tonkin. Religious workers' contributions to Sinology research extended into the second half of the 20th century: François Houang (Houang Kia-tcheng, 1911–1990) translated the *Tao Te Ching*（道德经）in addition to works on **Buddhism** and Christianity and a translation of Yan Fu's **dissertation**.

❼ The study of philosophy and religion was once the exclusive domain of French Sinology. Considerable research has been conducted in **Taoism** and Buddhism, while the research on **Confucianism** has been **obscure** at best, aside from some relevant research triggered by the **revival** of Confucianism at the end of the 20th century. Located somewhere along the **spectrum** between philosophy and mysticism, *The Book of Changes* (易经) is the most widely discussed subject in French Sinology, and at least nine works are devoted to this. Scholars have also devoted considerable attention to Chuang-Tzu's teachings. The relationship between literature and philosophy is still a subject that **merits** continuous attention, and Paul Demiévile was a pioneer in this field.

❽ Later on, literature became the subject of many researches. Beginning in the 1920s, and especially in the 1930s, literature began to occupy a position outside mainstream university research on legal or diplomatic relations. At that time, such research was mainly carried out by Chinese students who studied in France. George Soulié de Morant (1878–1955) and Georges Margouliès (1902–1972) authored the first introduction to Chinese literature written by non-Chinese persons, followed by in-depth studies on a particular work or author. Generally speaking, literary studies have occupied an important position in French Sinology since the 1950s. We must also mention the Jesuits' and Scheutistes' pioneering role in research on modern Chinese literature. Considering the difficulty of the original texts, French Sinologists' achievements in translation are quite impressive. In the early 20th century, poetry and short stories were the main objects of translation. In the late 1960s, translators expanded their **repertoire** to classical novels. The translation of ancient classics began with Serephin Couvreur's (1835–1919) versions of *The Book of Rites* (礼记), *The Book of Songs* and *The Four Books* and Edouard Chavannes' version of *Historical Records*. At the end of the 20th century, the translations of the two were republished, and some new versions were also introduced to the French public, such as *Liezi* (列子), *Xunzi* (荀子), *Han Feizi* (韩非子) and *The Spring and Autumn Annals* (春秋).

❾ Throughout the 20th century, in addition to poetry and **vernacular** novels, the most frequently translated texts tended to be philosophical classics, such as *The Book of Changes*, *The Analects* (论语), *Chuang-Tzu* (庄子), and *Sun-Tzu* (孙子), each having multiple complete and selected translations. The prize for the most significant contribution to the translation of classical literature or philosophical works goes to the Connaisance de L'Orient.

❿ Throughout the past century, French Sinology has undergone a continuous evolution. At the beginning of the century, it was closely linked to French forces in Indochina and China, scientific expeditions, and missionary work. French Sinology exists to a large extent in the form of field study Sinology. By the second half of the 20th century, it had been essentially transformed into a university-oriented academic discipline. In the 1920s and 1940s, research on China's influence on France was **confined** to doctoral-level **theses** produced by Chinese students studying abroad in France. However, from the 1960s to 1970s, as more and more French students began learning Chinese, French students and later Sinologists took up higher-quality research.

(1,127 words)

 Glossary

vestige	/ˈvestɪdʒ/	n.	残留部分；遗迹
Sinophile	/ˈsaɪnəˌfaɪl/	adj.	喜爱中国的，亲华的

missionary	/ˈmɪʃənri/	n.	传教士
chinoiserie	/ʃinˈwaːzəri/	n.	中式风格艺术
lacquer	/ˈlækə(r)/	n.	漆
bibliographic	/ˌbɪbliəˈgræfɪk/	adj.	目录的
Sinology	/saɪˈnɒlədʒi/	n.	汉学
amass	/əˈmæs/	v.	（尤指一段时间内大量）积累，积聚
sensibility	/ˌsensəˈbɪləti/	n.	鉴赏力，感受能力
Enlightenment	/ɪnˈlaɪtnmənt/	n.	（18世纪欧洲的）启蒙运动
looting	/ˈluːtɪŋ/	n.	（暴力事件中发生的）抢劫，洗劫
ransacking	/ˈrænsæk/	n.	洗劫，劫掠
Manchu	/mænˈtʃu/	n./adj.	满族人；满族的；满族语的
Tartar	/ˈtɑːtə(r)/	n./adj.	鞑靼人；鞑靼（人）的
Oriental	/ˌɔːriˈentl/	adj.	东方的；东方人的
emanate	/ˈeməneɪt/	v.	发源于；从……发出
dialect	/ˈdaɪəlekt/	n.	方言，土语，地方话
usher	/ˈʌʃə(r)/	v.	开创；开始；开启
archaeology	/ˌɑːkiˈɒlədʒi/	n.	考古学
hamper	/ˈhæmpə(r)/	v.	妨碍；阻止；阻碍
Dunhuang Grottos			敦煌石窟
cohort	/ˈkəʊhɔːt/	n.	（有共同特点的）一群人，一批人
ethnographic	/eθnəˈgræfɪk/	adj.	人种志的，人种论的；人种志著作的
Buddhism	/ˈbʊdɪzəm/	n.	佛教
dissertation	/ˌdɪsəˈteɪʃn/	n.	专题论文；（尤指）学位论文
Taoism	/ˈdaʊɪzəm/	n.	道家
Confucianism	/kənˈfjuːʃənɪzəm/	n.	孔子学说；儒学，儒教
obscure	/əbˈskjʊə(r)/	adj.	无名的；鲜为人知的
revival	/rɪˈvaɪvl/	n.	复兴；再流行
spectrum	/ˈspektrəm/	n.	（看法、感觉等的）范围，各层次
merit	/ˈmerɪt/	v.	值得（表扬、关注等）
repertoire	/ˈrepətwɑː(r)/	n.	全部剧目，全部曲目

vernacular	/vəˈnækjələ(r)/	n.	本地话，方言；白话
confine	/kənˈfaɪn/	v.	把……局限在，限制
thesis	/ˈθiːsɪs/	n.	论文；论题，命题；论点

Task 1

Directions: *Please read the text and fill in the blanks in the timeframe.*

The Influence of Ancient Chinese Cultural Classics in France
Late 17th century: • Louis XIV sends Jesuit (1) _____ to China, initiating a cultural exchange.   • French Jesuit priest Joachim Bouvet brings back over 50 books from China, forming the (2) _____ of French (3) _____.
18th century: • Chinese literature was introduced to France through Yuan Dynasty play.   • (4) _____ philosophers draw inspiration from China.
19th century: • French (5) _____ focused on Sinology research were founded.   • Old Summer Palace was looted in 1860.   • Significant advancements in Sinology research.
Early 20th century: • Exploration era begins with contributions from Sinologists.   • The First World War affects progress but (6) _____ discovery inspires further research.
Mid-20th century: • Missionaries and scholars contribute to Sinology research.   • Study of philosophy and religions expands, with a focus on (7) _____ and Buddhism.

(Continued)

The Influence of Ancient Chinese Cultural Classics in France
Late-20th century:
• (8) _____ of Confucianism triggers relevant research.
• (9) _____ becomes a major focus, with translations of classical texts.
• French Sinology evolves into a university-oriented academic (10) _____.

Task 2

Directions: *Please read the text again and match the contributions to French Sinology in Column B with the key figures in Column A.*

Column A	Column B
1. Joachim Bouvet	a. authored the first introduction to Chinese literature written by non-Chinese persons and conducted in-depth studies on particular works or authors in the mid-20th century
2. Paul Pelliot, Edouard Chavannes, and Victor Segalen	b. pioneered the study of the relationship between literature and philosophy in French Sinology
3. François Houang (Houang Kia-tcheng)	c. sent Jesuit missionaries to the imperial court of Emperor Kangxi, initiating cultural exchanges between France and China in the late 17th century
4. Père Alfred Liétard	d. brought more than 50 books from China to France in 1697, forming the foundation of the Royal Library's Sinology collection
5. George Soulié de Morant and Georges Margouliès	e. completed several studies on non-Han ethnic minority groups in China in the late 19th and early 20th centuries
6. Serephin Couvreur and Edouard Chavannes	f. conducted in-depth ethnographic studies on the Axi Yi people in the early 20th century
7. Paul Demiévile	g. contributed to archaeological explorations and Sinology research in the late 19th and early 20th centuries, particularly in Dunhuang

8. General Henry d'Ollone h. showed early signs of Sinophile tendencies, indicating the beginning of French interest in Chinese culture

9. Michel de Montaigne i. initiated the translation of ancient Chinese classics into French in the early 20th century

10. Louis XIV j. Translated the *Tao Te Ching* and works on Buddhism and Christianity, extending religious workers' contributions to Sinology research into the mid-20th century

Task 3

Directions: *Please translate the following five sentences into English using the words or phrases in the parentheses.*

1. 全球化加速了世界各国之间的交流与合作，促进了文化、经济和政治的互动与发展。（globalization）

2. 在跨文化交流中，理解对方的文化背景和价值观是促进沟通和合作的关键。（cross-cultural exchanges）

3. 中国文化在海外传播的过程中也不可避免地吸收当地的文化元素。（incorporate）

4. 法国汉学家致力于探索中国文化的深层内涵和价值观念，以促进中法文化交流和理解。（commit）

5. 在 17 世纪，中国文化和艺术品在法国的传播仅限于皇室和贵族范围之内。（exclusive）

Task 4

Directions: *The year 2024 marks the 60th anniversary of the establishment of Sino-French diplomatic relations. Please make an investigation on the mutual influence of Chinese and French culture in modern times and finish a mini-report, approximately 300 words. You are encouraged to refer to other resources for the report. You can use the following table to help you organize ideas.*

Chinese Culture Influence in France	French Culture Influence in China
e.g.: China's silk in France	e.g.: French wine in China

(Continued)

Chinese Culture Influence in France	French Culture Influence in China

Part II Drilling for GC Skills

How to Give a Formal Presentation (II)

1. How to Speak Appropriately in a Presentation

(1) How to Overcome Fear and Anxiety in a Formal Presentation

Nervousness or anxiety in certain situations is normal, and public speaking is no exception. Fear of public speaking is a common form of anxiety. It can range from slight nervousness to paralyzing fear and panic. Many people with this fear avoid public speaking situations altogether, or they suffer through them with shaking hands and a quavering voice. But with preparation and persistence, the fear of public speaking can be overcome. The following steps may help:

- Know your topic. The better you understand what you're talking about, and the more you care about the topic, the less likely you'll make a mistake or get off track. And if you do get lost, you'll be able to recover quickly. Take some time to consider what questions the audience may ask and have your responses ready.

- Get organized. Carefully plan out the information you want to present ahead of time, including any props, audio or visual aids. The more organized you are, the less nervous you'll be. Use an outline on a small card to stay on track. If possible, visit the place where you'll be speaking and review available equipment before your presentation.

- Practice. Practice is never too much. Practice your complete presentation several times. Do it for some people you're comfortable with and ask for feedback. It may also be helpful to practice with a few people with whom you're less familiar. Consider making a video of your presentation so you can watch it and see opportunities for improvement.

- Visualize your success. Imagine that your presentation will go well. Positive thoughts can help decrease some of your negativity about your social performance and relieve some anxiety.

- Focus on your material, not on your audience. People mainly pay attention to new information—not how it's presented. They may not notice your nervousness. If audience members do notice that you're nervous, they may root for you and want your presentation to be a success.

- Don't fear a moment of silence. If you lose track of what you're saying or start to feel nervous and your mind goes blank, it may seem like you've been silent for an eternity. In reality, it's probably only a few seconds. Even if it's longer, it's likely your audience won't mind a pause to consider what you've been saying. Just take a few slow, deep breaths.

Task 1

Directions: *Please read the adapted passage taken from* Harvard Business Review, *and discuss the following questions with your partner.*

Most of us—even those at the top—struggle with public-speaking anxiety. When I ask my clients what makes them nervous, invariably they respond with the same answers:

"I don't like being watched."

"I don't like the eyes on me."

"I don't like being in the spotlight."

And it follows that when they get up to speak, nearly all of them initially avoid making eye contact with members of the audience. Therein lies the problem: While avoiding direct eye contact may seem like an effective strategy for coping with speaking anxiety, it actually makes you even more nervous.

To understand why, we need to go way back to prehistoric times when humans perceived eyes watching us as an existential threat. Those eyes were likely predators. People were literally terrified of being eaten alive. In response to that prehistoric reality, the amygdala, the part of our brain that helps us respond to danger, kicked into full gear. And when our fight-or-flight response gets triggered, we understandably feel intense stress and anxiety. What does this have to do with public speaking? Our brains have transferred that ancient fear of being watched onto public speaking. In other words, public-speaking anxiety is in our DNA. We experience public speaking as an attack. We physiologically register an audience as a threatening predator and mount a comparable response.

So today when we speak in front of a group and feel the eyes watching us, we feel painfully visible, like a caveman exposed in daylight. And because our brain is telling us that we are under attack, we do whatever is necessary to protect ourselves. We construct walls between ourselves and the source of danger—in this case, the audience—to repel the attack and blunt any danger.

What do these walls look like? We focus on our slides. We look down. We retreat into our notes. In the process, we disregard the people in front of us, wishing them into invisibility. Even the most confident speakers find ways to distance themselves from their audience.

Fortunately, there is a solution: human generosity. The key to calming the amygdala and disarming our organic panic button is to turn the focus away from ourselves—away from whether we will mess up or whether the audience will like us—and toward helping the audience.

Studies have shown that an increase in generosity leads to a decrease in amygdala activity. Showing kindness and generosity to others has been shown to activate the vagus nerve, which has the power to calm the fight-or-flight response. When we are kind to others, we feel calmer and less stressed. The same principle applies to public speaking. When we approach speaking with a spirit of generosity, we counteract the sensation of being under attack and start to feel less nervous. Start with these three steps:

When you're preparing, think about your audience. When we start preparing for a presentation, the mistake we all make is starting with the topic. This immediately gets us inside the details—and makes it harder to break down the wall between us and others. Instead, start with the audience. Before diving into the information, ask yourself: Who will be in the room? Why are they there? What do they need? Be specific in your answers. Identify the audience's needs, both spoken and unspoken and craft a message that speaks directly to those needs.

Right before you speak, refocus your brain. You are the most nervous right before you speak. This is the moment where your brain is telling you, "Everyone is judging me. What if I fail?" And it is exactly at this moment that you can refocus your brain. Remind yourself that you are here to help your audience. Be firm with your brain. Tell yourself, "Brain, this presentation is not about me. It is about helping my audience." Over time, your brain will begin to get it, and you will become less nervous.

While you're speaking, make eye contact. One of the biggest mistakes we make is speaking to people as a group. We scan the room—trying to look at everyone at once—and end up connecting with nobody.

In reality, each person in the room is listening to you as an individual. And so the best way to connect to your audience is by speaking to them as individuals. How? By making sustained eye contact with one person per thought. By focusing on one person at a time, you make each person in the room feel like you are talking just to them.

We know the power of generosity to give us a sense of fulfillment, purpose, and meaning. Generosity is just as powerful in speaking. It turns a nerve-wracking and even painful experience into one of giving and helping others. A generous speaker is calmer, more relaxed, and—most importantly—more effective at reaching the audience and making the desired impact.

Questions for discussion:

1. According to the passage, why don't most people like the feeling of being in the spotlight?

2. Various opinions are given on how to overcome the fear of public speaking, do you think the suggestions like "Focus on your material, not on your audience" and "When you're preparing, think about your audience" are contradictory?

3. Apart from eye contact, can you list any other body language that is often used in giving presentations?

4. Share some of your personal experiences about how to overcome fear in public speaking. What are your tips?

(2) Language Style in a Formal Presentation

Language of the presentation used on formal occasions, such as academic conferences, business negotiations, international summits, etc., should be formal in style, but it is less formal than written English in such contexts. Formal language is characterized by the use of standard English, more complex sentence structures, infrequent use of personal pronouns, and a lack of colloquial or slang terms.

Take academic context for example. A presenter needs to connect with their audience more directly than they would as the author of a paper on the same topic. Written academic language has a formality that is particularly stylized and unnatural to most speakers of English. It is a style that does not really exist outside the limited realm of academic publications. It would be very unnatural for someone to speak using that language, and a presenter needs to be natural in order to make that connection with the audience. wTherefore, the presenter needs to use an appropriately natural form of language to communicate with them. However, academic presenters also need to retain their credentials as credible academics, and experts in their field, so they can't "dumb down" the content or avoid using language that is important to maintain that credibility within their field.

There are several tips for presenters to make their language appropriate in formality. First, reversing the expressions can help with making the spoken language less formal. Addressing the audience as "you" and talking about the research in the first person is an important step to make the presentation more personal and less formal than written English, by which the presenters are highlighting that there is a connection between the audience and themselves. It engages the audience by including them in the presentation. Second, good presenters will also ask questions of the audience, rather than phrasing the question as a statement. Rhetorical questions again involve the audience in the presentation by encouraging them to consider for themselves the issues that the presenter is addressing, or by allowing them to relate the presenter's experience to their own. Third, a further strategy is to use contractions and less formal words, like phrasal verbs, which are often edited out of academic writing style. It would sound very unnatural for a speaker to pronounce each word, rather than use a contraction.

Task 2

Directions: *Compare the three groups of sentences and decide which of them are appropriate for presentations on formal occasions. Then summarize the differences between formal spoken English and formal written English.*

Group 1

A) Because the jobs are even more complex, programs to train people will take longer.

B) The increased complexity of tasks will lead to the extension of the duration of training programs.

Group 2

A) The use of this method of control unquestionably leads to safer and faster train running in the most adverse weather conditions.

B) You can control the trains this way and if you do that you can be quite sure that they'll be able to run more safely and more quickly than they would otherwise, no matter how bad the weather gets.

Group 3

A) Improvements in technology have reduced the risks and high costs associated with simultaneous installation.

B) Because the technology has improved, it's less risky than it used to be to install them at the same time, and it doesn't cost so much either.

Group 4

A) It is believed that the Global Civilization Initiative stands as a robust response to concepts supporting the estrangement, clash, or superiority of civilizations.

B) I believe that the Global Civilization Initiative will exert lasting influence on the current international environment that is characterized by estrangement, clash, or superiority of civilizations.

	Formal Spoken English	**Formal Written English**
Choice of words	More verbs	
		More lexical words
	Relatively simple words	
Sentence structure	More coordinate clauses	More subordinate clauses
	More adverbial	
		"It is… that" structure

(3) Typical Functional Language Used in Presentations

Introduction is a crucial part of any presentation. There are many functions that the presenter can achieve:

Expressing the purpose:

- The objective/aim/purpose of the presentation/talk today is…
- What I want to present this morning/afternoon/today is…
- I'm here today to share/give…

Giving the structure:

- There are four parts in this presentation/talk. They are…
- This talk is divided into four main parts. To start with/Firstly, I'd like to look at…

    Then/Secondly, I'll be talking about… Thirdly… My fourth point will be about…

- For this talk, I'd like to start with the concept of… Then I will analyze the problems of… Lastly, I'd like to share some possible solutions and personal reflections.

Giving the timing:

- My presentation/talk/lecture will take/last about 20 minutes.
- I will finish the presentation in about 20 minutes.

Handling questions:

- At the end of my talk, welcome questions from you.
- I'll be happy to answer any relevant questions you have at the end of my presentation.

(4) Transitional Language in Presentations

A vital part of any presentation is transitioning or moving to a new section. It is crucial because of the difference between listening and reading. When you are reading, you can easily see where one section (or paragraph) ends, but this is not the case in listening. Therefore, good academic speakers need to give cues to signal the end of a section. This helps the audience understand the structure of the presentation and follow the main points. The following patterns and expressions can be used in transition.

Transitional sentence patterns

- Let's now move on to/ turn to the next part…
- Now I want to go on to the next point…
- This leads/brings me to my next point, which is…
- I'd now like to move on to/ turn to…
- So far we have looked at…Now I'd like to…

Giving examples

- Let me give you one example about…
- A good example of this is…
- I'd like to share some cases that have been applied in…

Summarizing

- What I'm trying to say is…
- Let me just try and sum that up before we move on to…

- So far, I've presented...

Concluding

- I'd like to finish the presentation by emphasizing...

- In conclusion, I'd like to end the presentation by sharing...

- Thanks for your attention/time. If you have any questions or comments, I'll be happy/ I'll do my best to answer them.

2. How to Use Visual Aids and Non-verbal Language in Presentations

(1) Visual Aids in Presentations

Visuals can spark interest, build emotional connections, clarify your words, explain abstract ideas, help draw conclusions and increase understanding. Done well—simple, visible, relevant, memorable, and audience-focused—visual aids can have a profound impact on the audience. Visual aids can be an important part of conveying the presenter's message effectively since people learn far more than through hearing or seeing alone. The brain processes verbal and visual information separately. By helping the audience build visual and verbal memories, they are more likely to be able to remember the information at a later time.

A visual aid is what the audience can see, helping the audience follow the spoken presentation. In addition to aiding understanding, visual aids can also help keep the audience's attention and interest by adding variety to the presentation style.

The most common types of visual aids in presentations are PowerPoint, whiteboard/blackboard, and handouts.

Various types of information can be used in the visual aids, including texts, images, charts (bar charts, pie charts, etc.), graphs/diagrams, and audio-videos.

Remember that visual aids must be visual, and the visual aids must aid your presentation. Slides must show the key points that you want to make. You will add comments while you speak, but if the audience can see your main points, this will help them follow what you are saying. The following ten tips can be constructive in preparing visual aids:

- Make sure you have a slide showing the structure/table of contents of your presentation;

- Keep text information concise, use bullet points rather than complete sentences/paragraphs or even passages;

- Keep the bullet points parallel in hierarchy, and avoid over three levels of bullet points;
- Follow the six-by-six rule, which means a maximum of six lines, with a maximum of six words per line;
- Make the bullet points grammatically correct and consistent in wording;
- Make sure all images/pictures used are relevant to the presentation topic;
- Make sure the font/size of the text on the slide is suitable for those at the back of the presentation room;
- Keep a proper slide style, avoiding too creative and decorative use of colors or images in the slide;
- Keep the table/graph/diagram used on slide clear and informative, meanwhile avoiding over-complicated diagrams;
- Keep your audio/video clips proportionate (if you use any) in your presentation and explain it while necessary.

Task 3

Directions: *Discuss with your partners if the following presentation slides have any problems, and identify them if they have any.*

Slide 1

> If we look at heart disease, for example, and the drugs we take to regulate or "cure" it, we can see that the number of prescriptions issued by doctors has almost quadrupled—increased by just under 400%—in the last 20 years. This includes drugs to lower blood pressure and to reduce cholesterol. So we really are becoming a nation of pill takers but—and this is the point that I want to emphasize—we are not attacking the underlying causes of heart disease. One major cause of heart disease is physical inactivity. And, in the UK, we are becoming more inactive; we are doing less physical exercise. If you have a look at the statistics on your handout, you will see that these illustrate that since the 1970s the average number of miles traveled on foot has dropped by around a quarter, just about 23%, and the number of miles traveled by bike has dropped by one-third. In other words, we are walking less, we are cycling less. By contrast, the number of miles people drive has increased by 70% over the same period of time. So, more use of the car and less physical exercise is the overall picture.

Unit 10　A Community of Shared Future for Mankind (III)

Slide 2

How to use bullet points:
- Make sure all items in the list are related to each other
- Use the same font and margin width in each bulleted point
- Keep bullet points short, preferably no more than three lines long
- Begin all items with the same part of speech and make sure they are in parallel form
- Make all bullet points approximately the same length
- Make sure the format is consistent within each list
- Emphasize the beginning of each bullet point to make the list skim-friendly
- Use periods at the end of each line only if they are complete sentences
- Use neutral bullet points if all items in a list are equal
- Indicate sequence or importance with numbers or letters

Slide 3

Roadmap

WHAT
- CM definition

HOW
- traditional method
- corpus-based method

WHAT FOR
- conceptual analysis
- semantic analysis
- experimental analysis
- cultural analysis

ELIN & MetaEmo projects

Slide 4

Aim

The aim of the study is to investigate the general opinion of first-year graduates in the Foreign Language Department in BUAA on their Academic Writing Course. Feedback of the action research will be delivered to the course instructor as well as the department, in order to help solve the problems emerging from this course.

Slide 5

Advantages for researchers:

- Lab time limited
- Finds relevant data
- More accurate results

(2) Non-verbal Language Used in Presentations

Much of our communication is non-verbal. Between verbal and non-verbal communication, it's probably the latter who speaks louder. Non-verbal language is a more natural, unconscious language that reveals our genuine feelings and intentions. By non-verbally expressing an open and positive attitude during presentations, the presenter can encourage a supportive and collaborative atmosphere between him/her and the audience. Below are different ways you can communicate non-verbally and positive indicators for each.

Face

Facial expressions not only comprise a huge aspect of non-verbal communication, but they are also the only non-verbal behavior where the meanings don't significantly vary across cultures.

Positive indicators:

- Establish eye contact with your audience but don't stare or make them uncomfortable;
- Smile often as this indicates openness, warmth, and friendliness.

Posture

Be aware of your posture and what it silently communicates.

Positive indicators:

- Avoid turning your back from the audience while presenting;
- Stand up straight but keep your body relaxed;
- Keep your arms and hands open with palms up to show trustworthiness and honesty;
- When directly speaking to someone in the audience, lean slightly forward towards him/her or tilt your head slightly towards hsi/her direction to convey interest;
- When having to move, move slowly and walk with confidence. It's one way to portray you're relaxed, focused, and calm.

Gestures

It is a highly important way of communicating, for presenters often make lots of movements and signals unconsciously. For the audience, some subtle gestures presenters unknowingly make may appear deliberate.

Positive indicators:

- Limit repetitive movements, for they can be distracting to your presentation;
- Use hand gestures to reinforce the message, and make sure the hand gestures look natural so that it can make the presenter seem more authentic and genuine;
- Be intentional with gestures or design some proper gestures to take advantage of them to communicate meaning without words, but avoid over-rehearsing gestures, for it may create a speaker who is artificial and robotic.

Paralanguage

Paralanguage refers to the non-verbal elements of speech that convey meaning and emotions, such as the tone of voice, pitch, volume, tempo, and rhythm. It includes the vocal cues and characteristics that accompany spoken language and play a significant role in communication. Paralanguage can greatly influence the interpretation of a message and the emotional impact of a conversation. It is particularly important in interpersonal communication because it can provide additional context, clarify meaning, and reveal the speaker's emotional state. Understanding paralanguage is crucial for effective communication, as it helps in interpreting messages accurately and empathetically. Here are some key components of paralanguage:

- **Tone of voice:** This refers to the emotional quality of one's voice. In a formal presentation, the presenter is supposed to speak in a friendly, calm, and firm tone.

- **Pitch:** Pitch is the highness or lowness of the voice. A rising pitch often indicates a question, while a falling pitch can signal a statement. In presentations, the pitch usually fluctuates with what the presenter intends to deliver.

- **Tempo:** The speed at which someone speaks can convey excitement (fast tempo) or relaxation (slow tempo). Tempo also fluctuates with the content of the presentation.

- **Rhythm:** The pattern and cadence of speech, including pauses and emphasis on certain words, can influence the message's meaning. In presentations, effective pausing or silence is one of the most powerful non-verbal cues that you can use to emphasize some points or motivate the audience.

- **Articulation and pronunciation:** Clear or mumbled speech, as well as proper pronunciation, can affect the audience's comprehension and impression. Non-English speakers may unavoidably speak with some accent, but make sure it is articulated fluently and clearly.

Task 4

Directions: *Read the following statements and decide whether the following behaviors are appropriate for presentations.*

1. Knowing the key to conveying friendliness is to smile, the speaker wears a smile throughout the presentation, even when he is talking about something quite serious.

2. The speaker appears serious during a neutral presentation to conform to the formality of an academic presentation.

3. The speaker tries to copy the facial expression of a well-known talk show host.

4. The speaker practices his facial expression in front of a mirror, asking himself "Do they match my words?"

5. The speaker wears a smile even before he begins.

Task 5

Directions: *Please watch a TED talk entitled "How Books Can Open Your Mind" (2013) by Lisa Bu and discuss with your partner the following questions.*

1. What do you think of the visual aids used in this talk?

2. Talk about the non-verbal language used in this talk, for example, the speaker's facial expressions, eye contact, body gestures, tone of voice, rhythm, etc.

3. What can you learn from the speaker in the presentation, including the design of major points as well as personal style in delivering the information?

3. How to Handle the Question-and-Answer Session in Presentations

(1) How to Ask Questions

The question-and-answer session is an essential part of a formal presentation, such as an academic presentation at a conference or a business talk on a formal occasion, etc. Good questions stimulate the audience intellectually and create better atmosphere for communication.

Usually the audience ask questions when they didn't understand some points in the presentations, and such questions can also enhance the comprehension of the entire audience. In more specific occasions like scientific presentations, scholars/researchers also ask questions even when they are not expecting any definite answers. Such "questions" can be an advice for the presenter, a suggestion of an alternative hypothesis, or a problem raised to the entire audience. In other words, questions and answers serve to deepen the understanding of all members of the audience and to encourage the exchange of ideas among everyone at the venue.

For many audiences, coming up with significant and innovative questions is a big challenge. A key is to be active listeners—do not simply absorb information, but continuously compare the information being presented with what you have in your brain, and try to make connections between them. Once you develop this habit, you will find that questions begin to come up automatically. More importantly, by asking questions you will gain not only the information you requested, but also the ability to think critically, and the recognition of other audience or your peers. Here is a list of advice for those who think they are not good at raising a good question.

- What is the key/central question of this presentation?

- What is the most important supporting evidence? Is the evidence relevant and strong?

- Can you think of any other ways to interpret or explain the data and experimental results if it is a scientific presentation?

- Predict what will come next—what kind of effect/changes will be triggered by the current measures/policies?

- Is the presenter's conclusion or interpretation on some key points consistent with what you know to be fact or consensus?

Questioners can first express a positive attitude towards the presenter or presentation, and then signal their intentions for the question.

To request detailed explanations for contents you didn't understand or would like to hear further explanation about.

- Thanks for your wonderful/impressive talk, Professor XXX. I don't quite understand what you mean by saying "XXX". Can you explain that point further?

- Thanks for your wonderful/impressive talk, Professor XXX. I didn't follow how you reached that conclusion. Could you elaborate on that?

- Thanks for your wonderful/impressive talk, Professor XXX. I am quite interested in xxx that you mentioned in the talk, but I am a beginner in this field. Do you have any recommendations or suggestions?

- Thanks for your wonderful/impressive talk, Professor XXX. You mentioned very briefly about xxx, can you share more personal insights/judgment on XXX?

To ask about the major points/supporting evidence/interpretations that you don't agree or even suspect.

- Thanks for your informative talk and insights on XXX. Based on my recent reading, I learned that some researchers/organizations hold a different opinion on XXX, which is... What do you think of their opinions?

- Thanks for your talk and I was particularly enlightened by your interpretations in the second part of your talk. From my perspective, the issue on XXX is far away from reaching a consensus. What can be done further in order to…?

- Thanks for your talk. You mentioned the case/experiment about XXX to support your argument. I wonder if factors like XXX weren't taken into account in your experiment/case analysis? If we take XXX into account, will there be a different conclusion?

To ask questions on future directions or less directly relevant questions to the major points.

- Thanks for the insightful talk. XXX is a hot topic currently in various fields. What would be future development of xxx according to your expert judgment?

- Thanks for the impressive talk. What I am interested in is probably not the main focus of the talk. But I am just curious about what the possible results would be if we…?

- Thanks for the wonderful talk. It reminds me of a scenario/question in a well-known book/film which is *XXX*. Do you think the proposals in your talk can be a solution to this question?

(2) How to Answer Presentation Questions

Whether the presenter can handle the questions well is extraordinarily important for the presentation itself and his/her professional career. Be it at a conference, a job seminar, or a research grant interview, the audience will scrutinize the way in which the presenter deals with questions. This is because the response to questions is a direct reflection of the person's expertise on certain topics, attitude, as well as vision. People will judge the presenter by examining how he/she handles questions. While preparing for presentations, it is important to make a habit of thinking about potential questions. Here are some tips on how to answer questions:

When you don't understand a question, confirm it. If you are not confident that you have fully grasped the question, do not hesitate to confirm it before offering an answer. It is often difficult to infer the motivation behind a question. State clearly that you didn't understand the question and ask the questioner to repeat it. When you have some ideas about what the questioner is asking, a better strategy is to rephrase/paraphrase the question in your own words and confirm it with the questioner. This is much more effective than having the questioner repeat the question in exactly the same way or in another similarly confusing rewording. It will also give the audience the impression that you are rather experienced in fielding questions. The following expressions can be used in this situation.

- I am not sure if I fully understand your question. Could you rephrase your question?

- I am afraid I didn't quite catch what you're asking. Are you asking about…?/What you would like to know is…?

When you need time to answer a question, ask for it. When you receive an unexpected question that requires some time to compose a response, give an indication that you have understood the question, but you need a moment to think about the answer, rather than respond with silence, for the audience has no idea how to interpret your silence. They may assume that you have not understood the question, and the questioner is likely to begin rewording and repeating the question. To avoid this kind of uncomfortable situation, the following expressions can be used:

- That's a really difficult/challenging question to answer. Let me think about that for a second.

- Thanks for the enlightening question. I hadn't actually thought of that point before. I'd like to investigate that point further and share with you my findings later.

When the question is very technical or detailed, offer the audience some background or communicate with the questioner after the presentation. During the question-and-answer session, someone in a field closely related to the presenter may raise a very specific or technical question that is unfamiliar to most of the audience. What is likely to follow is an intense dialog between the questioner and the presenter, leaving the rest of the audience in the dark. While such a discussion is a part of the objective of giving a presentation, you must remember that the Q&A is for the entire audience, and you are supposed to respond in a way that everyone can benefit from your answer. If you receive a very technical question that is unlikely to be understood by most of the audience, restate the question in simpler terms and add background information to aid the audience's comprehension. Your expressions can be like this:

- That's an important and technical question. Before sharing my opinions, I'd like to mention some background information about XXX, and then I will talk about my understanding from the perspective of XXX.

- Glad to see your interest in XXX. The question is very technical and deserves a very detailed answer. Would it be OK to discuss this with you after the presentation?

If you have any additional information to support your claim, provide it. Some questions are intended to challenge the conclusions and interpretations proposed by the presenter. Pointing out logical gaps or suggesting alternative interpretations falls into this category. Such questions may sound aggressive, but the aggressiveness mostly is not directed to the presenter but to the content of the presentation. The point is that the questioner intends to know how concrete the new result or idea that the presenter has delivered is. In such a case, the presenter doesn't have to limit the answer to the point that has been asked directly by the questioner, and any additional results that support the claim can be a valid response to the question. This can include the presenter's own preliminary results, results of related work by others, or loosely related information. The following are expressions that can be used to introduce the supportive information:

- The idea/claim is highly personal, but it is also supported by an extra dataset which wasn't presented in this talk for the sake of…

- We actually did another survey/experiment to…, and the preliminary results shows that…

- There is another piece of evidence from recent research made by XXX, which shows similar conclusions/results.

Task 6

Directions: Watch a TED video entitled "How Great Leaders Inspire Action" and think about what questions you would like to put forward.

Part III Notes from China

Nishan Forum on World Civilizations[1]

The Nishan forum, which focuses on dialog among different civilizations, has increasingly become an important platform for promoting traditional Chinese culture, promoting common values for mankind, and strengthening international cultural exchanges and cooperation since its inception in 2010. The broadening scope of discussions in Nishan—from academia to international politics, culture and traditional Chinese medicine—underlines an urgent need for shared global values vital for addressing multifaceted global challenges.

The Ninth Nishan Forum on World Civilizations was held in the hometown of Confucius at Nishan Mountain in Qufu, Shandong Province from September 26 to 28, 2023, bringing together more than 1,600 participants of politicians, representatives from international organizations, diplomats, experts, and scholars, including over 330 foreign guests. Under the theme of "Common Values for Mankind and a Community with a Shared Future for Mankind—Strengthening Exchanges and Mutual Learning Among

---

1 The text was adapted from the CGTN and Xinhua news websites.

Civilizations to Jointly Address Global Challenges", the forum featured a number of activities, including a main forum, high-level dialogs, keynote speeches, etc.

Addressing the opening ceremony of the event, Shohrat Zakir, vice Chairman of the Standing Committee of the 14th National People's Congress, said that the Global Civilization Initiative is a significant guideline for the development and progress of human civilizations, injecting a powerful impetus into the modernization process of human society. He stressed the importance of respecting the diversity of human civilizations, actively upholding its progressiveness, promoting its inclusiveness, and vigorously advocating for the common values of humanity to build a global community of shared future and create a better world.

International Olympic Committee (IOC) president Thomas Bach said the Nishan Forum shares the same objective with the Olympics, which is deepening the understanding among the civilizations of the world through respectful dialog and exchange.

To forge a better understanding of the world and truly workable common values is a long and rocky road, Jeffrey D. Sachs, president of the United Nations Sustainable Development Solutions Network, said at the forum. "It will have to come through collective interaction over many years of discussion, debate, encounter and realization of our commonality as human beings and our common interests on the planet," he said, adding he believes that ancient wisdom can play a tremendously important role in enabling us to find common values for the 21st century.

Participants agreed that the diversity of civilizations is the source of human progress. Civilizations keep flourishing through exchanges and mutual learning. In a world where countries are increasingly interdependent and share weal and woe, respecting diversity is key to cooperation and obtaining win-win outcomes.

(420 words)

Directions: Read the passage above and finish the following assignments.

1. How much do you know about Confucius and Confucianism? Please focus on one particular point (for example, the notion of harmony) about Confucius or Confucianism and tell one story about it.

2. Please make an investigation on the mutual cultural influence between China and another country or region in the current world. You are suggested to choose specific culture areas as your targets, such as Chinese tea culture in America vs. American sports culture in China.

Glossary

A

abate	/əˈbeɪt/	v.	减弱，减轻
abatement	/əˈbeɪtmənt/	n.	减少；减轻；减弱
accelerate	/əkˈseləreɪt/	v.	加速；（使）加速；加快
accessible	/əkˈsesəbl/	adj.	可使用的；可接近的；可到达的
accolade	/ˈækəleɪd/	n.	荣誉
accountability	/əˌkaʊntəˈbɪləti/	n.	责任，责任心
accurate	/ˈækjərət/	adj.	精确的，准确的
administration	/ədˌmɪnɪˈstreɪʃn/	n.	行政；政府；行政部门；管理部门
advisory	/ədˈvaɪzəri/	adj.	咨询的；顾问的
advocacy	/ˈædvəkəsi/	n.	拥护，提倡
advocate	/ˈædvəkeɪt/	n.	拥护者，提倡者
affiliation	/əˌfɪliˈeɪʃn/	n.	紧密联系；官方联系
afforestation	/əˌfɒrɪˈsteɪʃn/	n.	植树造林
agenda	/əˈdʒendə/	n.	议题，议事日程
agglomeration	/əˌɡlɒməˈreɪʃn/	n.	集聚
aggregate	/ˈæɡrɪɡət/	adj.	总计的，合计的
agro-product	/ˈæɡrəʊ ˈprɒdʌkt/	n.	农产品
align	/əˈlaɪn/	v.	使一致
allocation	/ˌæləˈkeɪʃn/	n.	分配
allowance	/əˈlaʊəns/	n.	（定期发给的）津贴，补助
amass	/əˈmæs/	v.	（尤指一段时间内大量）积累，积聚
ambulatory	/ˈæmbjələtəri/	adj.	非固定的，可移动的
amplify	/ˈæmplɪfaɪ/	v.	放大；增强
anecdotal	/ˌænɪkˈdəʊtl/	adj.	轶事的，传闻的
annually	/ˈænjuəli/	adv.	一年一次地
approximately	/əˈprɒksɪmətli/	adv.	大约，近似
arbitrary	/ˈɑːbɪtrəri/	adj.	任意的；武断的；随心所欲的
archaeology	/ˌɑːkiˈɒlədʒi/	n.	考古学
array	/əˈreɪ/	n.	一长列（物品）

articulate	/ɑːˈtɪkjələt/	adj.	善于表达的
associated	/əˈsəʊʃieɪtɪd/	adj.	有关联的，相关的
astroturfing	/ˈæstrəʊˌtɜːfɪŋ/	n.	营销操控
at stake			有风险；处于危急关头
atrocious	/əˈtrəʊʃəs/	adj.	极坏的；残暴的
autonomous	/ɔːˈtɒnəməs/	adj.	自治的，自主的
avenue	/ˈævənjuː/	n.	选择；途径；手段

B

bibliographic	/ˌbɪbliəˈɡræfɪk/	adj.	目录的
bilateral	/ˌbaɪˈlætərəl/	adj.	双边的
biodiversity	/ˌbaɪəʊdaɪˈvɜːsəti/	n.	生物多样性
biosecurity	/ˌbaɪəʊsɪˈkjʊərəti/	n.	生物安全性
blueprint	/ˈbluːprɪnt/	n.	计划蓝图；行动方案
boost	/buːst/	v.	推动，使增长
broadband	/ˈbrɔːdbænd/	n.	宽带
Buddhism	/ˈbʊdɪzəm/	n.	佛教
budgetary	/ˈbʌdʒɪtəri/	adj.	预算的

C

campaign	/kæmˈpeɪn/	n.	运动，活动
capacity	/kəˈpæsəti/	n.	能力；生产量；生产能力
capitalize	/ˈkæpɪtəlaɪz/	v.	利用
cargo	/ˈkɑːɡəʊ/	n.	货物
catalyze	/ˈkætəlaɪz/	v.	催化；使起催化作用
catastrophic	/ˌkætəˈstrɒfɪk/	adj.	灾难性的
ceramic	/səˈræmɪk/	n.	陶瓷制品，陶瓷器；制陶艺术
certificate	/səˈtɪfɪkət/	n.	证明书；结业证书
chinoiserie	/ʃinˈwɑːzəri/	n.	中式风格艺术
citizenship	/ˈsɪtɪzənʃɪp/	n.	公民身份，国籍
closure	/ˈkləʊʒə(r)/	n.	结尾
coercion	/kəʊˈɜːʃn/	n.	强迫，逼迫

cohort	/ˈkəʊhɔːt/	n.	（有共同特点的）一群人，一批人
collaborate	/kəˈlæbəreɪt/	v.	合作，协作
collaboration	/kəˌlæbəˈreɪʃn/	n.	合作
collective	/kəˈlektɪv/	adj.	集体的，共同的
collision	/kəˈlɪʒn/	n.	碰撞，相撞
committed	/kəˈmɪtɪd/	adj.	尽心尽力的；坚信的；坚定的
committee	/kəˈmɪti/	n.	委员会
commons	/ˈkɒmənz/	n.	共享资源
community	/kəˈmjuːnəti/	n.	社区；社会；团体
competent	/ˈkɒmpɪtənt/	adj.	能胜任的
compromise	/ˈkɒmprəmaɪz/	v.	妥协，折中，和解
concerted	/kənˈsɜːtɪd/	adj.	一致的
conducive	/kənˈdjuːsɪv/	adj.	有助于；便于
confine	/kənˈfaɪn/	v.	把……局限在，限制
conflict	/ˈkɑːnflɪkt/	n.	冲突，争论
conformity	/kənˈfɔːməti/	n.	一致性；（对社会规则的）遵守
confrontation	/ˌkɒnfrʌnˈteɪʃn/	n.	对抗；对峙；冲突
Confucianism	/kənˈfjuːʃənɪzəm/	n.	孔子学说；儒学，儒教
connectivity	/ˌkɒnekˈtɪvɪti/	n.	互联互通
connotation	/ˌkɒnəˈteɪʃn/	n.	内涵意义，隐含意义，联想意义
consensus	/kənˈsensəs/	n.	共识；一致的意见
consortium	/kənˈsɔːtiəm/	n.	联盟
constellation	/ˌkɒnstəˈleɪʃn/	n.	一系列（相关的想法、事物）
consultative	/kənˈsʌltətɪv/	adj.	咨询的，顾问的
consume	/kənˈsjuːm/	v.	吃，喝
contributor	/kənˈtrɪbjətə(r)/	n.	做出贡献者
conversion	/kənˈvɜːʃn/	n.	转换，转化
coordinate	/kəʊˈɔːdɪneɪt/	v.	使协调，使调和
coordination	/kəʊˌɔːdɪˈneɪʃn/	n.	协作；协调；配合
corridor	/ˈkɒrɪdɔː(r)/	n.	走廊
cost-effective	/ˌkɒstɪˈfektɪv/	adj.	成本效益好的
council	/ˈkaʊnsl/	n.	委员会，理事会，顾问委员会
coverage	/ˈkʌvərɪdʒ/	n.	覆盖

culminate	/ˈkʌlmɪneɪt/	v.	以……告终；结果成为
culvert	/ˈkʌlvət/	n.	涵洞
cumulative	/ˈkjuːmjələtɪv/	adj.	累积的
cybersecurity	/ˌsaɪbəsɪˈkjʊərəti/	n.	网络（空间）安全

D

decarbonization	/ˌdiːkɑːbənaɪˈzeɪʃn/	n.	脱碳（作用）
deem	/diːm/	v.	认为；相信
defamation	/ˌdefəˈmeɪʃn/	n.	诽谤，中伤
demographic	/ˌdeməˈɡræfɪk/	adj.	人口的，人口统计的
deploy	/dɪˈplɔɪ/	v.	部署，调动
derailment	/dɪˈreɪlmənt/	n.	脱轨
deregulation	/ˌdiːˌreɡjuˈleɪʃn/	n.	撤销管制，解除控制
designate	/ˈdezɪɡneɪt/	v.	指定，指派
designation	/ˌdezɪɡˈneɪʃn/	n.	名称；头衔
determinant	/dɪˈtɜːmɪnənt/	n.	决定因素；决定条件
detriment	/ˈdetrɪmənt/	n.	伤害；损害；造成伤害的事物
dialect	/ˈdaɪəlekt/	n.	方言，土语，地方话
diplomacy	/dɪˈpləʊməsi/	n.	外交；外交手段
discipline	/ˈdɪsəplɪn/	n.	（尤指大学的）学科，科目
discredit	/dɪsˈkredɪt/	v.	使丧失信誉，败坏名誉
discriminate	/dɪˈskrɪmɪneɪt/	v.	歧视
disparity	/dɪˈspærəti/	n.	明显差异
disposition	/ˌdɪspəˈzɪʃn/	n.	性情
disrepair	/ˌdɪsrɪˈpeə(r)/	n.	破败；破损
disruption	/dɪsˈrʌpʃn/	n.	中断；扰乱；混乱
dissertation	/ˌdɪsəˈteɪʃn/	n.	专题论文;（尤指）学位论文
domain	/dəˈmeɪn/	n.	（知识、活动的）领域，范围，范畴
dominant	/ˈdɒmɪnənt/	adj.	占支配地位的
dovetail	/ˈdʌvteɪl/	v.	吻合，切合
dox	/dɒks/	v.	公布（某人）的个人信息
dropout	/ˈdrɒpaʊt/	n.	辍学者，退学者

dual	/ˈdjuːəl/	adj.	双重的
Dunhuang Grottos			敦煌石窟
dynamic	/daɪˈnæmɪk/	adj.	充满活力的；发展变化的
dynamics	/daɪˈnæmɪks/	n.	动力学，动力

E

e-commerce	/ˌiːˈkɒmɜːs/	n.	电子商务
economy	/ɪˈkɒnəmi/	n.	经济体
elaborate	/iˈlæbərət/	v.	详尽阐述；详细描述
eligible	/ˈelɪdʒəbl/	adj.	符合条件的；合适的
elimination	/ɪˌlɪmɪˈneɪʃn/	n.	排除，根除
elucidate	/iˈluːsɪdeɪt/	v.	阐明；解释；说明
emanate	/ˈeməneɪt/	v.	发源于；从……发出
embankment	/ɪmˈbæŋkmənt/	n.	路堤
emblematic	/ˌembləˈmætɪk/	adj.	象征的；可当标志的
embodiment	/ɪmˈbɒdimənt/	n.	体现
empower	/ɪmˈpaʊə(r)/	v.	使能够
empowerment	/ɪmˈpaʊəmənt/	n.	授权，赋权
encompass	/ɪnˈkʌmpəs/	v.	包含，包括
Enlightenment	/ɪnˈlaɪtnmənt/	n.	（18世纪欧洲的）启蒙运动
entail	/ɪnˈteɪl/	v.	牵连；导致
enterprise	/ˈentəpraɪz/	n.	企业；公司
entity	/ˈentəti/	n.	实体
entrepreneur	/ˌɒntrəprəˈnɜː(r)/	n.	企业家
entrepreneurial	/ˌɒntrəprəˈnɜːriəl/	adj.	具有企业家素质的
envoy	/ˈenvɔɪ/	n.	特使，使节
epidemic	/ˌepɪˈdemɪk/	n.	（疾病的）流行
equitable	/ˈekwɪtəbl/	adj.	公正的，合理的
equity	/ˈekwəti/	n.	公平，公正
equivalent	/ɪˈkwɪvələnt/	adj.	相同的；相等的
eradicate	/ɪˈrædɪkeɪt/	v.	根除，消灭
eradication	/ɪˌrædɪˈkeɪʃn/	n.	根除

escalate	/ˈeskəleɪt/	v.	加剧，逐步升级
essential	/ɪˈsenʃl/	adj.	基本的；重要的
estrangement	/ɪˈstreɪndʒmənt/	n.	疏远；分离
ethnic	/ˈeθnɪk/	adj.	民族的，种族的
ethnographic	/eθnəˈɡræfɪk/	adj.	人种志的，人种论的；人种志著作的
eventually	/ɪˈventʃuəli/	adv.	终于；最终
exacerbate	/ɪɡˈzæsəbeɪt/	v.	恶化，加剧
exclusive	/ɪkˈskluːsɪv/	adj.	专用的，专有的；独占的
expertise	/ˌekspɜːˈtiːz/	n.	专业知识；专门技能
extension	/ɪkˈstenʃn/	n.	延伸，延展
extensive	/ɪkˈstensɪv/	adj.	广泛的

F

facilitate	/fəˈsɪlɪteɪt/	v.	促进；使便利；促使
faculty	/ˈfæklti/	n.	全体教员；（高等院校的）系，院
feasible	/ˈfiːzəbl/	adj.	可行的
flagship	/ˈflæɡʃɪp/	n.	旗舰
flexibility	/ˌfleksəˈbɪləti/	n.	灵活性，弹性，适应性
flourish	/ˈflʌrɪʃ/	v.	繁荣；兴旺
forge	/fɔːdʒ/	v.	锻造
forum	/ˈfɔːrəm/	n.	论坛，讨论会
fragility	/fræˈdʒɪləti/	n.	脆弱
fragmentation	/ˌfræɡmenˈteɪʃn/	n.	破碎；分裂
fundamental	/ˌfʌndəˈmentl/	adj.	基本的，根本的

G

galvanize	/ˈɡælvənaɪz/	v.	使振奋，激励
gauge	/ɡeɪdʒ/	n.	（铁道的）轨距
gender-inclusive	/ˈdʒendər ɪnˈkluːsɪv/	adj.	性别包容的
generate	/ˈdʒenəreɪt/	v.	产生，引起
good	/ɡʊd/	n.	用处；好处，益处

governance	/ˈɡʌvənəns/	n.	管理方式
grassroots	/ˈɡrɑːsruːts/	n.	基层；草根
groundwork	/ˈɡraʊndwɜːk/	n.	基础

H

hallmark	/ˈhɔːlmɑːk/	n.	标志；特征
halve	/hɑːv/	v.	把……减半
hamper	/ˈhæmpə(r)/	v.	妨碍；阻止；阻碍
harassment	/ˈhærəsmənt/	n.	骚扰，侵扰
harness	/ˈhɑːnɪs/	n.	控制
headcount	/ˈhedkaʊnt/	n.	人数统计
herdsman	/ˈhɜːdzmən/	n.	牧人
hinterland	/ˈhɪntəlænd/	n.	内陆
holistic	/həʊˈlɪstɪk/	adj.	整体的；全面的
hospitality	/ˌhɒspɪˈtæləti/	n.	殷勤款待，好客
humanitarian	/hjuːˌmænɪˈteəriən/	adj.	人道主义的；博爱的
hydrological	/ˌhaɪdrəˈlɒdʒɪkəl/	adj.	水文学的

I

ideology	/ˌaɪdiˈɒlədʒi/	n.	思想（体系）；思想意识
illicit	/ɪˈlɪsɪt/	adj.	非法的
illustrative	/ˈɪləstrətɪv/	adj.	说明性的；解说性的
immense	/ɪˈmens/	adj.	广大的，巨大的
immerse	/ɪˈmɜːs/	v.	使专心于
immersive	/ɪˈmɜːsɪv/	adj.	拟真的；沉浸式的
imperative	/ɪmˈperətɪv/	adj.	命令式的，强制式的
imperative	/ɪmˈperətɪv/	n.	重要紧急的事
impersonation	/ɪmˌpɜːsəˈneɪʃn/	n.	冒充，伪装
impetus	/ˈɪmpɪtəs/	n.	动力，促进
implementation	/ˌɪmplɪmenˈteɪʃn/	n.	实施；执行；完成；贯彻
implication	/ˌɪmplɪˈkeɪʃn/	n.	可能的影响（或作用、结果）
import	/ˈɪmpɔːt/	n.	输入，引进

impoverish	/ɪmˈpɒvərɪʃ/	v.	使贫困
incentive	/ɪnˈsentɪv/	n.	激励，刺激
inception	/ɪnˈsepʃn/	n.	（机构、组织等的）开端，创始
inclusion	/ɪnˈkluːʒn/	n.	包含；被包括的人（或事物）
inclusive	/ɪnˈkluːsɪv/	adj.	兼收并蓄的
inclusiveness	/ɪnˈkluːsɪvnəs/	n.	包容性，兼容并蓄
incorporate	/ɪnˈkɔːpəreɪt/	v.	包含，合并
incremental	/ˌɪŋkrəˈmentl/	adj.	增加的，递增的
indiscriminate	/ˌɪndɪˈskrɪmɪnət/	adj.	任意而为的
indivisible	/ˌɪndɪˈvɪzəbl/	adj.	不可分的
inevitablely	/ɪnˈevɪtəbli/	adv.	必然发生地
infrastructure	/ˈɪnfrəstrʌktʃə(r)/	n.	基础设施，基础建设
inhospitable	/ˌɪnhɒˈspɪtəbl/	adj.	不适宜居住的
initiative	/ɪˈnɪʃətɪv/	n.	倡议
innovation	/ˌɪnəˈveɪʃn/	n.	创新；改革
inscribed	/ɪnˈskraɪbd/	adj.	记名的
inscription	/ɪnˈskrɪpʃn/	n.	（石头或金属上）刻写的文字，碑文
installation	/ˌɪnstəˈleɪʃn/	n.	安装；设置
instill	/ɪnˈstɪl/	v.	逐渐灌输
integrated	/ˈɪntɪɡreɪtɪd/	adj.	融合的，各部分密切协调的
integration	/ˌɪntɪˈɡreɪʃn/	n.	整合；一体化；融合
intensify	/ɪnˈtensɪfaɪ/	v.	（使）增强，加剧；强化
inter-civilization	/ˌɪntərˌsɪvəˌlaɪˈzeɪʃn/	n.	文明之间，跨文明
interconnect	/ˌɪntəkəˈnekt/	v.	相联系；相互连接
interference	/ˌɪntəˈfɪərəns/	n.	干涉；干预；介入
intermediary	/ˌɪntəˈmiːdiəri/	n.	中间人，调解人
internalize	/ɪnˈtɜːnəlaɪz/	v.	使……内在化
interoperability	/ˌɪntərɒpərəˈbɪləti/	n.	互操作性；互用性
intervention	/ˌɪntəˈvenʃn/	n.	干涉

J

jurisdiction	/ˌdʒʊərɪsˈdɪkʃn/	n.	司法权；审判权；管辖权

| justice | /ˈdʒʌstɪs/ | n. | 正义，公正 |

L

lacquer	/ˈlækə(r)/	n.	漆
landmass	/ˈlændmæs/	n.	大陆，陆块，地块
legislation	/ˌledʒɪsˈleɪʃn/	n.	法律；立法
legislative	/ˈledʒɪslətɪv/	adj.	立法的
legitimate	/lɪˈdʒɪtɪmət/	adj.	合法的；法律认可的；法定的
leverage	/ˈliːvərɪdʒ/	v.	充分利用
liberalization	/ˌlɪbrəlaɪˈzeɪʃn/	n.	自由主义化；自由化
likewise	/ˈlaɪkwaɪz/	adv.	同样地
linkage	/ˈlɪŋkɪdʒ/	n.	联系
literacy	/ˈlɪtərəsi/	n.	读写能力
literature	/ˈlɪtrətʃə(r)/	n.	文献
lockdown	/ˈlɒkdaʊn/	n.	封锁，禁闭
locomotive	/ˌləʊkəˈməʊtɪv/	n.	机车；火车头
logistical	/ləˈdʒɪstɪkl/	adj.	物流的；后勤的；组织管理的
logistics	/ləˈdʒɪstɪks/	n.	物流
looting	/ˈluːtɪŋ/	n.	（暴力事件中发生的）抢劫，洗劫

M

macro-objective	/ˈmækrəʊˌəbˈdʒektɪv/	n.	宏观目标
mainstream	/ˈmeɪnstriːm/	v.	使主流化，使成为主流
malaria	/məˈleəriə/	n.	疟疾
Manchu	/mænˈtʃu/	n./adj.	满族人；满族的；满族语的
mandate	/ˈmændeɪt/	n.	授权；强制执行；委托办理
mangrove	/ˈmæŋɡrəʊv/	n.	红树林
mechanism	/ˈmekənɪzəm/	n.	机制；方法
mediate	/ˈmiːdieɪt/	v.	调解
mediation	/ˌmiːdiˈeɪʃn/	n.	调解；仲裁
medicinal	/məˈdɪsɪnl/	adj.	药用的
mentor	/ˈmentɔː(r)/	n.	导师

mentorship	/ˈmentɔːʃɪp/	n.	导师制；指导关系
merit	/ˈmerɪt/	v.	值得（表扬、关注等）
migrate	/maɪˈgreɪt/	v.	迁徙
migration	/maɪˈgreɪʃn/	n.	移民，迁徙
minimum	/ˈmɪnɪməm/	n.	最小量；最低限度
ministerial	/ˌmɪnɪˈstɪəriəl/	adj.	部长的；大臣的
minor	/ˈmaɪnə(r)/	n.	辅修课程
minoritize	/maɪˈnɒrɪtaɪz/	v.	成为少数派，使成为少数派
minority	/maɪˈnɒrəti/	n.	少数
misinformation	/ˌmɪsɪnfərˈmeɪʃn/	n.	提供虚假信息
misogynistic	/mɪsɒdʒɪˈnɪstɪk/	adj.	厌恶女性的，憎恨女性的
mission	/ˈmɪʃn/	n.	使命；任务
missionary	/ˈmɪʃənri/	n.	传教士
mitigate	/ˈmɪtɪgeɪt/	v.	减轻；缓和
moistened	/ˈmɔɪstənd/	adj.	弄湿的
momentum	/məˈmentəm/	n.	势头；冲劲；动力
multidimensional	/ˌmʌltɪdaɪˈmenʃənl/	adj.	多维的；多面的
multilateral	/ˌmʌltiˈlætərl/	adj.	多边的；多国的
multilateralism	/ˌmʌltiˈlætərəlɪzəm/	n.	多边主义
multiple	/ˈmʌltɪpl/	adj.	多个；多重的
muted	/ˈmjuːtɪd/	adj.	（声音）压低的，减弱的

N

normative	/ˈnɔːmətɪv/	adj.	规范的，标准的
notoriety	/ˌnəʊtəˈraɪəti/	n.	知名度
nutrition	/njuˈtrɪʃn/	n.	营养；滋养

O

obscure	/əbˈskjʊə(r)/	adj.	无名的；鲜为人知的
omission	/əˈmɪʃn/	n.	疏忽
Oriental	/ˌɔːriˈentl/	adj.	东方的；东方人的
outpatient	/ˈaʊtpeɪʃnt/	n.	门诊病人

outreach	/ˈaʊtriːtʃ/	n.	伸出，展开；能达到的范围
overlap	/ˌəʊvəˈlæp/	v.	重叠，与……重合
overwhelming	/ˌəʊvəˈwelmɪŋ/	adj.	数量巨大的；压倒性的

P

parameter	/pəˈræmɪtə(r)/	n.	界限；范围；参数
paramount	/ˈpærəmaʊnt/	adj.	首要的，至为重要的；至高无上的
participatory	/pɑːˌtɪsɪˈpeɪtəri/	adj.	参与的
partisan	/ˌpɑːtɪˈzæn/	adj.	盲目拥护的
partnership	/ˈpɑːtnəʃɪp/	n.	伙伴；合伙公司
peak	/piːk/	v.	达到高峰，达到最大值
pension	/ˈpenʃn/	n.	养老金，退休金
perceive	/pəˈsiːv/	v.	感知；认为
perpetrator	/ˈpɜːpətreɪtə(r)/	n.	犯罪者，行凶者
perpetuate	/pəˈpetʃueɪt/	v.	使永存，使持续存在
persistent	/pəˈsɪstənt/	adj.	持续的；固执的
pillar	/ˈpɪlə(r)/	n.	支柱；核心，基础
pluralistic	/ˌplʊərəˈlɪstɪk/	adj.	多元的
pool	/puːl/	v.	集中（资源、钱财等）以备共用
populous	/ˈpɒpjələs/	adj.	人口众多的，人口稠密的
porcelain	/ˈpɔːsəlɪn/	n.	瓷；瓷器
preeminent	/priˈemɪnənt/	adj.	卓越的；优秀的
prefecture	/ˈpriːfektʃə(r)/	n.	辖区，省，县
preferential	/ˌprefəˈrenʃl/	adj.	优惠的，优待的
prerequisite	/ˌpriːˈrekwəzɪt/	n.	先决条件，前提
prioritize	/praɪˈɒrɪtaɪz/	v.	优先处理
priority	/praɪˈɒrəti/	n.	优先事项，首要事情
proactively	/ˌprəʊˈæktɪvli/	adv.	主动地
problematic	/ˌprɒbləˈmætɪk/	adj.	成问题的
proclamation	/ˌprɒkləˈmeɪʃn/	n.	宣言；公告；声明
proficiency	/prəˈfɪʃnsi/	n.	水平
profound	/prəˈfaʊnd/	adj.	深刻的；极大的

progressively	/prəˈgresɪvli/	adv.	逐步地
propagation	/ˌprɒpəˈgeɪʃn/	n.	（观点、理论等的）传播
prosperity	/prɒˈsperəti/	n.	繁荣；成功；兴旺；昌盛
protocol	/ˈprəʊtəkɒl/	n.	国际议定书；协议
provision	/prəˈvɪʒn/	n.	规定
proximity	/prɒkˈsɪməti/	n.	接近，靠近
punctuate	/ˈpʌŋktʃueɪt/	v.	强调
pursuant	/pəˈsjuːənt/	adj./adv.	依照（的），按照（尤指规则或法律）（的）

R

radical	/ˈrædɪkl/	adj.	重大的；彻底的
ranger	/ˈreɪndʒə(r)/	n.	护林员
ransacking	/ˈrænsæk/	n.	洗劫，劫掠
rationalize	/ˈræʃnəlaɪz/	v.	合理化；进行合理化改革
rebate	/ˈriːbeɪt/	n.	退还款
referral	/rɪˈfɜːrəl/	n.	移交，送交
refreshing	/rɪˈfreʃɪŋ/	adj.	使人精神振作的
relief	/rɪˈliːf/	n.	救济；解救，解围
relocate	/ˌriːləʊˈkeɪt/	v.	搬迁，重新安置
remedy	/ˈremədi/	n.	解决方法；治疗方法
remuneration	/rɪˌmjuːnəˈreɪʃn/	n.	报酬
reorient	/ˌriːˈɔːrient/	v.	重定，再调整
repertoire	/ˈrepətwɑː(r)/	n.	全部剧目，全部曲目
reposition	/ˌriːpəˈzɪʃn/	n.	使复位
repository	/rɪˈpɒzətri/	n.	仓库；存放处；贮藏室；智囊
representative	/ˌreprɪˈzentətɪv/	n.	典型人物；代表他人者
reserve	/rɪˈzɜːv/	n.	保护区
resettlement	/ˌriːˈsetlmənt/	n.	重新定居，移居，重新安置
resilience	/rɪˈzɪliəns/	n.	恢复力，复原力
resiliency	/rɪˈzɪliənsi/	n.	弹性；跳回
responsiveness	/rɪˈspɒnsɪvnəs/	n.	响应性；响应度
restitution	/ˌrestɪˈtjuːʃn/	n.	归还

restoration	/ˌrestəˈreɪʃn/	n.	恢复，修复
revitalization	/riːˌvaɪtəˈlaɪzeɪʃn/	n.	复兴，振兴
revival	/rɪˈvaɪvl/	n.	复兴；再流行
rigorous	/ˈrɪgərəs/	adj.	严格的
robust	/rəʊˈbʌst/	adj.	强劲的；富有活力的

S

sanction	/ˈsæŋkʃn/	n.	制裁；惩罚
sanitation	/ˌsænɪˈteɪʃn/	n.	卫生；卫生设施体系
scrap	/skræp/	v.	放弃，抛弃（计划、体系）
secretariat	/ˌsekrəˈteəriət/	n.	（大型国际组织、政治组织的）秘书处，书记处
sectoral	/ˈsektərl/	adj.	不同行业的；某一经济部门的
sedentary	/ˈsedntri/	adj.	需要久坐的
sensibility	/ˌsensəˈbɪləti/	n.	鉴赏力，感受能力
sensitize	/ˈsensɪtaɪz/	v.	使敏感；使有知觉
serene	/səˈriːn/	adj.	平静的；宁静的
sewage	/ˈsuːɪdʒ/	n.	（下水道的）污水
signify	/ˈsɪgnɪfaɪ/	v.	表示；意味着
simultaneous	/ˌsɪmlˈteɪniəs/	adj.	同时的
simultaneously	/ˌsɪmlˈteɪniəsli/	adv.	同时；联立
Sinology	/saɪˈnɒlədʒi/	n.	汉学
Sinophile	/ˈsaɪnəˌfaɪl/	adj.	喜爱中国的，亲华的
slash	/slæʃ/	v.	大幅降低
sophisticated	/səˈfɪstɪkeɪtɪd/	adj.	复杂巧妙的；先进的，精密的
sovereignty	/ˈsɒvrənti/	n.	主权
specialty	/ˈspeʃəlti/	n.	特色食品，特产
spectrum	/ˈspektrəm/	n.	（看法、感觉等的）范围，各层次
spillover	/ˈspɪləʊvə(r)/	n.	溢出
spur	/spɜː(r)/	v.	刺激；促进，加速
stakeholder	/ˈsteɪkhəʊldə(r)/	n.	股东；利益相关者
stalk	/stɔːk/	v.	跟踪；悄悄接近
steering	/ˈstɪərɪŋ/	adj.	操控的；控制的

stewardess	/ˌstjuːə'des/	n.	女乘务员
stipulate	/'stɪpjuleɪt/	v.	规定；明确要求
stoke	/stəʊk/	v.	煽动；激起
stretch	/stretʃ/	v.	延续
stride	/straɪd/	n.	大步，阔步；步伐
stringent	/'strɪndʒənt/	adj.	严格的
subsequently	/'sʌbsɪkwəntli/	adv.	随后，后来，之后；接着
subsidy	/'sʌbsədi/	n.	补贴；津贴
subsistence	/səb'sɪstəns/	n.	生存，存活
substantial	/səb'stænʃl/	adj.	大量的
suffragist	/'sʌfrədʒɪst/	n.	妇女政权论者
superintendent	/ˌsuːpərɪn'tendənt/	n.	主管，负责人
supremacy	/suː'preməsi/	n.	至高无上；最大权力；最高地位
sustainability	/səˌsteɪnə'bɪləti/	n.	耐久性，可持续性
sustainable	/sə'steɪnəbl/	adj.	可持续的
swamp	/swɒmp/	n.	沼泽
synergy	/'sɪnədʒi/	n.	协同作用

T

tackle	/'tækl/	v.	处理，解决
tailor	/'teɪlə(r)/	v.	定做；定制；使适应
Taoism	/'daʊɪzəm/	n.	道家
targeted	/'tɑːgɪtɪd/	adj.	精准的
Tartar	/'tɑːtə(r)/	n./adj.	鞑靼人；鞑靼（人）的
temporarily	/'temprərɪli/	adv.	暂时地
therapeutics	/ˌθerə'pjuːtɪks/	n.	治疗学
thesis	/'θiːsɪs/	n.	论文；论题，命题；论点
thoroughfare	/'θʌrəfeə(r)/	n.	要道
threshold	/'θreʃhəʊld/	n.	界限，阈；门槛；开端
thrive	/θraɪv/	v.	繁荣；蓬勃发展
traffick	/'træfɪk/	v.	贩卖，交易
trafficking	/'træfɪkɪŋ/	n.	非法交易

transaction	/træn'zækʃn/	n.	交易；处理；业务；买卖
transcend	/træn'send/	v.	超越，超过
transfer	/træns'fɜː(r)/	v.	转移
transformation	/ˌtrænsfə'meɪʃn/	n.	（彻底的）变化，转变
transition	/træn'zɪʃn/	n.	过渡；转变；变革；变迁
transparency	/træns'pærənsi/	n.	透明性
transparent	/træns'pærənt/	adj.	透明的；显而易见的
trauma	/'trɔːmə/	n.	精神创伤，心理创伤
traverse	/trə'vɜːs/	v.	穿过
trinity	/'trɪnəti/	n.	三位一体
troll	/trɒl/	v.	（在网络上）留下恶意信息

U

ultimate	/'ʌltɪmət/	adj.	最终的，终极的
undermine	/ˌʌndə'maɪn/	v.	逐渐削弱
underpass	/'ʌndəpɑːs/	n.	地下通道
undertake	/ˌʌndə'teɪk/	v.	从事；承担
unevenly	/ʌn'iːvnli/	adv.	不均衡地
unilateralism	/ˌjuːnɪ'lætrəlɪzəm/	n.	单边主义
uninhabitable	/ˌʌnɪn'hæbɪtəbl/	adj.	不适合居住的
universal	/ˌjuːnɪ'vɜːsl/	adj.	全体的，普遍的
unleash	/ʌn'liːʃ/	v.	发泄；突然释放；使爆发
unparalleled	/ʌn'pærəleld/	adj.	无与伦比的；空前的
unprecedented	/ʌn'presɪdentɪd/	adj.	前所未有的
unveil	/ˌʌn'veɪl/	v.	为……揭幕；推出
usher	/'ʌʃə(r)/	v.	开创；开始；开启

V

vaccine	/'væksiːn/	n.	疫苗
variation	/ˌveəri'eɪʃn/	n.	变化，变动
verify	/'verɪfaɪ/	v.	核实，查清
vernacular	/və'nækjələ(r)/	n.	本地话，方言；白话

vestige	/ˈvestɪdʒ/	n.	残留部分；遗迹
viaduct	/ˈvaɪədʌkt/	n.	高架桥
vocational	/vəʊˈkeɪʃənl/	adj.	职业的
vulnerable	/ˈvʌlnərəbl/	adj.	脆弱的，易受伤害的；易患病的

W

well-groomed	/ˌwel ˈɡruːmd/	adj.	梳妆整洁的

教师服务

感谢您选用清华大学出版社的教材！为了更好地服务教学，我们为授课教师提供本学科重点教材信息及样书，请您扫码获取。

≫ 最新书目

扫码获取 2024 **外语类**重点教材信息

≫ 样书赠送

教师扫码即可获取样书